Matt and Martin Rogan are a father-and-son team.

Matt Rogan has worked in and around professional sport for 15 years. He is Group Board and Commercial Director at Lane4, a performance development consultancy with a heritage in Olympic sport. Having graduated from Fitzwilliam College, Cambridge University, Matt's career has involved roles at NBA (US Basketball league), running the European Sponsorship division for MTV and strategy consulting for British television networks, cable operators and Premier League football clubs. Matt is also a Board Director of the European Sponsorship Association and a regular media commentator and speaker on the sports industry. He plays County level tennis and is an Ironman triathlete. He lives in Oxfordshire with his wife Claire, a regional level hockey player, son Conor and daughter Niamh.

Martin Rogan has been involved in British sport for 50 years – as participant in his own right (football and marathon running), father to three sporting children and an avid fan at the elite level. Now retired after a senior career at Nortel, he combines writing, helping his less than able children do up their homes, running daily and a keen interest in family genealogy. Martin's wife, and Matt's Mum, Marion has taught tennis to local juniors for 20 years. Together Martin and Marion have more than 40 marathons to their names.

Britain and the Olympic Games

PAST, PRESENT, LEGACY

Matt Rogan and Martin Rogan

Matador
5 Weir Road
Kibworth Beauchamp
Leicester LE8 0LQ, UK
Tel: (+44) 116 279 2277
Email: books@troubador.co.uk
Web: www.troubador.co.uk/matador

ISBN 978 184876 575 7

British Library Cataloguing in Publication Data.
A catalogue record for this book is available from the British Library.

Typeset in 11pt Sabon by Troubador Publishing Ltd, Leicester, UK
Printed in the UK by MPG Biddles Bodmin and Kings Lynn

Matador is an imprint of Troubador Publishing Ltd

This book could not have been created without the family and friends who have debated, discussed and shaped its contents along with us. We dedicate it to Marion and Claire, without whose support and love it would have remained a pipe dream.

CONTENTS

FOREWORD

In 1976, when I was 12, I saw David Wilkie win 200 metre breaststroke gold in Montreal. That was critical for me. It was the first time I had connected what I did with something so big. I thought, 'I do the same stroke as him. Wouldn't it be good if I could achieve that, too?'

A year later, David was hosting swimming clinics around Britain and he held one in Liverpool which my parents took me along to. He took us through his gold-medal race and, I can't remember whether I've made this up or whether it actually happened, but I'm pretty sure he asked: 'Who of you here wants to win at the Olympic Games?' He suggested it would be hard work, but it was possible. It made it real and for me that was a defining moment. I realised my goal in Seoul, but the iterative journey towards it began for me with that one question.

I am involved with the London 2012 Olympic and Paralympic Games on a number of levels, but most actively in my role as Managing Director of Lane4. As a business we believe passionately that the Games are far more than a sporting event. They will touch every area of the British way of life and perhaps, in a quiet moment, offer each of us a chance to challenge our own thinking about our lives inside and outside of work. So much of my early life was influenced and shaped by Olympic sport. In the run up to London 2012 I now have the pleasure of seeing the Games make a difference to so many more lives on a daily basis.

Matt and Martin's book offers you the chance to make the Olympic and Paralympic Games of London 2012 more real for yourselves. While it may be a little too late for a David Wilkie-type moment of inspiration for some of us, I hope it challenges you to think just a little differently about what London 2012 might mean for you, and what your own personal legacy might be.

Adrian Moorhouse MBE
Olympic Gold Medallist, 100 metre Breaststroke, Seoul 1988
Managing Director, Lane4

ACKNOWLEDGEMENTS

We have both grown up playing, watching, debating and reading about sport. Despite this, it was hardly in our minds to write a book on 6 July 2005 as Trafalgar Square erupted in celebration. Instead, the idea of writing a book on the genesis of Britain and the Olympic Games grew slowly and over time.

There were some specific turning points along this journey – a Lane4 Client Conference where we tested some of the content; the encouragement of our family to push on with the research beyond this point; the support and friendship of Marzena Bogdanowicz along the way; the creativity and energy of photographer Helen Turton who designed our front cover and the empathetic commitment and challenge of Martin Cloake, our editor. We would also like to thank Karen Earl, Dominic Mahony and Steve Hacking who took the time to offer us feedback on some early versions of our book.

We have been fortunate enough to be able to capture insights from so many inspirational and engaging people as we have researched and written this book. You will meet them along the way; however, a full list of their names and roles are given as part of the reference material after the main body of the book. Thanks to all of them for being so giving of their time, and in particular to Sylvia Disley and John and Dorothy Parlett, all of whom competed in London 1948 and were both kind and inspirational company.

We have also gained ideas and insight from many of the team at Lane4 on this journey, several of whom feature in these pages. Those who do not, but have been no less instrumental in our journey, have been Clare Hopkins, Fran Nash, Natalie Benjamin, Austin Swain and Tom Smith.

We have also had access to some very helpful other sources through the course of our writing this book, and would encourage you to dip into the Bibliography if you are looking for further reading. In particular, we were able to gain significant insight into the 1948 story from the work of Janie Hampton and Bob Phillips and access to the British Olympic Archive.

If Britain reacted with delight and surprise when Jacques Rogge read the word 'London' from the all-important envelope in 2005, it is nothing compared to the surprise and sense of pride we feel in publishing this title. On one level we have modest ambitions for it. We do not imagine that it will inspire many to choose sport in the first place, as the Olympic and Paralympic Games themselves surely will. We would, however, hope to offer more context and insight to those of you who, like us, already have 27 July 2012 marked down on your calendars. See you there.

INTRODUCTION

This is the story of how Britain shaped the modern Olympic Games and of how the modern Olympic Games shaped Britain. This deep and lasting relationship between an iconic city and an iconic event is continually evolving to set the template for a new and challenging world.

Through extensive archive research, interviews with athletes who competed in the London 1948 Olympic Games and privileged access to many of the current leading figures in British sport, business and the British nation's journey to London 2012 we aim to paint an unapologetically positive picture of the power of the partnership between Britain and the Olympic Games in promoting change for the better.

The pages of this book are populated with innovators, entrepreneurs, visionaries and characters whose sheer determination moved mountains. It is not just the tale of the great and the good, but also those whose less high-profile efforts behind the scenes continue to drive a sustained legacy in our country. Tracing the history of sport in Britain from the earliest age, we take a journey which finishes at three key points – all in London, and all at the site of an Olympic Games. In 1908 London breathed new life into an ancient and noble ideal; in 1948 it reshaped the Games to lay the foundations of the modern Olympic and, importantly, Paralympic movement in a British nation in desperate need of hope and new direction. Now, London 2012 is changing the model for winning, staging and driving a deep enduring legacy from a major sporting event in a new, more connected but similarly challenging world.

Britain's bid to stage the Olympic Games and Paralympic Games in 2012 was not, as had been the model previously, focused on technical excellence. Instead, it was steeped in references to the past and hopes for a better sporting future. Lord Sebastian Coe, in his now renowned speech to the International Olympic Committee in Singapore which was key to winning the bid, made specific reference to this.

'In the past, London and the Olympic Movement have come together when there were serious challenges to be faced,' he said. 'In 1908, London delivered the Games and the first purpose-built Olympic Stadium to the tightest of schedules. In 1948, our predecessors reunited a devastated world through sport. And their legacy was the first volunteer programme, an idea still at the heart of the Games. Today, London is ready to join you in facing a new challenge. And to provide another enduring sporting legacy. Today's challenge is tough. It's more complex. We can no longer take it for granted that young people will choose sport.'

This was an altogether new approach to selling a host nation's candidacy. It talked to Britain's ongoing role as a catalyst in the Olympic movement and how the London 2012 team as a whole, and Coe in particular, believed Britain could help the IOC redefine the role of the Olympic Games beyond 2012.

'My heroes were Olympians,' Coe said. 'My children's heroes change by the month. And they are the lucky ones. Millions more face the obstacle of limited resources and the resulting lack of guiding role models. Today we offer London's vision of inspiration and legacy. Choose London today and you send a clear message to the youth of the world: more than ever, the Olympic Games are for you.'

The speech worked and as we shall demonstrate has had a lasting impact on the way host cities view the Olympic Games, and the way the Olympic Committee itself views its major asset. After London's victory, Jacques Rogge paid tribute in the media to Sebastian Coe. 'Most of the London winners today have had a long journey in the Olympic movement,' he said. 'I met Seb for the first time on the steps of the Olympic restaurant in Moscow in 1980 when he had won gold. Someone introduced us and we could not have believed at that time that we would be signing the host country contract now.'

Britain's role in the re-birth of the Olympic Games did not start in Singapore. It did not even start with London 1908 and 1948. The British love affair with sport has contributed on any number of levels to the way our world understands modern sport today, and the Games in particular.

Greg Searle, Olympic gold medallist in Barcelona and a current member of the British rowing team for London 2012, a mere 20 years on from his Barcelona victory, talks about the importance in his return to rowing of 'going slow to go fast'. It was critical for him to relearn the fundamentals of technique and base fitness (going slow) before focusing on developing a cardiovascular engine capable of racing once again (going fast).

Similarly, it is very difficult to truly understand Britain's role in the Olympic Games without first building a base of knowledge which begins long before Olympic competition itself. Almost everyone can conjure up a picture of the Ancient Olympic Games and most will feature the image of a perfectly-formed athlete hurling a discus or engaged in some form of combative sport. This was the image which inspired the re-creation of what we now recognise as the greatest international sporting contest in the world – the modern Olympic Games.

Britain's history is intrinsically connected with this process of recreating the Olympic Games. It was a series of interventions by British leaders which have shaped the spectacle we know today, to the extent that Britain could even stake a reasonable challenge to Athens as being the birthplace of the modern Olympic Games.

As Seb Coe illustrated in his Singapore speech, the contribution Britain has made to the Olympic movement demonstrates both a national sporting obsession and an ability through this obsession to reinvent the Olympic movement itself. In 2012 London becomes the only city to have staged the Olympic Games three times. In order to do justice to the context for this latest London Games and the British influence on the Olympic movement, we first have to understand the role of games and sport in British culture.

We begin our journey 30,000 years ago. This might seem a strange and distant place to start a book on the Olympic Games and yet the core themes from those early days are still valid today. Searle's words, 'go slow to go fast', ring particularly true for us on our journey in this first section.

Having shared the context for Britain's relationship with sport in general, and the Olympic Games in particular, we go on to focus on the remarkable similarities and stark differences between London 1948 and London 2012 respectively. We do this not only because it is a fascinating exercise in comparison and contrast, but also because it is important to understand how London 1948 set the operating model for the Olympic Games for the following

60 years. Once we understand this, we can truly grasp how different London 2012 really will be. We hope to show what successful delivery of London 2012 would mean to our society, our children and the Olympic movement.

Just as Britain has shaped the Olympic Games in some critical moments over the last 400 years, so the Olympic Games will shape our own society in 2012. So, in turn, will our delivery of London 2012 shape the Olympic movement for the next 100 years ahead. Let the time travel begin.

PART ONE

An Historic Undertaking

'I cannot bring my Muse to dropp Vies
Twixt Cotswold, and the Olimpicke exercise'
Ben Jonson

1

Sport and Games in Britain to 1945

Sport in Britain has always been about far more than what actually happens on the field of play. The story of the relationship between the sporting and social fabric of life in Britain is one of gradual progress but constant tension. From the very start, sport was used as a means of preserving political power, the social status quo and even norms of morality. There are cameo roles in this journey for gambling, the role of the Church and even alcoholic drink, all as omnipresent in the backdrop to sporting competition hundreds and even thousands of years ago as they are today.

We start our journey in a cave, some 30,000 years ago. Paintings known to have adorned the walls of dwellings in this era offer some indication of the role of exercise and sport at this time – with depictions of animals being hunted for food but also for sporting enjoyment. There are paintings of the hunting of woolly rhinoceros, which would certainly have been hunted for sport rather than sustenance. As society gradually became more sophisticated, demonstrating personal power and superiority over one's acquaintances through the sport of hunting rather than mortal combat was seen as a more progressive means of establishing rank. Right from the beginning of our journey as a civilisation, sport has helped society to develop its unwritten rules and afforded those who compete a sense of prestige, profile and, let's not forget, pure enjoyment.

Sporting festivals, too, come to the fore very early in our journey. Both Tim Harris in *Sport* and Melvyn Watman in *The History of British Athletics* identify the most ancient of these to have been the Tailteann Games, which are believed to have been started in 632 BC, although some put its origins as far back as 1829

BC. These were effectively an Olympic Games of the age, staged in County Meath in Ireland every three years. The Games were held on the Feast of Lughnasa, now traditionally the first day of August. Contests in horse and chariot racing were held, as well as swimming, spear throwing, running, vaulting, high-jumping, putting the stone and throwing the wheel. There was even a team game broadly equating to what we know today as the Irish sport of Hurling. A legendary hero of these Games was a character named Setanta, a name familiar to many of us today as the adopted brand name of the Irish Pay TV sports channel.

These Games continued until the Norman invasions brought them to a halt in 1168, some 2-3,000 years after their inception, a period which puts the longevity of the modern Olympic movement into perspective. While there is no evidence to confirm that sporting festivals of this kind extended from Ireland to Britain during this period any more successfully than Setanta did a few years ago, it is certain that less active games were enjoyed in Britain at the time. Druid graves discovered near Colchester suggest board games were a common feature of Celtic times. Discovered neatly organised in these Colchester graves, beneath the bodily remains, was a board game with glass counters laid out ready to play, as well as some sort of herbal brew, perhaps enjoyed at the same time!

Brief Roman governance left Britain a language in Latin and a religion in Christianity. Latin was never a common tongue with which to bond the people, but rather a means of defining an elite social class through its usage. Anglo-Saxon times saw the nation geographically divided into separate kingdoms. These regions shared a common language and similar customs but were divided under many different kings. Succession to the kingdom depended on the amount of support that could be bought in influential circles. Gifting land, treasure and slaves was generally the way to retain popularity, and winning battles the route to securing a plentiful supply of this currency. Given this context, it is unsurprising that fighting was the critical physical pursuit of the age. Sport and pastimes such as horse racing and hunting were derivative of the fight. Dice and board games, such as a form of chess, were also prevalent.

Once in situ, kings aimed to outlaw anything which had the potential of causing uprising against their rule. The Church was often their principal means of doing so, and it was heavily involved in the regulation of sport. Sport for the masses was often perceived as threatening to the status quo, and was heavily controlled.

As Ireland had already demonstrated through the popularity of the Tailteann Games, there was certainly early evidence that sport could have a broader entertainment as well as participation value. Between 1120 and 1300 the era of knights on horseback arrived and with them the early stages of commercialised sport. The original tournaments were not the classic Hollywood joust, but rather freeform scraps that gained rules as they went along. By 1200 a typical tournament lasted two days, with an initial day of jousting and skirmishing followed by the charge and breaking of lances, before the competing armies broke up into a melee. A good fight between roughly equal sides was in everyone's interests, for an unequal battle would discourage defeated knights from competing again and mean less booty for the victors. This worry is echoed in some quarters today as unease grows that audiences may dwindle, as an elite group of rich clubs in football's Premier League become increasingly dominant.

The experience on tournament day itself also invited comparison with a Premier League match day. Tournaments of this type were the defining spectator sport of the age, with audience chants, team colours and big salaries for the knights themselves. Although all sorts of foul play seemed standard practice, common sense usually prevailed. Tricks of the trade included such strategies as cost cutting (reducing ransom price in the field, or even releasing a captured knight to earn his ransom in the field fighting for you) and agreeing profit sharing from the competition in advance of the action unfolding. In many ways these tricks are very similar to the kinds of activities which remain commonplace in professional cycling. Prizes for performances were also given. There is also record of English Knight William the Marshall being awarded one after the day's events had concluded. Tim Harris's *Sport* suggests William was unable to pick up his prize in person as he was with his blacksmith having his 'battered pot helm removed from his head.'

Although these events were usually on a smaller scale in Britain than in France, they were a welcome diversion and source of income for the locals. However, their increasing popularity meant that they risked sparking local riots and the resultant extensive destruction. Navigating this tension continued to be challenging and in 1194 Richard the Lionheart reorganised jousting and set up five licensed sites. Much like Formula One teams today, tournament teams were funded for the prestige they brought their benefactors. As well as wages and prizes, expensive transfer fees were paid for star performers. When William the Marshall moved to the team of Phillip of Flanders, he was 'transferred' in exchange for one quarter of the rents of the port of St Omer.

Following Richard's death, the main competition sites were one near Dunstable and another at Hounslow Heath, now Heathrow Airport. It is strange to think that most of the international sporting elite will arrive in Britain for London 2012 by landing on one of the country's very first commercial sporting sites!

Jousting continued to evolve, with a wooden enclosure soon used to define the area of competition. In many cases the contest was used to decide 'justice' as opposed to a more regular form of earthly judge. Both Smithfield and Cheapside in London became centres for these events. Much of the sporting participation of this time in London is captured in the *Liber Costumarum*, a Latin document dating from around 1175, which can still be read to this day in the Corporation of London library. Although it reads at times like a public relations exercise on behalf of the London of the day it does make one less favourable comment on the city.

'I cannot think of any city more commendable for the habits of its citizens in attending church, in observing the divine festivals, in giving alms, in providing hospitality, in formalising betrothals, in contracting marriages, in celebrating weddings, in throwing banquets, in keeping guests entertained, as well as in attention to the burial and funeral needs of the deceased,' opined the writer. 'The only problems that plague London are the idiots who drink to excess and the frequency of fires.'

There is little mention of the London commoner in the 12th Century in historical records, and for many hundreds of years afterwards, unless there is some record of domestic unrest. As a result, the historical reputation of our national sport is somewhat patchy and chequered, usually mentioned only in court or legislation reportage. The sport that was to become football had an image problem from the very early days. The *Liber Costumarum* actually mentions 'the famous game of ball' held on Shrove Tuesday. London was certainly becoming a centre for sporting innovation, however social tension was never far below the surface. Whenever war seemed imminent, sporting bans were not far behind in case the activities were to the detriment of archery practice. In 1314, with war against the Scots looming, the Lord Mayor of

London issued a proclamation forbidding 'rumpuses with large footballs', or more colourfully in Norman French, 'rageries de grosse pelottes de pee'.

An additional sideshow to the evolution of sport in Britain began with the return of armies from the Crusades. The troops had occupied themselves during the long campaigns by gambling and gaming and their return sparked a significant increase in these activities. In response to the trouble and violence these pursuits engendered, Richard legislated to restrict gambling to the nobles and control stakes. This was the start of 600 years of restricting the general population from participating in such activity, a measure aimed to focus them on working for a living. In the following century the council of Worcester tried to stop even the clergy gambling. Richard II added legislation to this effect in 1388.

While we may tend of think of Princess Anne and Zara Phillips as our first sporting royals, this is far from the truth. In the Tudor era, Henry VIII dominated the sporting scene as a competitor. Secure in his throne, from an early age he had attended the May Game in the Royal Park, riding the great courses and taking part in hunts and jousts. Henry's various palaces became the sports centres of their day. The first rule-making sporting body to be set up in Britain was the Ancient Maisters of the Science of Defence, founded in 1540. Their elaborate martial arts code involved the mastery of various different weapons. Contestants competed in sword fighting, boxing cum wrestling, and cudgeling. The inherent prejudice in favour of the noble and wealthy could not have been more obvious given that street football was again banned in 1541, but sword fighting deemed perfectly reasonable as long as the participants were of the correct social status!

Here, then, is the background to sporting participation in Britain. From Druid board games to folkball, the commercial sports leagues of the knights to the relative sporting stardom of the Monarch of the day, the British population had long demonstrated a significant appetite to watch and play sport. However, this was never far from some broader social undercurrents. Tensions between the role of the Church (as a tool for the social elite) and sport were clear. Sport became a device to protect the noble from the general population and emphasise the importance of productivity among the working population. The notion of sport as entertainment was continually linked with the dangers of alcohol, rowdy crowds and violence. Sport was also a political lever for the leaders in society and a means for social aspirants to better themselves. This was the backdrop for the very first Olympic Games in England.

The first modern Olympic Games occurred above the Cotswold village of Weston-sub-Edge in 1612. It was the brainchild of Robert Dover, who based his ideas on the epic accounts handed down from the Greek poetry of Pindar. Just as Dover took his inspiration from poetry, so our understanding of the background to Dover's Games is taken from poetry, in this case a book named *Annalia Dubrensia*. Although Dover's inspiration was Classical Greece, his creation shows almost as many similarities with the modern Games as we know them.

England in the early 17th Century was a fractured nation. The increasing influence of the Puritan movement restricted any opportunity for those working six days every week to indulge in many of their formerly encouraged sporting and leisure activities. Dover, a lawyer by profession and a supporter of the Royalist cause, established Robert Dover's Cotswold Olimpick Games with the earnest intent to recreate the benefits of healthy sporting contest for those 'living in the wold, or in the vale'. It is extraordinary to think that exactly 400 years before the forthcoming London Games, there was already a British Olimpick event focused on a legacy of sporting participation and health.

In order to initiate an event of this type Dover required the permission, or sponsorship, of King James I. This took the form of an (old) set of regal finery presented by the King which Robert wore at the event to signify royal support. The winner of each contest was presented with coloured ribbons for their cap or coat, knotted in a manner that distinguished their achievement in very clear tones. The fall of the monarchy saw the suspension of the annual event, but it recommenced after the Restoration in the mid 1650s and continued until the 1850s. Two hundred years represents a far longer life span than the current Olympic Games.

Just as with the ancient Olympic Games, so we can learn from Robert Dover's Olimpick Games through the drawings and poetry associated with the event. *Annalia Dubrensia*, published in 1636, was created 'Upon the yearly celebration of Mr Robert Dover's Olimpick Games upon Cotswold Hills'. This was possibly generated from a 'commonplace book' compiled over the early years of the Games. This depicts many of the activities which formed part of the competitions.

It is very clear from the work that there were two levels of sporting contest conducted in the Cotswold Games, echoing the theme of social exclusion and class divides in British sporting history to this point. The familiar foot races, jumping and throwing events feature, as does a form of fencing with each competitor wielding two swords or sticks. Wrestling is also among the list of those pursuits for the 'lower' levels of society. For the nobility and gentry, without whose support the Games could not have succeeded, there was horse racing on a course over several miles, and coursing, both with hounds and greyhounds. Dr Francis Burns says in his *History of the Olimpick Games*, 'For the gentler souls there were dancing contests, games of skill and chance such as chess, the card game cent and an Irish game resembling backgammon.' As we shall see, class divides persisted deep into the history of the Olympic movements.

The level of interest in the Games is hinted at by the fact that some well-known and respected poets of the day such as Michael Drayton, Ben Jonson and Thomas Heywood contributed to the recording of the events. The underlying themes of the poems equate the Games specifically with the original Hellenic Olympic Games tradition and also take the opportunity to criticise the Puritan attitude to games which was never far from the surface.

Two hundred years of popular and well-intentioned sport passed successfully until by the 1850s the event was attracting vast crowds. Unfortunately this also resulted in some poor behaviour among spectators and the local authorities used this as the rationale for calling them to a halt. This decision coincided conveniently with the division of the lands used for the Games amongst the local landowners. Sport at this stage was very clearly subservient to political power. The Games were discontinued.

The remaining original section of pasture and fields was only saved from the ravages of development in 1929 by the intervention of a local artist who risked significant funds to purchase the area before organising local subscription and transferring ownership to the National Trust. This Cotswold site is where the Games are held to this day and competitors and spectators are invited to convene at Dover's Hill each June for the event. Unlike the 2012 event in London which require years of commitment and effort to ensure a place on the starting line, entries for Dover's Games are accepted on the day!

It is worth taking a minute to consider the bare facts of Dover's achievement. Wanting to recreate the Olympic ideal in order to promote health through sporting participation, he created an event which endured for 200 years. One wonders quite what the Olympic Games would look like today if Dover's initial creation had survived the greed of local landowners and problems of crowd disturbance.

Certainly as the Cotswolds propelled the Olimpick movement onwards, sport across Britain was also growing significantly – and with it the popularity of gambling. The sport of the age in Tudor times was tennis. While it would strike fear into those running today's ATP Tennis Tour, recently rocked by betting scandals of the twenty-first century kind, betting on every single point was not unusual for the Tudor crowd! Horse racing also offered gambling opportunities around the country, as did martial arts contests featuring rounds of boxing cum wrestling, cudgeling and fencing. Many of these bouts were staged in front of crowds inside the inns around London. Bowling alleys were another big earner for those same inns, although great efforts were made by the authorities to close them down.

The arrival of the Stuart dynasty meant the passion for sport as a vehicle for gambling continued unabated. As we have seen, horse racing was the primary passion amongst the gentry, only briefly interrupted by Puritan Parliamentary rule. Echoing many a domestic horse racing meet from the present day, prizes for victory were relatively small but wagers were vast. The relaxation of the drinking laws meant towns turned to race meetings as an alternative to the traditional fairs.

Sporting stardom was also on the rise, harking back to the days of the knights. Running footmen, who accompanied their masters on dangerous roads, competed in races. Samuel Pepys records a footrace in St James' Park between Lee and Crow, one of whom had recently left the employ of Lord Claypoole to make his fortune on the track. One of the first recorded boxing matches was between the Duke of Albermarle's footman and his butcher!

By the 18th Century gambling had become one of the most important social and political issues of the day. In some areas the lack of focus on more serious matters it was perceived to cause was even blamed for one of the most humiliating defeats of British Imperial history, the loss of America. By the end of the 19th Century political flyers began to circulate in London demanding that an axe be taken to gambling, suggesting somewhat hysterically that it was the root of all of the British problems of the day.

Horse racing remained the most popular gambling sport but racing aristocrats, fearing that control of 'their' sport was passing to the growing number of smaller courses and the general population, persuaded Parliament to ban races with prizes under £50. The result of this was that many of the smaller courses were forced to close. These same individuals who dominated the horse racing scene in Britain owned vast tracts of the land in the country. Not only did they dominate professional sport but, as the century went on, also made further fortunes from industry, the colonies and speculation. In many ways our Premier League football clubs today are taking us back to this realm of rich individuals owning the most popular sporting institutions of the day.

Cricket was catching up at this time as a major gambling sport, with large amounts to be won or lost. This tradition continues to this day in Asia with scandal never far behind it in recent years. The benefit of cricket as a subject of betting at the time lay in the fact that the rules were agreed only as the game commenced. From a gambling perspective cricket seemed to avoid both the cost and crookedness of the racetrack. As bigger bets were staked and demand increased for more cricket there was employment for professionals. In 1744 the rules of cricket were finally published leading to fewer disputes.

The era also gave rise to many handicap matches to support the incessant demands of gamblers – single wicket contests, 11 against 22 and, on at least one occasion, the suggestion that one team would play with one hand tied behind their backs! In 1748 it was ruled that cricketers could only play for goods, not money, and professionalism became more complex. Certainly some of these innovations put the furore around the launch of 20-20 cricket and its supposed diversion from the pure heritage of cricket into perspective.

Even bare-knuckle boxing drifted towards the realms of circus as a result of the gambling craze. In 1720 British Champion Bob Stokoe and his wife took on Ned Sutton and the 'Kentish Heroine' at Figg's Amphitheatre in Marylebone, London. There were prizes of £40 for the most sword cuts and £20 for the most cudgel hits. Around 1750, bare-knuckle boxing was declared illegal. This was not, as one might have thought, because of damage to protagonists but instead due to the propensity of the spectacle to attract large and potentially unruly crowds. It was not until 1867 that boxing was once again made 'respectable', when the Queensbury Rules created a more controlled environment in the ring.

The picture we have is therefore of Britain's favourite sports being subject to several concurrent threats – trivialisation in the hands of a British addiction to gambling, restricted access to all but a social elite who were determined to keep all of the fun for themselves and total shut-down due to the sheer weight of excitable audiences. Ironically the Napoleonic Wars (1795-1815) briefly quelled several of these threats because fear of invasion created a need to 'build up muscles to fight the foe.' Boxing was once again encouraged. Foreign military Allies were invited to attend competition events. This illustrates the uneasy and shifting relationship between the establishment's fear of the crowd's martial tendencies and its willingness to use that spirit to suit its purposes, a theme which has continued throughout British history. The war disrupted sports other than boxing, however, and in the countryside there were protests over enclosure, wartime taxation and poor harvests.

Once the Napoleonic war was over, the aristocracy started to claw back sporting ownership for the nobility. The waters now safe, another aristocratic club took control of its sport with the formation of The Yacht Club. Royal patronage was obtained which ensured that the minimum limit for membership was a vessel of 30 tons or more, so ensuring membership for the elite classes only. The Game Act in 1831 enabled owner hunting and fishing rights to be sold and facilitated subscription hunts. This was shortly followed by the Gaming Act in 1845 which made sporting bets unenforceable in law, handing over control of all on-course betting to the Jockey Club. The set-up of off-course listers attractive to the lower classes was soon closed down by Parliament after some particularly scaremongering speeches from the floor of the House.

To add to the scandals of the day, almost for the first time, women were also increasingly emerging as gambling addicts as well as men. By the middle of the 19th Century not only the Church but also the emerging middle class had the vice of gambling in their sights. They saw the aristocratic upper classes as profligate and the 'lower orders' condemned to poverty by their increasing addiction. As a result, they were able to look down on both. The popular middle class view was that work was the way to make money and gambling on sport was for degenerates. The moral compass was set to that of Middle England.

Football remained a target for the Authorities. The 1835 Highways Act fined any street footballers who could be caught. There was a crackdown on folk football and a severe limiting of Public Holidays. This meant the game could only really thrive in spacious private grounds such as those of the public schools.

In direct contrast to a general perception that sport was somehow morally dubious, Victorian parlour games designed to teach basic behaviour became popular. These included Goose, Snakes and Ladders, and Ludo. Many were themed on the British Commonwealth, both in terms of geography and historical events. A six-sided spinning top replaced the dreaded dice which retained connotations of the evils of gambling.

This, then, was the prevailing mood of the day which led to the end of Robert Dover's Olimpick Games. The sponsorship of the aristocracy which had helped Dover create the Games was a relic from 200 years past and the health agenda which inspired him was now viewed as secondary to preserving the social status quo and economic prosperity of the day.

Despite the demise of the Dover ideal in the 1850s, renewed stirrings of the Olympic ideal emanated from a Victorian Doctor, William Penny Brookes, of Much Wenlock in Shropshire. Brookes was anxious to improve the lot of the working man and having first formed a reading society to improve their minds in his local area, he then looked at improving their bodies. There is some evidence that he was familiar with Joseph Strutt's book, *Sports and Pastimes of the People of England,* which had included details of Dover's exploits in an earlier age. In 1850 he formed the Wenlock Olympian Class, holding the first games that year. They have continued annually until the present day.

Although the opportunity for travel at that time was limited to a wealthy few, the cosmopolitan nature of Britain ensured Dover's evangelical message spread quickly. Immigrant communities were well represented when the first National Olympian Games were held in London. The Capital already had some links with international as well as British sporting excellence in that the global headquarters of the gymnastics Turnvereine Movement were already based in the Turnhalle, now restored as the German Gymnasium in St. Pancras.

While the Much Wenlock Games were still largely a local event, Brookes also made contact with the Greek campaigners for a modern Olympic Games. The minute books of the Olympian Society record a letter of thanks dated 1860 from the Greek authorities for 'The Wenlock Prize' contributed by the Wenlock Committee at the first revived games in Greece, assigned to the 'best runner in the longest race.' In 1890 Brookes hosted Baron De Coubertin, holding a Wenlock Games in his honour. It is widely acknowledged that this was part of the inspiration for De Coubertin's own Games in Athens in 1898. More recently, then-IOC President Juan Antonio Samaranch paid homage at Brookes's grave in Much Wenlock.

Brookes's Wenlock Olympian Class stated its objective was to 'promote the moral, physical and intellectual improvement of the town and neighbourhood.' Just as Dover did before him and the London 2012 team would do after him, Brookes started with a central idea that the Olympic tradition could somehow enable social progress. He not only instilled this thought in Britain, he handed it to De Coubertin. The 'legacy' promise to Wenlock's citizens above seems strikingly similar to the goal of the regeneration and restoration of East London through London 2012.

With a perfect symmetry, London's naming of the Olympic mascot as Wenlock takes the forthcoming Games back to the very beginnings of Brookes's initiative. While there could hardly be larger differences between the 1850 and 2012 iterations of the event, the objectives are strikingly similar. Brookes would no doubt be proud that Much Wenlock has recently opened a brand new school in his name, the William Brookes School, and of the existence of the Wenlock mascot. At the heart of the school, and the new focus of the annual Olympian Games, is a brand new tartan athletics track.

The relationship between Britain and the Olympic ideal has long been part of a far broader social context for the development of the country. Social exclusion through sport was at the forefront of this. The sporting world in which the privileged operated was far removed from the rest of society. Whenever possible, the upper classes restricted access to the fun they were having, sporting or otherwise. Slowly, the distinction between amateurism and professionalism became the principal means by which this social difference could be upheld.

Many of the class distinctions at the end of the 19th Century were reinforced by the restriction of sporting club membership to the affluent and influential. Many clubs had insisted on opening membership purely to those able to vote. Voting itself was reserved for property owners, and therefore the upper echelons of society. However, since the Reform Act did away with that particular restriction for voting rights, another rule was needed to preserve sports club membership purely for the social elite. Since subjective rules were difficult to enforce, the definition which many clubs chose to retain control over the membership became whether or not you played for wages. Those who competed for wages were excluded from membership, which meant that the social elite (who did not need to earn money themselves) were able to continue their lives of sporting privilege. In this sense amateurism was initially nothing more than a convenient way of preserving sport for the elite.

This had quite an impact on many Olympic sports and clubs. For example, for the Leander Club in Lambeth the use of professionals as rowing partners, coxes or coaches had formerly been part of the negotiation before the race, with boring, blocking and other hard nut river tactics all regarded as part of the game. Now a new division between gentlemen amateurs and professional boatmen, who worked on the water, had been created. Styles began to change. Even rowing style became important as a barometer of sporting, and therefore social, background. Long elegant strokes became fashionable – the professional 'anything goes' style was frowned upon. Gradually the rules of entry began to be tightened at major events like Henley, to exclude all but the university or public school crews. What had traditionally been a morally neutral sport became loaded with a set of Victorian values. There was no suggestion that this was intended as anything other than a deliberate social divide. When Henley's restrictions were breached by a Canadian crew which won its race easily, further rules were imposed to prevent 'artisans, labourers or mechanics' competing. The impact of this decision was to reduce the potential talent pool for British rowing considerably, which damaged its international standing in the sport for decades. In effect the use of sport as a means of social class divide was being seen as primary to the pursuit of sporting excellence. The impact of this was still being felt at the London Olympic Games in 1948.

In cricket there was a clear distinction between gentlemen and the professional players. The players were hired hands rather than club members with different changing rooms and even different levels of food provision. By now 'real' cricket had come to mean the three-day game, which conveniently enough no working man could contemplate for fear of the impact on his wages. International tours were undertaken by professionals, who needed to earn a living in the close season somehow. The aristocrats had better things to do than take extended journeys to play commoners in the colonies, after all.

Subsequently the first visiting side was from Australia in 1867. By the 1870s, MCC members were taking cricket to the Empire.

As we have seen, throughout British sporting history football has been the sport of the masses. It is no surprise then that in 1863 football was the first to break the mould of self elected members' clubs deciding who could and could not play any specific sport. The Football Association was formed as an association of equal members. Its stated aim, toasted after their first match at Battersea in 1864, was to welcome competitors 'regardless of class or creed', an aim realised with the creation of the FA Cup competition in 1871. This recalls the tradition of 'folkball' from early British sporting history. The first 11 FA Cup Finals were won by gentlemen; however, in 1883 Blackburn Olympic were the victors and by 1890 Blackburn Rovers had won it for the third time running. Its players were free to enjoy Saturday afternoons of sport at last, thanks to a succession of Factories Acts. Football had the mindset of inclusion, but only government intervention was able to truly set it free to flourish.

Athletics, too, chose to exclude professional influence by outlawing financial gain through the winning of prize money. This was intended to keep the sport 'pure' – the winning of prize money now being perceived as somehow dirty. This missed the point entirely. Actually it was the influence of betting on the creation of 'circus-style' events and the throwing of matches which was corrupting most sports at the time, not the earning of money or prizes through victory. The solution athletics proposed, although deeply flawed and often breached even in its early days, was to form the basis of Baron de Coubertin's Olympic definition.

Sport as a discipline at the time was very much an inter-club contest. Less active games, however, already had a broader international competition dimension. The Great Exhibition of 1851 was held with the aim of reinforcing Britain's industrial and economic supremacy. At the exhibition Howard Staunton, the English chess master generally regarded as one of the world's strongest players at that time, demonstrated the power of taking control of the definition of rules and administration of sport. Chess had originated in India around the 8th Century and was known throughout world in various forms. Staunton held a tournament at the exhibition between the world's greatest players, establishing a common set of rules and pieces which have remained the standard ever since. In fact, few in the modern world recognise it was ever otherwise.

The lessons of the Great Exhibition were not missed by those wishing to take control and influence in the broader international arena. Subsequent World Fairs around the world and ultimately de Coubertin's Olympic Games were to learn from their success. The British propaganda message was principally intended for domestic consumption as much as for the broader world audience. That said, the wealth and prosperity the Exhibitions presented provided an uncomfortable contrast with the issues of poverty and famine of the day.

2

The Rise, Fall and Rescue of the Early International Olympic Games

Born in 1863 in Paris to an aristocratic family and educated under the guidance of the Jesuits, Pierre de Coubertin chose a career as an intellectual, studying and later writing on a broad range of topics. His particular interest was educational development. Throughout the 1880s, his primary educational objective was to introduce a strong 'athleticism' to the French schooling system. He was enamoured of examples he discoverered in the British system, in particular its strong classical Greek influences. Encounters at various conferences had put him in touch with individuals such as Thomas Arnold and William Penny Brookes. Brookes, as we have seen, was also an advocate of the broader value of sport as a vehicle for promoting education and health.

In the spring of 1894, four years after his visit to Much Wenlock under Brookes's hospitality, he gathered a group of like-minded friends and aristocratic acquaintances at the Sorbonne to discuss his dreams of a modern revival of the Olympic Games of ancient Greece. Earlier Pan-Hellenistic sporting events had failed to maintain momentum, but when Pierre de Coubertin presented his ideas the outcome was a resolution calling for competitions along the lines of the ancient Games to be held every four years. Three 'Olympiads' followed shortly afterwards – Athens in 1896, Paris in 1900 and St. Louis in 1904.

The International Olympic Committee was inaugurated under the Greek Presidency of Demitrius Vikelas. De Coubertin had hoped to welcome in the new century with the first Games in Paris in 1900, but the Committee was impatient and after deliberating on various alternatives, selected Athens for the first Games in 1896. The resurgent domestic interest in the revival of the Olympic Games of ancient times received a timely boost with the recovery of the ancient stadium of Panathenaic at the instigation of King George of Greece.

At the time of the revival of the movement the Greek government was beset by financial and political crisis, much like today. Public enthusiasm was harnessed to raise funds and, with the support of Greek businessman George Averoff, the task of delivering the Games got underway. The majority of the participants were Greek, but many foreigners entered privately or were holidaymakers. In total 12 countries were represented competing in nine sports.

Track and field events were held in the Panathenaic stadium, re-modeled by Greek architect Anastas Mataxas to accommodate 70,000 spectators. A new sand running track was set down by Charles Parry in the available space around the existing U-shaped centre track. He was selected due to his success in building and maintaining an athletics track at London's Stamford Bridge, a facility which pre-dated the creation of Chelsea Football Club in 1905. Parry provided a 333-yard track, although this was accompanied by some difficulties. As a result of the shape of the track, runners were forced to walking pace at corners. The 200 metres event was abandoned as a result.

The stadium was luxurious compared to the facilities for the swimmers. Finances could only run to the building of a pier, so events were held in the sea. Competitors were dropped off at sea by boat in the unseasonably cold weather, with water temperatures of 13 degrees centigrade. Alfred Hajos, the Hungarian winner of the 100m, used his chilly experience in winning the sprint event to cover his body in a thick layer of fat before the 1,200m event, which he also won. He was quoted afterwards as saying, 'My will to live completely overcame my desire to win.' Fortunately nobody drowned, but sailing and rowing were cancelled as a result of the 12-foot high waves. Hajos went on to represent Hungary at football and won a further Olympic prize in the Olympic Art Contest in 1924. His real name was Alfred Guttmann, a surname the Olympic legacy of which was to develop still further some 25 years later.

Although not originally part of the Ancient Olympic Games, the marathon held an emotional appeal for the Greeks because of its historical significance. In their eyes it soon became the most important event at the Games. It still captures the imagination today. The victory by a Greek Shepherd, Spiridon

Louis, is probably the most widely-known result from the first modern Games. Lesser known is the fact that there was a degree of pressure for women to be able to join the men in competing right from the very beginning. In the Greek trials held just a few weeks in advance of the event a lady, Miss Melpomene, completed the course in four hours and 30 minutes and enrolled for the competition. She was not permitted to run by the authorities. The newspaper *Akropolis* criticised this decision, suggesting that 'her participation would certainly not have been queried by the male competitors'. Another lady, Stamata Revithi, is also reputed to have run the course the day after the event, this time in five hours and 30 minutes, although her motive is not clear. This seems extraordinary in our current sporting culture, in which the women's marathon is just as big an occasion as the men's run and ultra-running for women is now taken to mean 50 miles and upwards, a distance author Matt's sisters Emma and Louise both compete at regularly.

Athens 1896 was an age well before international team entries and the Greek trials for the marathon were the exception rather than the rule. Occasionally participation was a result of direct intention, at other times it was a case of accidental proximity. Edwin Flack, an Australian working in London, took holiday from his post at Price Waterhouse having seen a Thomas Cook advertisement for the games. Flack won both 800 and 1500 metre events and only dropped out of the marathon when the dust from the cavalry accompanying the leaders finally got the better of him. Thomas Cook is a partner of the London 2012 Games. While Flack made a deliberate trip to compete, John Boland, an Irish holidaymaker, represented Britain in tennis. He won both the singles and doubles, partnering a German. More dust, albeit metaphorical this time, was raised when he complained that the British rather than the Irish flag was used at the presentation ceremony.

Despite minimal media exposure outside Greece, the Games were deemed a great success. Greece looked forward more than most to the next celebration, which at the time it also had the expectation of hosting.

After a promising start in Athens, the two subsequent events were both put on as sideshows to other, larger events. This risked de Coubertin's Olympic dream ending in failure. In addition, the Baron faced difficulty deflecting the efforts of the Greek King to bond with his people by asserting their claim to make the event an exclusively Greece-based festival.

The Paris Games were staged on a makeshift grass course in the grounds of the Racing Club de France and received no publicity since they were regarded as a sideshow to the 1900 Paris Exhibition. Right from the beginning significant challenges presented themselves. The opening event was foolishly scheduled for Saturday 14 July, Bastille Day, which clashed badly with other more entrenched traditions of Parisian culture. Moves to delay to Sunday were opposed by Sabbath observers. The event went ahead on the Saturday in front of sparse crowds and still faced the problem of leading athletes refusing to participate in heats and finals on the Sunday.

The Field magazine (not necessarily an impartial observer) reported 'the whole series of sports produced nothing but muddles, bad arrangements, bad management, bad prizes and any amount of ill-feeling amongst the nationalities engaged.' After widespread excitement at the time of the initial event in Athens, only 13 nations competed in Paris. Few bothered to send representative teams. Almost the whole of the 55-strong American team came from the New York Athletic Club or from college teams. They dominated much of the track competition, despite never having competed on grass before.

As in Athens, the only home athletic winner at the Games, Michel Theato, was in the marathon. In temperatures approaching 102 degrees Fahrenheit, only three of the eight finishers broke four hours for the twisting, poorly-marked 25-mile course and there are lingering suspicions that Theato may not have run the full distance. The American Arthur Newton maintained he took the lead at halfway and was never overtaken. He was officially placed fifth, just over an hour behind the winner.

Britain broke the American domination of track and field by producing a clean sweep in the 4000m steeplechase, an event which included stone fences, a water jump, hurdles and other obstacles. Even the 400m hurdles required hurdling over telegraph poles set at the requisite height as well as the small matter of a water jump. There were also British victories in the 800m, 1500m and 5000m team race. From an athletics team of only five, Britain won nine medals, four of them gold.

Elsewhere, the first British woman ever to win an Olympic gold medal was tennis player Charlotte 'Chattie' Cooper, who was the Women's Singles Champion, going on later to also secure gold in the mixed doubles partnering Reginald Doherty. As Wimbledon Champion in 1895, 1896 and 1898 Cooper's success was not altogether a surprise, and she later went on to win Wimbledon again in 1901 and 1908. Reginald, on the other hand, was scheduled to play his younger brother Hugh in the Olympic semi-final, but 'stepped aside'. His brother duly won the men's singles against Harold Mahony of Ireland.

There is a danger of looking back on the Paris Games from a modern perspective of international competition, when the reality was that competition was by no means truly international at this stage and certainly not representative of the very best international talent any country could supply. One good example of this was the cricket competition. 'Britain' won gold, although represented by Devon and Somerset Wanderers Cricket Club, who beat 'France' in the final. The French team comprised mainly staff from the British Embassy!

The lack of enthusiasm and disorganisation of Paris was repeated once again in St Louis. The United States claimed rights to a home venue as a result of their successes at the 1900 event, and whilst Chicago won the right to stage the event, St Louis threatened to hold a competitive contest to coincide with its World's Fair that year. Chicago conceded defeat. It is ironic on the back of Chicago's surprise failure to land the 2016 Olympic Games that the city had an even nearer miss just over a century earlier. Rather than being outmanoeuvered by a South American city as in 2016, it was another American city which denied Chicago the chance to host the Games in 1904.

After the challenges of Paris, the Olympic authorities were well aware of the perils of running an event concurrent with an International Fair. Despite this, nothing was done. There was little public interest in or even awareness of the event. Many of the competitors were unaware of its significance, as many sporting events were staged over a four-month period. The decathlon and marathon were held in early July, while the track and field was held between 29 August and 3 September. Only nine nations attended, so it became almost an American interclub contest, with the most hotly-contested scoring being between American clubs rather than international nations.

No British team was sent on the grounds of expense, depriving the Games of the greatest distance runners of the day. Although there are records of a gold and bronze medal being won by Britain at the Games, it appears that the gold medal in the decathlon was won by an Irishman, Tom Keily, who paid his own way to the Games having refused to represent Britain. Despite this, his victory was written into the records as one for Britain at a later date. Additionally, a British-born, naturalised American by the name of Tom Hicks won the marathon, run in intense heat over a hilly, dusty course. A winner months earlier of the Boston Marathon in two hours and 39 minutes, he finished the Olympic marathon in three hours and 28 minutes, completing the final seven miles in a distressed condition on a diet of strychnine, raw egg white and the odd nip of brandy. He never ran again. Pierre de Coubertin, the IOC President of the day, chose not to attend the event. He was quoted as reflecting on the 1904 Games, 'We have made a hash of our work. It's a miracle that the Olympic movement survived that celebration.'

Much has been written of de Coubertin's positive influence on the development of the Olympic movement, notwithstanding his abandonment of the St Louis Games and of course his support for the 1936 Games in Berlin. Much of De Coubertin's personal legacy, stirred in Much Wenlock, lies in the sense of sport as an educational concept with a broader value for society, and the sense of fair play which underpinned this philosophy. This came to a head in London 1908.

The London Games of 1908 came to be characterised by the intense rivalry between Britain and the United States. The many frustrations reached a crescendo when the US 'winner' of the 400 metres was disqualified. It seems this occurred primarily as a consequence of a differing interpretation of the rules, but in truth barely a day went by without a dispute of one sort or another between the two nations. The controversies of the day preceding de Coubertin's mid-Games speech to the International Olympic Committee were the worst so far. He therefore chose to raise the issue of fair play as one of the essential characteristics of the Olympic movement.

'The Olympic idea is the conception of strong physical culture, based in part on the spirit of fair play and in part on a cult of beauty and grace,' he started. Conscious of the fact that the dinner was being hosted by the British Government, however, he could not just blurt out his disquiet at the antagonism between Britain and the US. He chose to broaden the reference to include the suggestion that 'fair play is in danger and this is due above all to the canker which has rashly been allowed to develop: the craze for gaming betting and gambling!' Once again, gambling was used as a foil for a deeper message about society.

De Coubertin went on to refer to a talk given the previous day at St Paul's Cathedral by the Bishop of Bethlehem (Pennsylvania), Ethelbert Talbot, who was attending the Lambeth Conference, and proceeded to quote a phrase from Talbot, 'The important thing in these Olympiads is less to win than to take part in them.'

In effect, de Coubertin successfully directed both the British and the Americans to the incident uppermost in their minds that day. However, the caution, obliqueness, and diplomacy with which he publicly reproached them is revealing of a statesman at his peak. The phrase lives on of course and was used iconically in London in 1948, spelt out on the scoreboard which met the athletes entering the stadium for the opening ceremony.

The subtleties of De Coubertin's actions have one further level. While he quoted the phrase as being from Bishop Talbot and Bishop Talbot certainly emphasised the sentiment the day before, it was actually de Coubertin's very own line. De Coubertin put the success of the movement before his own ego – to great effect. He had a potent ability to force change in his fledgling movement. After the early setbacks of the Olympic Games, many an organisation would not have made it to 1908 at all. London 1908 was to breathe life into a struggling Olympic movement.

It was not a straightforward decision for London to host the Games. The story of the London Olympic Games of 1908 is the subject of several excellent books, particularly Rebecca Jenkins's *The First London Olympic Games 1908* and *The 1908 Olympic Games* by Keith Baker. In brief, it came about as a result of the resourcefulness of just a few individuals. Their drive enabled Baron de Coubertin to withstand the disappointing effects of the second and third Olympiads in Paris and St Louis, coupled together with the last minute intervention of Mother Nature ruling out Rome, the originally-intended venue for 1908.

Probably at its lowest ebb since the high point of the inaugural Athens Games, the International Olympic Committee decided initially to award the 1908 Games to Rome. There followed months and years of bitter argument between other Italian cities about the proposed nature of the event, before the eruption of Vesuvius in 1906 meant a change of venue became essential. Ironically, the decision-making was done by the Olympic Committee while they attended an 'unauthorised' Interim Games. This was held in Athens in 1906, an attempt by the Greek authorities to convince the world that they alone should be the 'eternal' venue. It was a critical time for de Coubertin. Faced with one location in Greece which was desperate to host the Games, two others which had failed and a third which had agreed and then pulled out, the easiest option would have been to assent to Greece's wishes. However, de Coubertin was not a man given to take the easy option.

In the British fencing team at the time (nicknamed the Knights) was a multitalented aristocratic athlete named Willie Grenfell, later Lord Desborough. Public school and Oxbridge educated, the best man at his wedding had been the Prince of Wales, now King. When the Greek Government invited Government representatives from Britain to their Interim Games at short notice, Desborough was one of those named.

Desborough's presence in the team transformed the interest in the event in Regency London and, as luck would have it, the Royal Family was holidaying in Greece at the time of the event. The King's excursion to view his friend's fencing contest against Germany, which ended in a resounding British victory, set the seal on his fervour. He enthusiastically agreed to support a plan to bail out the IOC and hold the 1908 Games in London. Importantly, while the King offered to support the plan, he stopped short of providing financial assistance.

The second influential partner in securing the Games was the Reverend Robert de Coursey Laffan. Laffan became a friend of de Coubertin after an encounter in July 1897, when he addressed an Olympic conference at Le Havre in perfect French. He spoke regarding the moral uses of sport, arguing that it was the means whereby man came to know himself better. De Coubertin recognised he had found 'a collaborator of the most invaluable kind'. Laffan was a headmaster of a public school and classically-educated. Before he left Le Havre he had been co-opted onto the International Olympic Committee and would remain a member for the next 30 years.

Rebecca Jenkins describes him as, 'an eloquent Irish dreamer disguised as a slightly pompous man with an almost obsessive eye for detail.' The combination of big dreams and a focus on detail were huge assets given the need to reinvent an Olympic movement.

Armed with the monarch's endorsement and backed by the formidable organisational talents of Laffan, Lord Desborough returned home to seek agreement of all the sporting bodies who would be involved. He returned to confirm that Britain would accept the challenge to produce the necessary facilities within the 24 months at their disposal. If there was any contention regarding the take-up of the challenge, it was soon dispelled when the sporting bodies were indemnified against loss subject only to agreeing to hand over 75% of their takings during the two weeks of the Games. This was a critical vote of confidence.

The biggest issue for the British would be the absence of a venue sufficiently large and flexible to host the event. There was a school of thought that a World Fair could be a centrepiece, although this was just the flaw which had brought the Olympic Games to the brink at both the Paris and St Louis events. From a financial perspective the Games represented a huge risk for the British, but the British philosophy at the time was that there was almost nothing they could not achieve if they set their minds to it. Ultimately fortune favoured the brave and in a situation that would find an echo in London in 1948, opportunity threw up an entrepreneur who would rise to the challenge. His name was Imre Kiralfy. His very first contribution was to engineer the indemnity which ensured that the sporting bodies had nothing to lose in signing up to the Games.

Kiralfy was a master of spectacle having spent his youth performing acrobatic Magyar folkdances all over the world. Much like the Michael Flatley Riverdance phenomenon, Kiralfy built a name for himself in America as an impresario of vast dance-based spectaculars. He spent years in private planning for an ultimate spectacle and signature production and the opportunity came with the Anglo French Exhibition. The brief was to outstrip the 1851 exhibition at the Crystal Palace on a site seven times its size, a location still known as White City.

Plans were fairly well advanced for the 1907 Exhibition when Desborough and Kiralfy found one another. The outcome was agreement to move the exhibition to 1908, to create a purpose-built arena within the site and therefore create the opportunity to demonstrate what every true Edwardian believed, that the principles of sport had been forged on the playing fields of the English aristocracy. This might not have been the premise under which Dover and Penny Brookes innovated, but it was central to the delivery of the 1908 Games.

If we think about the British role in defining the rules of chess at the Great Exhibition, it is clear that the prize at stake in the case of London 1908 was control of the rules of many of the sporting games which so far had developed rather haphazardly. Almost the first action was the definition of the rules for all the events being undertaken. At a time when communications were improving on all fronts and most sports encountered regional differences at every turn, this was the opportunity for the British to provide definitions and rules for the Games for the world. Somewhat unsurprisingly, London 1908 was the first Games where competitors were truly defined as part of a national team.

Desborough's good fortune did not stop at meeting Kiralfy. The Pathé Brothers Cinematograph Booth was one of the sideshows in the Franco Exhibition grounds which housed the stadium. As a result, the Games were immortalised forever as the first where colour movies of the events were recorded. Their cameramen were reputed to have shot 80 miles of colour film from the Exhibition each day and events in the stadium formed part of that footage. Further still, international publicity for events at the Games was enhanced by the newspaper circulation war going on in the USA. Sports pages were expanding, with photos and cartoons prominent together in an increasingly vivid style of reporting on the progress of the American team.

There were several important legacies from London's first Olympic Games. The rules of the Games were established – not just the rules of individual sports, but also the premise of competition between international teams which continues to this day. London 1908 also gave birth to a broader form of news communication – beyond the domestic to the world at large via moving image and written word. Venues were created with an entrepreneurial zeal rather than as an after-thought. Finally, it also demonstrated that the Games could be used to demonstrate broader, more active and political messages to the world at large. This final legacy was initially positive in that it made other cities far more likely to want to stage the Games. However, it also represented a signficant weakness. It suggested the Olympic Games could, in the wrong hands, become a malleable entity which could be used for broader nationalistic means. This of course was not lost on Hitler's Germany in 1936 and several times subsequently.

Britain's sporting history has always been indelibly linked to its social conditions and, more recently, international standing. Its first three brushes with the Hellenic Olympic tradition ensured the revival of the tradition. At their most vibrant the Cotswold, Much Wenlock and London 1908 Games demonstrated the latent potential for the Olympic Games to ultimately become one of the world's biggest events. Most critically London in 1908 demonstrated (as in the Cotswolds and Much Wenlock before) that it was able to build a picture of what a different kind of Olympic sporting festival for the times might look like. In doing so, it had breathed life into a flagging Olympic movement which was one poor Games away from ruin.

Despite all this, and although emboldened by London 1908, in reality the Olympic movement before the Second World War remained little more than a political and sporting plaything of the aristocracy. After the disaster of Berlin 1936 and then the Second World War, the Olympic movement was once again on the verge of collapse. It was time for Britain to step in once again.

Our journey through time moves on now to London 1948. While we travel 40 years in doing so, many of the themes we have encountered over the first few thousand years of our journey travel with us. We will be reminded in 1948 of the political importance of sport; its ability to engage huge audiences amidst a culture of social division; its broader educational value and the scale of commercial opportunity it represents. These themes are just as central to the narrative of London 1948 and the evolution of sport in Britain as to the modern Olympic movement.

PART TWO

London in 1948

'The working man… is far more interested in sport than politics, and can't stand preaching or moralising.'

Ferdynand Zweig

3

Facing the Challenge

It would be all too easy to assume that the euphoria of the end of the War persisted through to 1948, amidst perhaps the odd economic difficulty. We could imagine the British population being swept along by a wish to demonstrate a British position as a world power once again through the hosting of the Olympic Games. Much of the writing at the time reinforced this view, supported by the Government of the day. Only many years later are the threads of background difficulties being fully understood and the extent of the domestic propaganda becoming a little clearer.

Post-war recovery was a path already well trodden by early 20th Century generations. Many recalled their experiences after the 1914-18 War, where the 'land fit for heroes' returned to the old order pretty quickly. The sense of 'old order' meant that the previous class divisions remained firmly in place and a depressed economy continued to fail those already existing on or below the poverty threshold well into the 1920s.

Recall of the demobilisation organisation after 1914-18 was still firmly lodged in the folk-memory of the day and served to haunt many of the four million whose demobilisation approached this time around. Government in the early 1940s was not unaware of the significance of the issue and while there was not consensus on to how to proceed, plans were in place to address the challenges which might arise. It would be questionable today whether modern Britain could cope with four million 'new' people being assimilated into the current infrastructure. While the soldiers were in fact citizens who had been away to fight and were now returning, often they were not welcomed back but viewed as an incremental burden on a society without enough food, jobs or infrastructure to comfortably absorb them.

Post-1945, initial feelings about the US's supportive intervention in hostilities soon dissipated as the interest rates on the huge loans they provided began to bite. These added to the difficulties of an economy already creaking under the strains of a worldwide depression. While delivering the war effort was the principal objective before 1945, there had also been an undercurrent of planning for the new world order surprisingly early on during the war. In many ways the Second World War was an altogether different sort of campaign, not least in that the large numbers of the troops necessary for combat spent extensive time waiting for the action to commence. Just as with an elite athlete preparing for competition, there was a limit to the amount of preparation that could be conducted without contributing to both mental and physical staleness. As a consequence, training courses were introduced for the troops which addressed more general issues of how a better future might be achieved. The intention was to boost morale. However, the impact was to raise aspirations of what might be possible in post-war Britain.

It was an unexpected success that undermined the planned orderly return to civilian national lifestyle. Victory in Europe in May 1945 meant the potential for some of the armed forces to swiftly return to civilian life. It had been anticipated that the war with Japan would continue for two years but in August 1945 the dropping of the atomic bomb on Hiroshima, and another subsequently on Nagasaki, meant the end of hostilities. This presented an almost insurmountable challenge for a British nation with high expectations of a post-war world, but no realistic plan for achieving them.

Four million service personnel were demobilised between June 1945 and January 1947. Pressure on housing was exacerbated by the fact that three quarters of a million units of the national housing stock had been destroyed or made uninhabitable. Of the planned 500,000 temporary prefabricated homes promised in 1944, only 155,000 were actually built between 1945 and 1949. Within two weeks of the cessation of hostilities, the US withdrew the Lend-Lease facility, the financial support which had underpinned Britain through the war.

The social implications of the returning heroes also hit hard on many fronts. Whatever the hardships they encountered, these individuals were returning from an organised lifestyle with bed and board a given to what was to all intents and purposes a foreign land. Finding somewhere to live was dependant upon the housing circumstances which had been available before the war remaining intact. The Olympic Games created an additional need for temporary accommodation for international visitors, which increased the resentment towards the Games in some quarters.

The greatest challenge for returning War heroes was to successfully reintroduce the person they had become to the people they left behind, who themselves had changed over the years of separation. Divorce rates doubled between 1939 and 1945, despite the social stigma which came with this. By 1947 divorces had reached five times the 1945 figure. Returning prisoners of war were directed to Civil Resettlement Units for 're-orientation and recovery'. Twenty centres were planned, handling 20,000 men over six months. Given the numbers held behind enemy lines were over 170,000, the Government described its plans as 'modest'. 'Insufficient' would have been a more accurate description. Understanding of psychological trauma was limited at best. In the US and the Commonwealth there was a far greater understanding of the problems that could be faced by ex-servicemen returning without any visible injury. As Turner and Rennel say in their book *When Daddy Came Home*, it was 'a sobering thought that the standards of treatment achieved by the Americans after the First World War were still beyond the British after the Second.'

Every war has its casualties and this one was no different. The story of the development of the Stoke Mandeville facility under Dr Ludwig Guttmann is covered later in this book. It is important to recall that the physical casualties of this war were really guinea pigs for his innovative treatment at such an early stage of the understanding of disability. They were certainly not the fortunate beneficiaries of public healthcare provision at the standard we recognise today. While we can look with the benefit of hindsight and suggest they were the luckier casualties of war, if such a thing exists, it was certainly not clear at the time that would be the case. Paraplegic and quadraplegic casualties generally failed to survive beyond a matter of months and were often hidden from the view of the general public.

Rationing was also a reality which continued to become harsher. The issue was not simply the paucity of nutritious food available for all, but also the sheer tedium and complexity of the process. Queuing was endemic, and local knowledge was required to achieve the best results. This made sporting preparation particularly challenging. Rations were smaller for civilians than for the military.

Promises made during the conflict were broken. In particular, a 'priority return' to jobs previously held before the war stumbled when faced with logistical impracticalities and local political influences. Finding a job which matched the skills honed in the forces usually proved impossible. Having a formal trade was no protection from the rigours of finding work, even in a nation rebuilding its infrastructure. The British Olympic Association archives relating to London 1948 provide an insight to the lack of financial benefit to having a trade. The papers for the Exhibition of Olympic Art which was held alongside London 1948 show the budgeted cost for a programme seller at £5 per week. The same budget outlines a cost for a carpenter at £1 per day. Despite the skills required to build the Games requiring years of experience, there was simply no financial benefit in having them if you could be hired and fired on a daily basis. Tom, the grandfather and father of authors Matt and Martin respectively, was a time-served carpenter living in London. The reality of his working life at that time was to wait outside the builders' merchant on a borrowed bike, carrying his tools. He followed any lorry carrying timber to its destination, recognising that they had not only the materials but also the necessary licences to offer the chance of work.

While the infrastructure work linked to London 2012 is creating thousands of jobs and making a meaningful contribution to the construction industry at a time of financial hardship, the use of existing venues in London 1948 did little or nothing to help a working population who were psychologically scarred, undernourished and under-utilised.

Within Britain there was an understanding that success could not have been achieved without the intervention of its most prominent ally. However, as the relationships became more frosty and the cost of the loans provided by America made deep inroads into the potential for speedy recovery, there was an underlying misgiving that too high a price had been paid already. All rights to British advances in radar, antibiotics, jet aircraft, and nuclear technology had been handed over without any prospect of compensation. Britain returned a socialist government with a resounding majority in 1945.

Initially the new UK government, without whose support the Games could not go ahead, were somewhat swept up in the general euphoria for a brave new world opening before them and therefore very enthusiastic about what the Games could do for the nation. The opportunity to regain centre stage on a world platform, 'seeking peace through sport' while earning much-needed foreign currency to contribute towards economic recovery was a great temptation. Cabinet Office archives record that in January 1946 Ernest Bevin, the Foreign Secretary, responded to BOA Chairman Lord Portal's plan to stage the games by indicating, 'I should warmly welcome this proposal.' This was just the beginning of the debate.

If Britain just about survived the test of war, it was certainly not clear that its society would be able to withstand the rigours of peace. One immediate solution to the challenges of the day was sport and entertainment. Sport offered the excitement of competition wrapped in the certainty of rules known and understood. While many elements of British society changed beyond measure after the Second World War, sport remained a constant.

David Kynaston in his book *A World to Build* records a unique study conducted by Ferdynand Zweig during this time. The study itself was 'conducted in pubs, parks, cafés, dog racing stadiums', wherever he could get men to talk freely. His work became a portrait of the English working class at the time. He suggests that, 'A working man is a great realist. He sees life as it is, with constant ups and downs.' In the vast majority of cases he found they believed 'life is what you make it'. Zweig discovered a world of little jealousy, and an attitude to money which was defined in terms of being able to afford the essentials – 'beer, smokes, and food'. He shows a class of British society that 'is far more interested in sport than politics, and can't stand preaching or moralising.'

In the post-war economy, sport and the cinema were about the only thriving elements. The British had a very varied sporting appetite but attended events in their droves. In August 1945 at White City Stadium, 40,000 were locked out as 50,000 attended an athletics meeting featuring Sydney Wooderson competing against two Swedish middle-distance runners. Meanwhile at Lord's the ground was full, with 10,000 locked out, ten minutes after the start of the Fourth Victory Test.

Football, since the days of 'volkball' the sport of the working man, resumed with the FA Cup in 1945/6. The Football League resumed in the 1946/7 season when the top three divisions attracted 35 million paying spectators. Numbers peaked at 41 million in the 1948/49 season. This compares to less than 30 million today. The visit of Moscow Dynamo attracted huge crowds, but all records were exceeded in 1947 by Great Britain versus Europe at Hampden Park in Scotland when 500,000 applied for tickets and 134,000 attended what was in reality simply an exhibition match.

On 16 July 1947 27,000 turned out to see a British and Empire Heavyweight Title boxing contest. A bout for the British Empire Featherweight Title broadcast by the BBC from the Royal Albert Hall clashed with a broadcast by Clement Atlee reporting on the state of the nation with predictable results. Subsequent surveys of those between 30 and 55 suggest most had opted for the boxing.

The public mindset regarding boxing in post-war Britain was a far cry from the current day. There was immense interest in the professional rather than Olympic amateur side of the game, with National and Commonwealth titles held in high regard. No sporting compendium of the period was complete without extensive coverage of the stars of the ring. It was regarded as a working class sport, but one which opened the doors for the lowest levels in society to achieve fame and fortune. The authors' own family experience perhaps lends an insight into the mood of the day.

Author Matt's maternal grandfather, Charles, was with the British forces which ultimately received the German surrender in Norway. He was based there for some months after the war while they assisted in the return to normality. During the period of occupation, they published a local forces newspaper, *The Arctic Times*, to boost morale. With the aim of 'fostering good relationships with the locals' there were a series of boxing events where service teams competed against locals. The sport was respected as a demonstration of strength, skill and courage on the part of the contestants and, by inference, also of those they represented. It would be hard to imagine British troops boxing locals in Afghanistan or Iraq today.

The crossover point between amateur boxing and the professional game was also a well-frequented space. Fairs that toured the country inevitably included a boxing booth, which was usually manned by teams of ex-professionals still well known enough to attract a crowd. The opposition was provided by locals who volunteered to take them on. These locals were rewarded (only) if they survived an agreed number of rounds. Our carpenter Tom hailed from the West of Ireland and on occasion would use the significant skills he learnt in Ballina Boxing Club to supplement his income during this tough post-war period by comfortably out-lasting the ex-professionals.

As time has passed, the esteem in which boxing is held has diminished and it has always seemed the least likely of the Olympic sports to survive into the 21st century. Perhaps its salvation is due to the fact it is often perceived as one of the few sports which remains truly amateur today. It continues to provide the least privileged with a platform at the Games. The entry of female boxing at London 2012 will provide another dimension. Dr Mike Loosemore has been British Olympic Boxing Team Doctor for the last three Olympic Games, and sat ringside as James de Gale boxed his way to gold. He says, 'The boxing guys are fantastic to work with. They don't have a lot and as a result are really grateful for the support they get. The opportunity boxing offers them is enormous. Tony Jeffries, who won a medal in Beijing, used to flip burgers at Sunderland – he is a huge football fan. After Beijing, he was invited into the Directors' box.'

While sport attendances were vast when a game or match was actually held, there were only limited opportunities to actually watch live sport in 1948. Power shortages and the bitter winter of 1947 resulted in a midweek ban on all sports. Most were lifted in the spring of 1948, but bans on midweek football remained until the end of the season, as did the ban for greyhound racing, the bête noire of the intellectual classes. This was particularly badly received in Britain as it was regarded as austerity for its own sake. Given this context, it was clear that attendance at the Games was never really in doubt, and that the events might bring a much-needed boost to morale on the back of a bitter winter, power shortages, sporting bans and the like. Attendances were more than just important to drive morale, however. As we shall see, the pent-up demand for entertainment in general, and sport in particular, gave London 1948's Organising Committee the belief they could deliver a Games which would still be financially viable in a time of such austerity.

4

International Instability and Domestic Crisis

There was a delicate balance of power between the once united Allies in the Post War period. Great Britain, the United States, France and the Soviet Union all had different nuances in their future planning and, in the case of the United States and the Soviet Union, opposing economic structures of capitalism and communism.

Against this backdrop Britain's international standing was becoming increasingly important in the decision making as to whether it really should host the Games. In a secret memorandum issued on 25 March 1947, Philip Noel-Baker, Secretary of State for Air, and Harold Wilson, Secretary for Overseas Trade, wrote, 'If the Games are to be held in this country, it is essential to our national prestige that they should be a success; and as we are committed to holding them here, the Government should give all possible assistance in assuring their success.' Inward investment was important but, just as in London 1908, so was international standing.

Germany was divided into quarters allowing each ally to run its division by a military government until a suitable national government could be devised. The divided Germany, under the supervision of the Allied Control Council or ACC, was to become the first battleground of the emerging Cold War between the United States and the Soviet Union. Berlin was particularly vulnerable, situated as it was in a position totally within the Soviet allocated area. Food rations in some parts of Germany were being cut to 900 calories a day, far below the recommended daily allowance for adequate nutrition.

In September 1947, the United States, Great Britain and France combined their zones into one military province with the aim of providing economic stability as the German recession worsened. In early 1948, a new four-power currency was proposed. The Soviets, however, refused to accept the new currency and their delegation stormed out of a meeting in March. Both sides waited for the other to make a move until finally, on 18 June, the other three sectors established their own currency. In an effort to push the West out of Berlin, the Soviets countered by requiring that all Western convoys bound for Berlin and travelling through Soviet Germany be searched. The Trizone, as it became known, refused to accept the right of the Soviets to search their cargo. On 27 June, a matter of days before doves were due to fly at Wembley to mark the opening of the Olympic Games, the Soviets cut all surface traffic to West Berlin. Shipments by rail and the autobahn came to a halt. A desperate Berlin, faced with starvation and in need of vital supplies, looked to the West for help.

To counter the blockade, the western powers organised and airlifted a total of 2,326,406 tons of food, coal, passengers, and other items into the city in a total of 278,228 flights. The mission was a success. The Soviets did not respond to the airlift by trying to stop it, probably because they believed that they would either have failed or triggered another war. At the height of the airlift, planes flew around the clock in four hour blocks, taking off and landing every 90 seconds. At any given time there were 32 aircraft in the air. The London 1948 Games Olympic Ceremony took place on 28 July 1948, just one month after the Berlin Airlift had begun.

The blockade of Berlin lasted 11 months. Berlin became a symbol of the Allied resolve to stand up to the Soviet threat without being forced into a direct conflict. At a time of significant national economic debt, the airlift had been carried out at a cost of $345 million to the Americans, £17 million to the English, and 150 million Deutschmarks to the Germans. The Soviets did not compete at London 1948. However, they travelled to London and watched avidly, noting what was necessary to ensure sporting success as they actively competed with Britain on an altogether different level thousands of miles away. Russia exploded onto the sporting stage in 1952. Their impact on the public and political mood at the time of London 1948 was arguably all the greater from thousands of miles away.

Even without ongoing international instability, things would have been little calmer at home. Behind the move towards socialism ignited by the 1945 General Election victory was an overwhelming desire to 'move the control of industry into the hands of the working man'. The new government forged ahead with nationalisation, believing it represented not only the solution to many of their ills, but also that they carried the populace with them. Unfortunately, it proved misguided on both counts. An example of the ills of the day can be found in the mining industry, one of the first industries to be brought under government control.

When the war started, the mining industry was 600,000 strong and a reserved occupation, but the option of military service was permitted. It speaks volumes that 36,000 immediately chose military service over mining, with the result that by 1943 conscription was used to fill the places of those who had departed to fight. Ten per cent of those conscripted between the ages of 18 and 25 were directed to the mines. Many were not released until some years after the war.

Despite the continued efforts of those miners, the country was still suffering from shortages of power. This impacted on far more than the sporting calendar. The socialist government initially hoped that output would receive a surge as a result of an emotional connection with political change, however this was never apparent. Other nationalised industries experienced the same industrial conflict and moderate productivity. The emotional estrangement from politics by the growing middle classes continued apace, in much the same way as Middle Britain today struggles to come to terms with modern day politics on the back of an expenses scandal that has arguably changed our perception of our public servants for years to come.

As the days and weeks passed, the political and economic situation continued to deteriorate. This created an increasing amount of pressure on the Olympic authorities. As Daphné Bolz's excellent paper *Welcoming the World's Best Athletes: An Olympic Challenge for Post-War Britain* describes, behind the scenes discussions between the government and the Organising Committee became increasingly fractious. The decision to use military buildings for athlete accommodation was met by unambiguous opposition from within the Ministry of Works. They objected to the level of priority being afforded to the work and materials needed to re-purpose the buildings, arguing this went completely against the emergency programmes being run throughout the country. A letter from the Ministry of Works to the Cabinet Office admitted that 'only the involvement of Government policy and national prestige had enabled agreement.'

Doubts continued to surface. In September 1947 Edwin Plowden, Chairman of the new Economic Planning Board, had written to the Board of Trade, who were responsible for the Games, informing them that the government had a policy of economic cuts and that it wished to re-examine all current building projects, including those of the 1948 Games. Plowden asked, 'What would be the consequences of closing down the building work in preparation for the 1948 Olympiad, including the effect of a decision that the Olympiad should not be held, should that be the logical corollary?' The investigation was abandoned on the direct instruction of the Cabinet when it told Plowden, 'We should be very much opposed to any suggestion that the 1948 Olympiad should not be held in this country. I am sure if it were now decided to abandon the Games, the blow to our prestige would be very considerable and I do not know that for the moment it stands so high that it can stand more knocks.'

Hosting the Olympic Games in 1908 had been chiefly a challenge of statesmanship and influence against the backdrop of a to-date-impotent Olympic movement. The situation for London in 1948 was far more challenging. The only certainty was that the British public would mostly engage with and attend the event. This was the dimmest of lights at the end of a very long tunnel.

PART THREE

This is the Modern World

'The Olympic Games have caused the right seeds to be planted, but the economic weather will determine the extent to which they grow.'

Morgan Garfield

5

The London 2012 Olympic and Paralympic Games in Context

The central themes of the build up to the London 1948 Games – a troubled society; financial crisis; public debt; political upheaval and international instability – map directly across to London 2012. Of course many of these have been constants over the last 70 years. That said however, the starkness of the current public debt figures and recession, the combination of Britain's ongoing involvement in armed combat, political instability and pressing social crisis have been unprecedented since 1948.

Early 21st Century Britain has seen a return to many of the societal challenges felt during the mid-20th Century. The gap between rich and poor has grown rather than reduced over the last 40 years. For example, data from the Institute of Fiscal Studies from 2007/08 reported that inequality rose to its highest level since comparable data began in 1961, surpassing its previous peak in 2000/01. Over the period since 2004 the IFS suggests incomes of the poorest fifth of households have fallen by 2.6% after inflation, while the incomes of the richest fifth rose by nearly 3.3% on the same basis. Alastair Muriel, IFS Research Economist, has been quoted as suggesting that 'the recession may see poorer households regain some ground… but if history is any guide, average income growth is likely to slow even further across the population.'

While significant government investment in healthcare has been widely welcomed, and average life expectancy in the UK is increasing, there is a sense in which our nation is sicklier than in previous decades. Lack of physical exercise and poor diet are contributing to more bronchial and heart disease.

The international dimension of our working and leisure lives has led to faster spread of global epidemics. This has yet to hit the UK with the force we might have predicted a few years ago. However, parts of the food chain have already been hit. Bird flu, swine flu and mad cow disease have all threatened our health in the last 15 years. Epidemics are expected to become more, not less, of a threat. There is a perception, rightly or wrongly, that we are living longer because of the standard of healthcare provision and despite our increasingly poor diets.

Data published in April 2010 by the Department of Health found that binge-drinking and obesity were increasing so-called lifestyle illnesses such as liver disease and diabetes, while deaths from cancer and circulatory diseases were continuing to fall. The same study suggested that one in four adults in the UK is now classed as obese, twice as many as in France, Italy or Holland.

Britain's population has continued to grow in absolute terms and age on average. In 2007 the number of pensioners in the UK outnumbered the number of children for the first time. By 2030, it is estimated that over 45% of our population will be over 50 years of age. Whilst it is possible for the UK to absorb increases in population, this will not be feasible if we rely exclusively on the existing infrastructure of houses, roads, shops, GP surgeries and schools.

The pressures on the National Health Service are significant, which renders even more important the London 2012 Organising Committee's intent to build an event which drives a participation and health legacy from the Games. Britain needs to develop its ability to use sport as a means of prevention, to ensure that the NHS does not crack under an ever increasing need to cure.

Andy McGrath, Associate Director of Performance at NHS South Central Strategic Health Authority, joined the NHS relatively late in his career. He says, 'I was in banking for 22 years. I was stirred by an advert asking if I would like to help the NHS heal itself. Now in the NHS, I can see we need to embrace the 'more for less' culture – to become more efficient and productive. The critical need is to redesign patient pathways across the whole health economy. We need collaborative working between GP's, hospitals and social services, which isn't something that comes naturally to us. We need to become more commercially aware and consider how we can reduce cost to serve in a safe way. A focus on quality and safety is also necessary to bring down costs.' Of course there is no more straightforward way to reduce costs than through reducing demand on the NHS in the first place.

Budgetary pressure has placed increased emphasis not just on controlling NHS spending but all areas of the public purse. While the current scarcity of public and affordable housing is not as pressing as in 1948, deeper investment in the areas of social as well as affordable housing options is required. Chief opportunities to add housing are in out-of-town areas where jobs available are either scarce or remain principally manual and low-paid. Rising house prices have made it harder and harder to step onto the housing ladder – which in turn has widened the gap between social classes in the UK.

This is not a uniquely inner city challenge but it has created a greater imperative for maximum usage of current urban space. One of the principal arguments behind hosting the Olympic Games in London, and the chief driver of the overall budget figures for the Games, has been the potential regeneration of a forgotten part of Greater London. The Olympic Village – the central hub of the Games – will accommodate 17,000 athletes and officials during the Olympic Games and 6,500 during the Paralympic Games. Afterwards, the buildings will be converted into 3,800 homes. Games chiefs have pledged that 30% of this figure will be affordable housing – ranging from apartments to maisonettes and mews houses.

The legacy of the village will also include an education campus providing 120 nursery places, 840 primary school places and 900 secondary school places. The Olympic Delivery Authority is also planning a 2,800 square metre primary healthcare centre – the legacy of the 2012 athletes' healthcare facilities. While these seem relatively modest numbers, they will be critical to ensuring that a sustainable community can start to emerge once the flame has departed.

Of course the Olympic Park itself is simply one piece of the jigsaw. Recently the East End has been a ghost town, far removed from its origins growing out from the commercial hub of the docks and devoid of the kind of institutional investors which develop and own buildings and so drive much of the regeneration in this country. Morgan Garfield is a partner at Ellandi LLP, a business that invests in UK commercial real estate and financial products underpinned by UK property. He says, 'Decades of underinvestment in East London created a practical opportunity for London 2012 as a project – where else in London could you have bought and cleared acres of land to create an Olympic Park only seven minutes by train from the City? The scale of the project has the potential to leave a legacy of infrastructure and seed investment that could reunite the East of London with the capital's mainstream property market'.

As soon as London won the Olympic bid in 2005 there was an immediate interest in acquiring property in the Olympic area to benefit from the regeneration effect that the Olympic Games will produce. Many developers hoped to develop offices, retail, leisure and residential property to open with great fanfare in 2012 – Westfield Stratford City being the biggest example. Garfield recognises that not all of these hopes will come to fruition, saying, 'The credit crisis has meant that many projects failed to find financing at the critical stage in 2008/09. However, there has been sufficient public and private investment in property and infrastructure. Let's not kid ourselves, the area needs a significant amount of regeneration. However it now has momentum and is no longer a no-go area for the institutional capital required to foster this. We are also already seeing that the glow of the Olympic flame carries a good distance – the positive sentiment toward Stratford and the Olympic Park is helping to attract real estate investment to the entire eastern quadrant of the M25 and beyond into Essex and the Thames Gateway.'

While signs are initially promising, this potential legacy is still threatened by the aftermath of the credit crisis which might yet cause further competition for finance in the market. Garfield says, 'Typically when capital becomes tight, an established location will always win over a regeneration area so there is a risk that the shortage of debt available from banks for real estate projects may freeze the progress being made. The good news is that the Olympic Games have caused the right seeds to be planted from a property perspective, but the economic weather will still dictate the extent to which they flourish and grow.'

Alongside property regeneration for decrepid areas of London, transport and environmental concerns are also back on our radar. If one-way streets were invented to alleviate the perceived overcrowding of London thoroughfares in the run-up to the London 1948 Games, a question remains as to whether Ken Livingstone's legacy investments in public transport, congestion charging and cycling infrastructure will be enough to release London from its current traffic challenges. Investment into the tube, rail networks such as the Javelin and a higher speed Eurostar connection with the Continent have continued. The question is to what extent the projects which sit outside of the ring-fenced Games budget will be concluded given our public debt figures.

Beyond the short term unpleasantness of traffic and pollution levels, we are now more aware than ever of the broader impact of our lives on the environment. Britain arguably occupies a middle-of-the-pack position in terms of the green debate – neither pushing nor resisting the environmental agenda. Green concerns are certainly a newer phenomenon moving into this Olympic Games. Beijing brought the tensions between the environment and the Olympic Games to the fore like never before and any event which brings people together from across the globe through air travel is now likely to encourage a great deal of criticism. LOCOG has attempted to handle this debate proactively along with its partners, many of whom have the green agenda front and centre not just of their marketing plans, but their entire business strategy.

Richard Hughes, B2C Commercial Director at EDF Energy explains, 'It is very important that the Olympic Games are more than an enjoyable summer of sport in London, but that the same passion and ideals leave a lasting legacy on the country's health and carbon footprint. I hope the sustainable approach and forward-thinking being applied to London 2012 will be a model for future events. There are many parallels in these aspirations to those of EDF Energy. One of our founding companies in the UK was the London Electricity Board and we continue to be the largest electricity supplier to homes and businesses across London. But like the Games themselves, our scope and aspirations are much wider and more enduring. In 2009 we purchased British Energy and its nuclear generation fleet, making us the largest low carbon electricity generator in the country as a whole. We are also investing billions in building new nuclear power stations and aim to leave a low carbon legacy, powering the homes, transportation and lives of generations to come. We hope to commence building nuclear power stations in 2012 – when our race really begins.'

Of course the construction of the Olympic Park itself is not without environmental implications. The Organising Committee understandably point out that the land which is being used was deeply polluted before the construction began and so they are contributing towards a better future for this area of London as well as putting on a global festival of sport. Games promotional films regularly show footage of whole cars which have long been submerged on the Olympic Park site being plucked out of dingy canals. Indeed, the project to clean and clear the Olympic Park site ahead of construction was awarded the 'Greatest Contribution to London' award at the 2010 ICE London Civil Engineering

Awards. Before any work started on the Olympic Park site, LOCOG produced an Environment Statement which was part of the approved planning application for the Olympic Park. This looked at the likely significant effects of the Olympic Park project on the environment and the measures necessary to manage them. The report considered issues such as air quality, noise, ecology, water quality, flooding and transport. Critically these are not simply conditions which they set themselves, but also drip down through every element of the supply chain when any construction or support work is tendered for. Each contractor and even sub contractor has to prove their green credentials as part of the tendering process.

LOCOG's sustainability work sits alongside its environmental stance. This has been central to the Games from bid stage onwards. LOCOG committed to use venues already existing in the UK where possible, only build permanent structures that will have a long-term use after the Games and make use of temporary structures for everything else. Policies around waste management, biodiversity and the management of greenhouse emissions sit underneath this, and decisions such as using Wembley Arena for badminton rather than building a temporary structure continue to support this objective while handily saving funds at the same time. Instead of being criticised for climbing down on their initial plans, LOCOG have generally received plaudits for the austerity in cost-saving ventures such as these.

It is useful to look again at the experience of the Vancouver 2010 Winter Olympic Games when considering the potential environmental impact of a London Games. The Winter Olympic Games is regularly faced with significant challenges in this area because of the terrain in which it must take place. It is one thing to put on an Olympic Games in a polluted and forgotten area of a metropolis, but another thing entirely to try to deliver an environmentally sustainable Games in an area of outstanding natural beauty. As anyone who has bought organic food in a supermarket will know, being green often comes at a price. Vancouver organisers were faced with this challenge when procuring a catering contractor for 2010. Their final two bids were from a local firm of caterers and a multinational. The local firm's proximity to the park and local knowledge was a real good news environmental story. However, it did not have the economies of scale and years of experience that the multi-national corporate was offering. In the end the Vancouver Organising Committee brokered a consortium approach between the two parties, securing the carbon footprint and know-how of the local provider, but the buying power and experience of the global supplier. Anne Duffy, Sustainability Office for Vancouver 2010, was able to claim that through smart thinking on their part 'we found it possible to make a difference… in carbon, in waste, throughout our supply chain.' While this was undoubtedly true, the economics of compromise can really never be far from the forefront in delivering an Olympic Games. For example, the taxpayer liability from widening the access to Whistler through a tunnel rather than overland route was judged too high, despite the fact that the overland route chosen came at an ecological price.

Environmental concerns, of course, are a relatively new piece of the jigsaw puzzle for an Olympic organiser. The principal driver of this has been our increased awareness of the impact our own behaviour has on gas emissions and global warming. This change has been championed by a new generation born between 1980 and 1990 which has driven a change in our stance on many things, not least the environment. The organisers of London 2012 are acutely aware of the need to deliver for this generation, one which is central to leaving a sporting participation legacy in Britain.

This new generation values personal expression and individuality, it is opinionated, less circumspect and more willing and able to identify with authentic emotions and expressions from leaders in our society. They also prize authenticity in the brands and trends they follow. As Professor Mike Beverland from the University of Bath says, 'the degree of authenticity of a brand is an increasingly important predictor of purchasing decisions. In order to succeed, marketers now need to imbue their brands with the warts and all humanity we now crave and use the tools at their disposal to tell, and help others tell, stories.' The increasing influence of this generational shift is changing the way we think as a nation. There is no longer as strong a desire to be 'delivered to' or guided as there was in 1948. Now the consent to be led or directed is increasingly only given on the condition that a degree of individual choice and influence is a part of the process – success is increasingly defined as creating your own identity and travelling your own path. Divisions between work and leisure time are falling away as individuals expect to be able to perfom any task at any time rather than divide their days and their lives into segments. This is not a generation that will respond well to being told they should not be watching the Olympic Games on their laptops during work hours.

Technology and communications will be one of the themes we cover in more detail later in this book. It is important at this stage to note the impact this has already had on participation in sport in this country. There is a view that the so-called PlayStation Generation play less sport than previous generations, with a resultant impact on health, emerging obesity and so on. There are already a significant number of schemes cropping up which are intended to drive active participation in sport. For example, the Government Bike to Work scheme (which provides tax breaks for employees who wish to buy bikes to cycle rather than drive to work) has proved extremely popular. At a local level a host of additional schemes are cropping up, such as the London Cycle Hire scheme which encourages people to rent bicycles for short periods in Central London as a means of driving health and the green agenda. Buckinghamshire has a project called Fit for Life which aims to encourage people to take part in physical activity and more specifically overcome the concerns that many older people face when looking to become more active.

While the evidence of the impact electronic games are having on our active society is compelling, there is also a sense that we may just be starting to see a reversal in this trend away from active pursuits. Nintendo has been very successful in launching the Wii Fit series of games, which require active movement and so encourage activity and fitness. Progress is logged and stored online. Private healthcare providers are also working hard to incentivise active participation in sport, recognising this will keep people away from the doctor's surgery. Pru Health supplies a Fitbug to its members which tracks the number of steps taken each day. The more regularly these steps are taken, the more the member can access a host of additional benefits and even earn cash back on his or her policy.

6

The Political and Financial Landscape

British society in 2010 is probably best described as dazed and confused. It is dazed by the challenges of public welfare provision, green concerns, coalition government and the gap between rich and poor in a creaking economy. Similarly, it feels confused by changing demographics and an emerging disconnect between different groups in our population. As in 1948, the current level of political and financial crisis is particularly unsettling and a constant theme in the run up to the Olympic Games. Each time Britain has attempted to deliver an Olympic Games it has been necessary to build a unique economic model in order to meet the global and domestic economic demands of the day.

From a political perspective, as we will see, Britain's Labour politicians played a critical role in winning the Games for the country. Many of the domestic themes playing themselves out as we write in the post-New Labour phase of coalition government replicate similar frustrations Clement Atlee felt during the aftermath of his election victory. Cracks in class infrastructure, a frightening balance of payments and growing disillusionment with the current financial predicament are all familiar. The additional challenge we face today is a sense of disengagement with the role of politicians and politics on the back of the 2009 expenses scandal and practical concerns as to the genuine impact of a coalition government.

In 1948 public net debt was in or around 200% of our GDP, whereas today we are currently expecting it to peak at around 72%. This statistic does come with a health warning, given that our economy has also spent the majority of the last 60 years with a core focus on GDP growth. While not as high as in 1948, 72% is the highest percentage Britain has sustained since 1969 and certainly not to be underestimated in the context of faltering global confidence in the British pound.

Unemployment, too, is raising its head again. The 2010 General Election was undeniably fought on an economic theme – the then Chancellor and Shadow Chancellors debating as regularly as potential Prime Ministers. Despite this, the lack of firm policy for navigating the frightening balance of payments and double dip recession continue to concern big business way beyond the election itself as the coalition government attempts to get to grips with making their economic cuts a reality.

British business also had its own leading role in the turmoil the global economy felt over the last few years. One of the current London 2012 partners, Lloyds Banking Group, is in the unusual situation of being a partly taxpayer-owned commercial sponsor of a partly taxpayer-funded event!

Initial signs are that while coalition government might ultimately slow the pace of change in British politics, some of the meatier concerns of the British public are to be met head-on. Equally the current budget cuts proposed for the Olympic project do not seem large enough to make any serious dent in the event. One of the London team's key strengths so far has been the amount of core cross party support for the Olympic Games and some of the key figures in British Sport have taken a very apolitical stance. For example, Baroness Sue Campbell CBE (the Chair of UK Sport and the Youth Sports Trust) is a cross bench peer.

We do have one signpost for the impact the transition from Labour to Conservative might have on the Olympic Games in London as Ken Livingstone has been succeeded by Boris Johnson. While the role of London Mayor is somewhat removed from front line party politics, Livingstone's support for the Games (ostensibly as an independent candidate, albeit with strong Labour leanings) was fundamental to being able to provide a credible bid for the event. He is quoted in Mike Lee's excellent book *The Race for the 2012 Olympic Games* as saying, 'for me at that stage I didn't think we had a cat in hell's chance of winning. But I was thinking that this was a good chance to get some more money out of the Government for Londoners. So I bid on that basis. It wasn't really until the Athens Games in August 2004 that I thought we could do it.' From that moment on, however, Livingstone was an increasingly critical piece of the bid team. Lee himself explains, 'Seb Coe did not have political problems. Of course, Tessa Jowell and Ken Livingstone wanted to put over their particular aims for the bid but they always fitted their comments into the general narrative or message. Nobody was trying to upstage anybody else. The French did not appear to have the same teamwork.'

Arriving into the Olympic environment as the new Mayor of London, Boris had nothing to gain politically by complimenting Ken on his work. There is a symmetry in the fact that before becoming Mayor Boris was actually MP for a host venue for the London 1948 Games at Henley-on-Thames. Initial complaints about mismanaged budgets and inefficient management teams have now ceased as Boris recognises he will be better set portraying himself as the White Knight of the Games and delivering the legacy component for London rather than bickering and haggling around Livingstone's legacy all the way to 2012. As an example of this, he has recently launched the plan for Central London at Games-time which will include The London Pedestrian Strip, planned to stretch from Nelson's Column to Covent Garden and Leicester Square, decorated throughout with Olympic flags and banners. The area will be home to cultural festivities, bands and artistic performances. Additionally there will also be 100,000 tickets a day available for the general public for the four live sites in Hyde Park, Victoria Park, Jubilee Gardens and Potter's Gate. These live sites will offer a more informal way of watching the Olympic action with huge screens showing the daily action and other activities including concerts.

Johnson and the other Olympic bosses know that engaging the locals and encouraging a spirit of national support for the athletes goes directly to the heart of whether the Games are judged a success or not. He wants everyone to have a good time whether they manage to get their hands on Olympic tickets or not. He also wants the city looking smart and has £32 million budgeted for 'the look of the Games'. We can certainly expect more shots of him on his bicycle over the rest of his tenure after he announced the London Cycle Hire project which will include the rather grandly-titled Cycle Superhighway routes. Intriguingly, however, Ken Livingstone has suggested that he will stand for re-election in 2012, just before the Games come to town.

Tessa Jowell's role in delivering the Games to London also cannot be underplayed. Appointed Secretary of State at the Department for Culture, Media and Sport after the 2001 election, Jowell played a significant role in defining the Government position and ultimately strong support for the London

2012 bid. If Tony Blair was central to the victory in Singapore, as Mike Lee acknowledges, Jowell was certainly central to getting him there in person. Jowell retained her Olympic Games portfolio when demoted in Gordon Brown's first reshuffle, holding it until the 2010 Election. Heavily criticised for cost over-runs relating to the Games she finds herself, much like Ken Livingstone and her former boss Tony Blair, having been a key part of bringing the Games to London and yet unable to share in the spoils of a potentially successful event on the world stage. As with all things political, there will be differing views on Jowell's legacy. That said, perhaps the most fitting observation was that on the evening of the decision in London's favour, Lee describes her as being one of the last to leave the dancefloor along with Seb and a few remaining stragglers from the bid team.

Perhaps the most concerning element of political change is not the delivery of a world class Games, but the delivery of the legacy plan in each area. This is already a hot potato in London. The Olympic Park Legacy Company, headed by chief executive Andrew Altman and Labour peer Baroness Ford, was formed last year to handle the long-term management of the park – a move that had taken some of the Games' legacy responsibilities from the London Development Agency. Before the General Election Hugh Robertson, now Minister for Sport and the Olympic Games, questioned the extent to which the legacy plans were on track. His task is now to deliver them.

Things are even less clear outside the M25. The new Government has thus far been very explicit in its desire to abolish all but the commercial influence of SEEDA – the South East England Development Agency. SEEDA has taken a very active role in delivery of legacy components for the Games in the region such as training and development for those skills which will be needed to deliver the Games and also for the business and procurement opportunities which should theoretically spread out across the region from the chiefly London-focused main event. It is still unclear as to how these components will be delivered if SEEDA is all-but-abolished.

It is ironic that the scale of the taxpayer investment in the banking sector has probably led to less media scrutiny of the London 2012 budget than we might have expected. Even stories of budget overruns have tended to relate to the impact of falling property prices on the total Games budget as opposed to focussing on mismanagement of any sort.

Despite this period of relative calm in the media, it would be dangerous to understate the potential threat of financial instability in Britain as we enter the delivery phase for the Olympic Games just because the budget is dwarfed by larger public debt concerns. As Morgan Garfield described, the potential threat sits chiefly with the legacy ambition for the Games – from the importance of affordable housing as part of legacy plans for the Olympic Park to the viability of building another Westfield Shopping Centre on the perimeter.

The need for austerity shapes the context to the London 2012 Games, just as in 1948. Against this backdrop the appointment of a Chief Executive with a sound financial background seems particularly prescient. Paul Deighton joined LOCOG after 22 years at Goldman Sachs. Chairman Seb Coe and Vice Chairman Keith Mills pushed hard for someone with a profile which was very different to a traditional Chief Executive of an Organising Committee. Rightly they decided to look for someone whose skillset might dovetail with their own. Paul leaves the politics to Seb and focuses on delivering LOCOG's commitments against the harsh current commercial reality. LOCOG has a budget of some £2bn, with between £650m and £700m to come from private sponsorship. The rest is made up of a share of broadcasting rights and worldwide sponsors' revenues, both of which flow from the IOC, in addition to domestic merchandising and ticket revenue. Deighton's role is to work alongside the Olympic Delivery Authority (ODA), which is in charge of building venues and acts as the regeneration body for the Olympic Park. Actually the overall publicised Games budget of £9.3bn (which comes partly from public funds through a combination of central taxation, council tax and lottery funds in addition to LOCOG's commercially generated contribution) includes a vast amount of legacy development of the local area, however this is not a newsworthy angle for the media.

Having wisely bitten the bullet with regards to the sizeable budget for the Olympic Games very early on, London has a little breathing room. However, ongoing financial pressures in the UK economy will take their toll and need to be planned for. A recent Government spending watchdog progress report warns 'previous experience shows that financial pressures and risks are likely to occur right up to the Games.' This could see further demands on the contingency fund. Last year £621 million of contingency funding was spent when construction of the Olympic Village and the media centre became entirely publicly funded after plans for private financing collapsed in the economic downturn.

Just as 1948 was a time of international instability despite the end of the Second World War, so we feel the same sense of uncertainty today. Britain continues to be at war in Afghanistan and pulled into an abstract conflict in Iraq – with little prospect of true resolution of either in the short term. There continues to be an impact on the British consciousness and conscience as the death toll and financial costs mount. While this clearly has nowhere near the same impact as the Berlin Airlift and emerging threat of Russia had after 1945, the fact that Britain is effectively at war with extremist terrorism in general, and Al Quaeda in particular, could yet have more propensity to play itself out in the events of the Games themselves. Increased security remains a significant additional expense for future Olympic Games and particularly for one to be held in London.

The security dimension of London 2012 requires an extraordinary level of planning and coordination at a national level with the Home Office, the Association of Chief Police Officers, the Metropolitan Police Service, the Government Olympic Executive (GOE), Department for Transport, London Fire Brigade and Ambulance and various other agencies involved in Central London safety and security. The events outside Central London also require liaison with police authorities in Dorset, Essex, Hertfordshire and the Thames Valley where events such as sailing, mountain biking, flat water canoeing and rowing will take place.

Even this of course is just the start. National teams will be arriving for training camps up and down the length of the country with the extra commercial opportunities and logistical pressure this can create at a local level. Usain Bolt and Jamaica are heading to Birmingham. Both Britain and Japan are heading to Loughborough. Each of these will bring increased local security and policing requirements. The United States, Iran, Iraq, North Korea and Afghanistan have yet to show their hands. That said, training camps bring with them a large amount of prestige and the interest from local authorities in hosting them has been significant.

Not every region can necessarily hope to host the biggest nations, because not every region has the benefit of such comprehensive facilities as Loughborough. Ian Barham, who manages the Buckinghamshire efforts for

London 2012 in partnership with Neil Gibson at Bucks County Council, has aspirations for his local area. He says, 'At the outset the Bucks 2012 group put significant efforts into ensuring that many of our venues were included in the official guide. We have worked to promote these venues to International Olympic and Paralympic Committees. This involves official launch events at the Beijing Olympic and Paralympic Games, hosting international visits by National Olympic and Paralympic Committee delegates and of course competitions at Buckinghamshire venues and by maintaining ongoing correspondence with interested nations. What has become increasingly apparent has been the desire of nations to ensure their athletes are made welcome and also get a rounded experience. In addition to the sporting facilities, they are also seeking access to educational opportunities, meaningful competition, places to visit and to practice their religious beliefs.'

Buckinghamshire has already secured nations as diverse as Papua New Guinea, Colombia, Finland, Uganda and Saudi Arabia, each bringing very distinct cultures and levels of policing challenge.

Away from the leafy Shires and back in London, the Metropolitan Police plan is very significant in scope. One of the big challenges is that the world does not stop when the Games come to town. In the Summer of 2012, the Metropolitan Police are also required to plan for a Diamond Jubilee, the Rathayatra Procession, Wimbledon tennis and the usual flood of Spring/Summer weekend music events in Hyde Park. All this stands on the calendar even before those connected to the Olympic Games themselves have begun. In July, World Pride, Party in the Park, the Respect Festival and Bermondsey Beat are core elements of the schedule. Not to mention the Notting Hill Carnival in the Olympic period itself and then the beginning of the 2012/13 football season. All Police leave during the Olympic and Paralympic Games has already been cancelled. The reality of the challenge dictates extraordinary measures.

Nothing can be left to chance come London 2012 and the detailed scenario planning is already well underway. The Met are working on a resource of 9,000 officers during the Games which they believe will be enough. Their busiest normal day of the year is the Notting Hill Carnival which requires a total of 6,000 officers to be on duty. They are already introducing some innovative schemes to increase resources, such as recruiting and training a corporate intake of UK PLC employees as Community Support Officers. They are actively targeting London-based businesses with this particular scheme on the basis that the skills learnt policing the Games will transfer back into the workplace. The current assumptions around policing numbers and hence budget reflect a security threat very common to the prevailing level post 7th July bombings, and the Met also have additional resources and plans at hand in case this rises further. Test events and incidents will form a significant part of their scenario planning for the Games themselves. One of the untold stories relating to the criticality of the sporting infrastructure delivering athletes and spectators on time is that the longer the authorities have to use them for test situations in advance of the Games, the safer the Games themselves will be.

As ever, the Games sit as a potential plaything on that fine line between international politics and international instability. Russia, the emerging political power in 1948, was not invited to the 1948 Games as it had declined to join the International Olympic Committee. An athlete of the day reflected the often brutal pragmatism of the competitor when suggesting: 'This was a very good thing for us non Russian athletes, because they were already capable of winning a significant number of medals four years before they actually did so in Helsinki.' Inevitably there will be boycott and security threats as the 2012 Games approach.

The principal Communist state in today's world is China. This vast nation and host of the 2008 Games will not only be invited in 2012, it will most likely top the medal table. Chinese growth has been stilted by financial instability in recent years, but only to the extent that GDP growth has been closer to 5% per annum than an incredible 10%. The inevitable tensions this creates against a backdrop of global recession are playing themselves out in areas such as the environment, but will increasingly dominate the international political agenda as we draw closer to the Games.

Even if the London Games are not boycotted, international tensions will still have have the propensity to make themselves evident in the day-to-day running of the Games, in particular in such an internationally diverse culture and democratic society as Britain. The London leg of the Beijing torch relay was just one which turned into chaos as a result of protesters against China's relationship with Tibet. Similar protests around Britain's recent international aggression in Iraq and Afghanistan appear inevitable.

The London 2012 Torch Relay will take the torch a significant distance across the UK and itself require sensitive management. The Relay starts with the flame being ignited at the site where the temple of Hera used to stand in Olympia, Greece. After five days in Greece, the torch will be transported to the UK for a total of 70 days between May-July 2012, ending with five days in London. The relay will spend four days in both Northern Ireland and Scotland and then a minimum of three days in each of the regions in England and Wales. Not only does the torch itself need to be policed, but just as critically also the evening events which are planned at each stop of the torch. The Met Police have been given the rather thankless responsibility for the security of the torch and local police forces will be responsible for the safety and security of the ceremonies themselves. These offer another opportunity for local areas to monetise Britain's hosting of the Games, something Canada did extremely successfully at Vancouver 2010.

THE SEARCH FOR OLYMPIC TALENT.

THE SQUIRE INSISTS UPON HIS CLAY BIRDS BEING THROWN BY HAND IN THE HOPE OF DISCOVERING A BORN DISCUS-THROWER.

Class has never been far away from the Olympic debate in Britain.
(© *Punch Magazine*, July 30, 1913)

Sylvia Cheeseman (now Disley) – from promising Sixth Form athlete to Olympic medallist, featured on a series of cigarette cards in advance of the London 1948 Olympic Games. (© *British American Tobacco*)

I

Official Poster of the London 1948 Olympic Games.
(© IOC / Olympic Museum Collections)

Crowds and uniformed competitors approach Elvin's own Olympic Stadium at Wembley in 1948 for the Opening Ceremony. The British population had been starved of live sport in the run-up to the Games.
(© *IOC / Olympic Museum Collections*)

The American cycling team on the deck of the SS America on the way to compete in London in 1948. The rollers used to keep cyclists in condition on the voyage are still used today. (© *IOC / Olympic Museum Collections*)

BBC cameras capture the action live in the Olympic Stadium in 1948.
(© IOC / Olympic Museum Collections)

A rare example of branding in the Olympic Stadium draws attention to OMEGA's
innovative timing technology, which was trialled in London 1948.
(© IOC / Olympic Museum Collections)

Shooting of Rank's Official Film of the London 1948 Olympic Games, an entrepreneurial innovation which paid dividends.
(© *IOC / Olympic Museums Collection*)

Early Pioneers – Archery, one of the very first sports to take place at Stoke Mandeville Hospital. (© *WheelPower*)

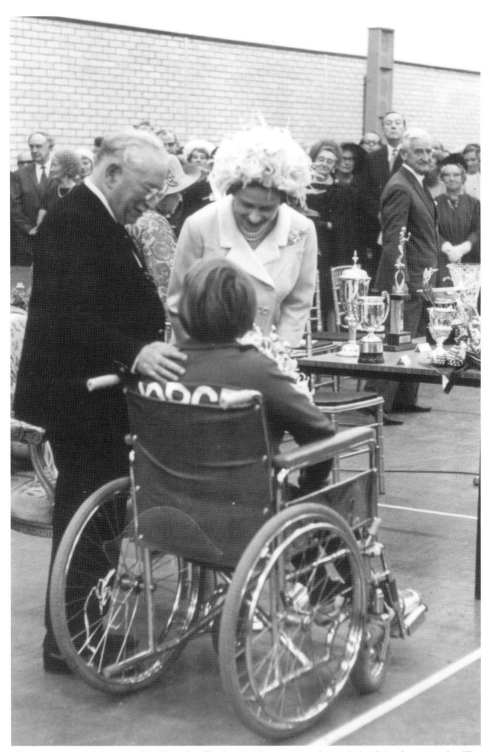

The Queen visiting Stoke Mandeville in 1969 to open the original Stoke Mandeville Stadium, seen here with an athlete and Sir Ludwig Guttmann. (© *WheelPower*)

After Stoke Mandeville intervenes at short notice to save the Paralympic Games of 1984, Iceland parade at the Opening Ceremony. (© *WheelPower*)

Competition begins in earnest in 1984 with the table tennis.
(© *WheelPower*)

7

The Question of Legacy

As we have seen, one of the drivers behind hosting the Olympic Games in London 1948 was to generate a short term diversion from the clear and present challenges at home and abroad through the medium of sport. While sport in itself might not have offered a solution, it did provide a release. Ultimately London 1948 kick-started some fundamental societal shifts, as we shall later see; however there is no real evidence that any of these were consciously intended outcomes of the Games themselves.

This points to a critical difference between London 1948 and London 2012. The reason that London decided to bid for the right to host the 2012 Games was its educated bet that sufficient long term sustainable benefits would be generated through hosting the Olympic and Paralympic Games in order to justify the investment. The bid was predicated on using the Olympic Games as an agent for long term social change rather than the short term mood lifting which was certainly evident with the hosting of our last major sporting event, Euro 2000 Football. The level of engagement which could be generated by elite sporting events was important – but only in so far as it drove the broader population to actively engage in playing sport and ensured the development of a stronger sporting infrastructure in Great Britain in general. Rehabilitation of a polluted and forgotten area of East London was a critical part of the plan. Similarly, since the onset of the bidding process, there has been a focus on spreading an economic investment legacy across Britain on the back of the biggest ever peacetime capital infrastructure project in this country. It is worth examining briefly each of these core objectives for the Olympic Games, and the role of sport in achieving them.

In 2007 the Olympic Board set out five priorities for legacy:

1) Making the UK a world-leading sporting nation;
2) Transforming the heart of east London;
3) Inspiring a new generation of young people to take part in volunteering, cultural and physical activity;
4) Making the Olympic Park a blueprint for sustainable living;
5) Demonstrating the UK is a creative, inclusive and welcoming place to live in, visit and for business.

The first of these is more complex than it may at first seem. The media would often have us believe that electronic games alone have destroyed the participation sport culture in Britain. Actually sporting participation was in decline way before the first Atari games console or Spectrum computer hit the marketplace in the early 1980s. There are many suggestions as to the trends which have driven this. Whenever figures on British obesity levels or national sporting failure are on the media agenda, we hear journalists decrying the decreasing emphasis on competitive sport in schools; disrepair and/or sell off of local public sports facilities and the proliferation of opportunities to engage with sport from the armchair (either on television or electronic games). Many sports coaches in the UK cite these three areas as impacting the participation agenda in the UK over the last 20 years. Fewer children are playing sport.

But these are not the only trends impacting on participation in sport. Active support from parents for their children to take part in sport away from the home has also declined. These are those same parents who were the very first to have computers at home during their childhoods. Many are the stories we have been told of children with great talent whose parents could or would not commit to the amount of travel needed to support the development of their child's pursuits. Matt's Mum and Martin's wife Marion has taught tennis to all levels of junior players from beginner upwards for 20 years. Her view is that, 'Children have very often not made the choice themselves to be coached in your sport. It is often a parent's choice based on what they think their child might be interested in. Equally it is often the case that the children are keen as mustard and really talented but their parents are just not prepared or financially able to support them at the level that is needed. Finding a talented child with willing parents does not happen every day.'

Alongside the crisis of dwindling numbers we are also seeing a fundamental change in the way even the sporting converts engage with sport in this country. Individual sports which can be fitted into busy personal diaries are on the rise. Running, cycling and gym attendance is increasing. This is often to the detriment of team-based pursuits and formal leagues. It is hard to think that it is a coincidence that exponential growth to saturation of the fitness and gym market has happened while participation in formal Saturday football leagues is shrinking.

Examining the remaining objectives of the London 2012 Games (rehabilitation of East London and economic legacy across Great Britain) sport itself clearly has a less direct role. That said, we depend on sport itself to create the compelling spectacle which will merit the television audience, the spectators, the sponsor dollars and the political imperative which will enable £9bn to be money well spent in this area. Given the level of public debt we now carry, this region of East London would have been waiting far longer for regeneration without the imperative of the Games. Baroness Sue Campbell, Chair of UK Sport, has estimated this length of time at 30 years.

It is already an amazing experience to journey past the Olympic Park and see the impact of some of the construction work on the area which has already been completed. Beyond the sporting arenas, the construction of the new Westfield Shopping Centre is underway. This will play a significant part in the ongoing regeneration of and traffic to the Olympic Village area and hopefully help the area to weather the potential instability in the financial markets which Morgan Garfield refers to, similar to the way the Shepherds Bush/White City Westfield location has achieved this in West London. The Centre itself will total 1.9m square feet, making it the largest urban shopping centre in Europe. Critical to the business plan is the catchment area which Olympic-driven transport plans provide. By the time of the Games, 6.7 million people (or more than 10% of the entire British population) will live within an hour's drive of the centre. Critically, too, Stratford is expected to be the fifth busiest rail station in Europe by then. Stratford's journey to this status from its position as a volatile outpost of Eastern London just ten short years ago is impressive.

Certainly the transport investment alone could ensure a significant part of the regeneration legacy for this area of East London. More than 800,000 spectators are expected to make their way to the Games each day. A footfall of 1.6 million people per day presents a special challenge to London and its transport network. London should certainly represent the best-ever connected Olympic Park with ten tube and rail lines with direct access. It is envisaged that one train will arrive every 15 seconds, with a capacity of 240,000 passengers per hour. Given this, it is expected that 80% of all spectators for the Park will travel by rail. This same level of infrastructure is the model which will be left for those residents who will be moving into the Village and the surrounding area once the Games are complete. A less extreme version of this public transport infrastructure is already operating successfully in Docklands, in particular in the Canary Wharf area.

Encouragingly there are also strong examples of London 2012 driving infrastructure investment and co-ordination across the country. A London 2012 partner, BT, is piloting a scheme in Buckinghamshire to connect various databases listing public facilities with disabled access up and down the country and to provide real time access to this at the touch of a mobile phone. This is part of an Accentuate programme launched on 3 December 2009 to mark the 1,000 day countdown to the Paralympic Games. The aim of the programme is to make a cultural change in the perceptions of people with disabilities. Buckinghamshire County Council is leading on the 'Paralympic Region' project, a key strand of this programme. In practical terms, the project has already been instrumental in getting significant access improvements worth almost £1million funded and completed at Aylesbury's public transport hubs. Neil Gibson is Strategic Director for Communities & Built Environment and simultaneously leads the Council's legacy plans for London 2012. He says, 'London 2012 is creating a real sense of momentum in Buckinghamshire now, not least when the London 2012 Paralympic Games mascot was recently named Mandeville! There is no doubt whatsoever that this event has inspired and mobilised all sections of Buckinghamshire's community, businesses and politicians to focus on making it a success and maximising the future legacy it can leave us. Already we are seeing improvements in infrastructure in the County that wouldn't otherwise have happened.' Buckinghamshire as the birthplace of the Paralympic Games is a very apt place for this progress. The county boasts both Stoke Mandeville

Stadium and Dorney Lake within its boundaries. The Coordination Group at the centre of this lobbied very early on for the funding to secure an Olympic role, which resulted in Ian Barham's appointment. One of Ian's key priorities has been the educational agenda. 'We identified very early on that we wanted to use the power of the Games to inspire young people,' he says, 'so have worked very closely with the London 2012 Education Get Set team to signpost Bucks schools to their exceptional resource network which offers all students the chance to take educational learning from the Games coming to town. Over half of all Bucks Schools are making great use of these resources, far higher than the national average.'

Timing was everything and the ring-fencing of Games-related funding has been critical to generating the possibility of business legacy from the Games. Without an Olympic Games commitment, there is no doubt that our construction industry today would be in even worse shape post recession. Corporates big and small up and down the country would certainly not have won work to deliver part of the infrastructure for the Games and 50-metre swimming pools would not be nearing completion up and down the country. The central London 2012 Procurement System Compete For framework has been successful in distributing contracts and commercial wealth from the Games across the country. Its stated vision is, 'To ensure the transparency and availability of London 2012 opportunities, maximising the number and diversity of businesses contributing to the London 2012 programme and create a legacy of increased capacity and expertise.' In Buckinghamshire alone, for example, as at 23 February 2010 some 23 Olympic contracts had been awarded to Bucks-based businesses through Compete For, most of these during extremely tough recessionary times between late 2008 and 2010.

While there will always be a certain degree of scepticism from within British small businesses when competing against the big boys in each industry sector, the data is initially impressive. As an illustration, Buckingham Group Construction won an open tender process against far bigger competitors to build the handball arena for the Games. One of their directors, Kevin Underwood talks compellingly about the challenges he went through. The bid process was a battle, even from the point of persuading his fellow directors to trade on their experience building MK Dons' new stadium and submit an initial application. His initial reaction, he says, when he picked up the procurement form was that 'we'll never tick all of those boxes.' He proceeded, however, on the basis that 'if you don't buy a ticket, you don't win the raffle.' They heard that through the Compete For process they had been shortlisted from 88 bidders to five, and ultimately they won the day. Kevin talks engagingly about the process of going through Compete For. 'It took us a while to fill in all of the forms and gather all of the data they were looking for, but it really helped us raise our game in terms of how we pitch for all of our work now, making sure we had our health and safety policies and so on absolutely up to date. The London 2012 work is the highest standard of specification I have ever seen for a builder, as you would expect of Britain's flagship project.'

Kevin's current experiences are a good example of the spill-over benefits of awarding contracts beyond the bigger suppliers. 'It is a £27m contract', he says, 'and of that £27m at least £20m goes elsewhere in our supply chain. Take the brickwork subcontractor. They buy from a builders' merchant, who buy their bricks from a brick manufacturer. That brick manufacturer will buy the raw materials from a quarry. We encourage all of our supply chain to operate under the terms and specifications of Compete For. That way we can ensure that we deliver the whole project to the highest standards.'

Some of the business beneficiaries of the Olympic halo effect are far away from the construction site. Hive Café in Burton Bradstock, Dorset is a great example of this. It is set some ten miles from the Weymouth sailing and windsurfing venue for London 2012. Owner Steve Attrill has built a location which serves great food and drink in an idyllic and secluded spot on the Jurassic coast. Although slightly off the beaten track, he has still engaged with London 2012 to the benefit of his business. He says, 'We learnt through local business networking that although the Games themselves bring in a lot of visitors from overseas, it is actually the following two to three years where the numbers of tourists really increase. We are therefore looking over the next five years to bring the rewards to our business and not just the four weeks of the Olympic and Paralympic Games. We entered the Team Dorset Legacy 2012 Award which rewards businesses who are looking to make the most of the Games as a catalyst for long term growth, and to our astonishment, we won. This has created even more impetus around our café, and we now have a much higher profile in the local business community. We were recently featured in a slot on prime time BBC TV South West News, where they are following the build-up to the Games and chose the Hive as an example of how businesses can prepare for the world coming to visit us. We are continuing to work closely with Gary Fooks and the 2012 Legacy Team for our area who are working hard to bring major benefits to the local region. For example, a communications upgrade for the region including faster broadband in every home, and a 'Sail for £5' Chesil Trust programme to drive active participation.'

The great irony, of course, is that despite all of these grand legacy plans which relate to the Games, history tells us that they do not define an Olympic Games in the memory of the population at large. That is the job of the home nation team. Australians recall Cathy Freeman's victory in the 400m as providing a national sentiment which continues to run far deeper than resentment at the white elephant of an Olympic Stadium in which she won that gold medal. Canadians in the aftermath of the Vancouver Games already find it hard to look beyond their victorious ice hockey team who beat the United States in the finale event.

The authorities are all too aware of this challenge and we will look in more detail at the plans they are laying to deliver a gold medal Games for Britain in London building on their success in Beijing. Of course the longer-term risk is that Britain peak in London only to fall off straight afterwards. As the Greek team are aware, this is a very real risk. Currently in England the responsibility for navigating this risk falls to Sport England. They are responsible for investing National Lottery and Exchequer funding in organisations and projects that will grow and sustain participation in grass roots sport and, ultimately, create opportunities for people to excel at their chosen sport. Sport England work in partnership with UK Sport, which has responsibility for elite success, and the Youth Sport Trust, which is focused on PE and school sport. National Governing Bodies of sport (NGBs) are at the heart of the strategy as it is their networks of community clubs, coaches and volunteers that make sport happen. Coalition policy is to integrate these three organisations as a cost saving device after London 2012, a decision which is certainly risky for the delivery of the legacy component of the Games given each of the organisations' plans have been built with their own independence in mind.

In addition to UK Sport funding, which is intended to fund the growth and development of British team members to 2012, NGBs also receive investment from Sport England to achieve targets around growth of the sport (numbers participating), the numbers staying in sport (in particular at the difficult 16 to 18 age) and then those individuals participating in talent development programmes before the elite levels. Each sport has developed a comprehensive plan that explains how it will use this money to achieve these targets. For example, the ways in which they will ensure that clubs actively get into the schools with their coaches to offer a welcoming 'bridge' from school sport to club sport, rather than the daunting move for any teenager that joining a club can often be. As it stands the future for governing bodies is to have greater autonomy over the decreasing four year public investment entrusted to them, but alongside this they will also have greater responsibility for effective delivery against Sport England's key targets. These efforts sit alongside efforts to develop the quality and quantity of coaching provision in the UK through Sportscoach UK.

Swimming provides one shining example of a brighter future. Total Swimming is run by Olympic 200 metre butterfly bronze medal winner Steve Parry. Steve became frustrated by the low attainment rates for Key Stage 2 among young children, by which point children would be expected to swim 25 metres. He says, 'We found out that some of these negative figures linked to areas of deprivation, ethnic minority groups or kids who did not have access to swimming pools.' With commercial partner British Gas, he has created a scheme to take temporary swimming pool structures to the schools rather than expect the kids to come to the pools. 'We want to provide five hours of quality teaching provision, on a ratio of one to seven,' he says. 'Our aim is to teach 25,000 kids in this way in 2010. Rather than paying their money to school coach providers to bus the children to the pools, the schools are spending their money on quality swim coaching.'

Creative models like this are going to be increasingly needed at the grass roots, notwithstanding the inevitable change that will be created by our change of Government in the UK and the shifts in the kinds of sports we enjoy playing as a nation. Perhaps the biggest challenge for our medal haul in 2016 and beyond is how NGBs are able to adjust to smaller levels of elite level funding beyond 2012. Corporate investment is likely to be required to cover the inevitable reductions in public sector funding which will follow. The elite performance end of many Olympic sports will be defined by the extent to which they are able to secure a groundswell of commercial support to sustain their current levels of activity beyond London 2012.

This is not a hopeless task. Kevin Roberts, Worldwide CEO of advertising giants Saatchi and Saatchi, has gone on record as saying that there will be commercial opportunities for sports who are prepared to be forward thinking. He has written in *Sportbusiness International* magazine, 'Small sports are expanding, particularly Olympic sports. In the US the Olympic Games and Olympians are highly respected. We are increasingly defining ourselves by the local. Events like the FIFA World Cup give us more than enough global competition but there is a trend towards localisation as the world retreats and begins to look inwards. There are people out there who are getting pissed off at what these [top level sportsmen] earn... I can see a resurgence based on an understanding that there is great value to be found in the second tier of sports.'

8

A Tale of Two Bids

Our journey so far has traced the history and context to London 1948 and 2012. On both occasions, many believed winning the right to host the Olympic movement represented the very last thing Britain needed at a challenging time. The two bid processes could hardly have been more different and yet close examination reveals the presence of the same heady cocktail of politics, economics and entrepreneurialism securing the right to host the Games. The next section of our journey looks behind the scenes at what winning the 1948 and 2012 Games really took.

As a nation going through an economic depression in the late 1940s, Britain had few emotional outlets except for sport. The potential morale boost of a major international sporting event lasting for two weeks was compelling. The authorities were happy to sell the Games in terms of being an amateur enterprise, with the implication that the 'man in the street' was participating. The reality as we have already seen was somewhat different.

Britain was a nation that could barely afford a full meal, let alone a new sporting infrastructure. Fortunately, its sporting appetite was intact and while the Government shied away from any financial investment in the London Games, others enthusiastically took up the cause. Sir Arthur Elvin and the Chairman of the British Olympic Association, Lord Burghley, championed the cause of hosting the Games, then provided the skills and the influence, the funds and the resources to deliver what they believed could be a focus for national pride and self respect if it were carried off correctly.

Wembley Stadium refurbishment had been achieved primarily with the proceeds from greyhound racing, an event which encompassed the excitement of horse racing without any of the elitist baggage occasioned by the need for midweek free time in order to attend. A night at the greyhounds also provided access to the on-course betting which was illegal elsewhere. The other popular regular pursuit at Wembley Stadium at the time was speedway. Wembley's owner, the very same Elvin, was both a fan and a shrewd businessman. Speedway at its peak was selling out the stadium on a regular basis, an even more staggering achievement when you consider that the capacity in those days of standing venues and minimal health and safety regulations was 125,000.

Arthur Elvin had been an observer in the Royal Flying Corps in the First World War at the age of just 17. He was shot down behind enemy lines, captured and failed to escape despite several attempts to do so. After the Armistice, before returning home, he led a team of POWs dismantling ammunition dumps in post-war France.

Elvin became the proprietor of a tobacco kiosk at the 1924 Empire Exhibition before taking over several other kiosks which were not turning a profit. In the aftermath of the Exhibition he made his money dismantling the redundant stands and rebuilding them elsewhere in the country. As with Kiralfy before him in 1908, this experience of dealing with large-scale events in London ultimately proved pivotal in successfully delivering the London Games. It is particularly ironic that the specific expertise that gave Elvin the grounding to lead London 1948 came from profitably selling-off the white elephant infrastructure left behind from 1924!

Just three short years after the Empire Exhibition, Elvin had purchased a tired Wembley Stadium from the receivers for £122,500 at 6.30pm on 17 August 1927. He did not take long to prove his entrepreneurial zeal, selling it to his backers at 6.31pm in the form of The Wembley Company for a total of £150,000. He took his profit in shares and was appointed managing director. His entrepreneurial skills brought him a knighthood in 1946, recognition of his success in rejuvenating one of the world's most famous sporting arenas.

Elvin might have acted quickly in securing Wembley Stadium but his desire for London to host the Olympic Games was a longer term project. He had established relations with the BOA as early as 1937 and when the IOC held its 1939 Congress in London, the last for seven years, Elvin put on an evening of dinner and entertainment at Wembley Stadium for the delegates. From the comfortable hospitality boxes they were entertained on the green pitch below by 7,000 members of the Women's League of Health and Beauty. During their London visit the IOC members were also treated to an indoor ice skating exhibition by Britain's European champions, Cecilia Colledge and Graham Sharp, and by six-year-old Jennifer Nicks, who would ultimately become an Olympic competitor in 1948 and 1952.

According to a report by Carl Diem, a German member, recorded in the IOC Bulletin of July 1939, 'the Congress was pervaded by an atmosphere of hospitality.' The delegates also attended the Aldershot Military Tattoo, the King's birthday parade along Whitehall and official dinners put on by Viscount Portal, the British Olympic Association and the Foreign Office. All this was a far cry from the process surrounding London's 1908 appointment as host, which had been akin to a face-saving mission for de Coubertin.

In the world of international sporting politics and also in the media Lord Burghley was the focal point of the Games. He believed passionately that Britain needed a fillip and that bringing the Olympic Games to London could achieve this, demonstrating to the rest of the world that post-war Britain was once again an international force. In many ways, his was the presence that we might stereotypically assume to have led an Organising Committee for an Olympic Games at that time – a politically astute, big picture British statesman. However, to genuinely make an Olympic Games happen in the aftermath of the Second World War needed more than statesmanship. It needed active leadership, innovation and entrepreneurial zeal. Once the political support was secured on the promise of financial return, this return had to be delivered.

The commercial power behind Burghley's throne was Elvin. In 1939 his hospitality and the demonstration of the facilities he had installed at Wembley Stadium ultimately proved instrumental in influencing the IOC Evaluation Committee to choose London for the 'next' Olympic Games in 1944. As a consequence, when 1944 was cancelled, London won 1948 on the nod of the IOC.

Despite having played a key role in the creation of the modern Olympic movement, and Britain's role in defining many of the rules of the Games in 1908, the prospect of bringing the 1948 Olympic Games to London faced much opposition from the most surprising quarter – elite British political circles. Ultimately, only the prospect of the hard currency it would bring into post-war Britain carried the day.

The domestic political and economic situation continued to deteriorate and by July even the BBC felt sufficiently exposed with regard to its commitment to the event to approach the Government with a request as to whether the Games 'might be abandoned or postponed'. The Cabinet response cited only the expected economic benefits of the projected dollar earnings.

Throughout the whole process, an at times utopian picture of progress was provided by The Olympic Newsletter. This was published monthly by the press department of the Organising Committee and distributed throughout the world to give the latest information about the progress of the preparatory work. It took pains to demonstrate the historic nature of the venues being prepared and their standing amongst the renowned international sporting stadia. It acknowledged that war had taken its toll on some, but said the opportunity was being taken to make the necessary restorations at once, in order to provide only the best facilities for all those visiting the Games. It also provided the perfect platform to reiterate that this would 'maintain a true sense of the importance of the occasion, and to keep the spirit of the movement as a Festival of Sport only.' The bitter experience of Berlin would, it said, be superseded.

In a sense Burghley and Elvin were the perfect team to deliver an Olympic Games that Britain was not sure it wanted. Burghley understood how to ensure that political support at the highest level continued even in the darkest days. Elvin's was an entrepreneurial zeal which did not just win the Games but understood how to deliver and commercialise it in a short time frame of just three years. Theirs is a powerful legacy.

If Britain inherited London 1948 having won 1944, securing London 2012 was certainly a tougher battle. Winning the right to stage the Olympic and Paralympic Games is probably now the biggest contract on earth any one organisation can win itself. No other deal carries with it the same heady mixture of political intrigue, financial risk, logistical conundrum, media scrutiny and sporting challenge. At the end of the process lies an incredible gift for the winner. Madrid's decision to bid once again for the Olympic and Paralympic Games in 2020 on the back of two successive defeats is a chastening reminder of the size of the commercial and social prize.

The decision-making process, too, is remarkably similar to the biggest business deals. In many ways it is akin to a large corporate acquisition of a successful, attractive target. The process of deciding who will host the Olympic

Games is theoretically played out based on pure logic – technical capability, transport logistics, funding structures and so on are all rigorously analysed and appraised by the IOC. The process is also intensively competitive. Points scored are only important in the context of how the other, equally able, bidders also scored. Ultimately though, the decision comes down to the behaviour of the various members of the IOC on one day – not in the years, months and weeks leading up to voting day. Despite all the due process in the world, this ultimately boils down to an emotional and individual decision. Not even Obama, still just about the most powerful man in the world, could sway the voting towards Chicago for 2016. The Games have become a catalyst for economic and social change, a sizeable investment and prize for first world governments around the world. Despite this, its destination is still decided by a population of elderly ex-athletes from around the world, whose own childhood sporting fires were likely fuelled by hearing of London 1948 and Helsinki 1952. In our modern, calculated world, only the election of the Pope in the Catholic Church retains a similar level of intrigue and unpredictability. As Tony Blair writes in his foreword to Mike Lee's book *The Race for the 2012 Olympic Games,* 'From the very beginning, until that nerve-tingling final ballot, London was never the favourite. In fact, if we had listened to some of the voices back home, we wouldn't have bothered putting in a bid at all.' As we shall see, the eventual victory was a victory of belief, good strategic thinking and creativity. It was ertainly a million miles away from the wining and dining involved with securing the Games in 1948.

It was critical for any London bid to host the Games in 2012 to learn from previous recent British bids. Of course, the start was not the beginning of the actual bidding process. Britain had failed comprehensively with bids for Manchester and Birmingham and (as IOC Member and now Member of the IOC Executive Board Sir Craig Reedie pointed out in his part of the final bid presentation in Singapore) had learnt its lessons in those defeats. Marzena Bogdanowicz was there from the start of the London bid as the Marketing Director of the British Olympic Association. Bid Chief Executive Sir Keith Mills has publically praised Marzena's role at this stage of the London 2012 bid. She tells of an extraordinary journey with modest origins which started in the 1990s.

'First of all, previous bids had taught us that it just had to be London!' she says. 'The BOA, as the National Olympic Committee of Great Britain, made a decision after the failed attempts by Birmingham and Manchester that if the

UK were to bid, it had to be London. And so it was. The journey began in 1997 with David Luckes, an Olympian himself as a former Goalkeeper for the British hockey team, on his own in the basement of the BOA working out the feasibility of the project. He wrote an amazing document that grew into what is now the Games plan. Back in those days, very few people believed it could be done, let alone won. It was just something we were trying to get sorted in our daily working lives. But when Ken Livingstone as Mayor of London said, 'You have my support for a Games in East London', that started to change things. Soon afterwards the Telegraph ran a front page story 'London Must Bid'. That was when it really got going!'

Evident in Bogdanowicz's words are the critical importance of media and governmental support from an early stage. Ultimately, of course, the latter is likely to follow if the former can be achieved. Much as in 1948, the story started with just a small few passionate individuals focusing on securing Government support.

'The key was to get the Government on side, which took a lot of hard work by many at the BOA. Once that was done the Bid team, led initially by Barbara Cassani, got underway. I remember helping David Luckes move into the offices of the Bid Committee. They were on the top floor of Canary Wharf at that time. There were just three staff, Barbara, David and a new chap, Charlie Wijeratna, who is still at LOCOG, along with some empty desks. Slowly we brought in all of David's files. That was the beginning...'

We hear a lot in business about the different skill sets and attributes of certain types of leaders. A start up leader does not necessarily make a great turnaround leader or FTSE Chief Executive. Equally many a FTSE Chief Executive would falter amidst the hurly-burly of daily start-up life. One of the key elements of any winning bid is that it has to start somewhere. Much like a long running soap opera, the cast list at the beginning of the show is often very different to the end. In the case of London 2012, as the clock ticks and protagonists come and go, it is easy to forget the number of individuals who were part of the initial team – Barbara Cassani, Ken Livingstone and Tony Blair among others. Without the support of all of these individuals, Britain would not even have bid for the Games. Cassani's contribution in particular has tended to be overlooked. Making her name with the start-up of Go – BA's budget airline – she led the start-up process for the London 2012 bid with the same zeal. Critically she also understood when the time was right to hand the baton on. She was well aware that in Lord Sebastian Coe she had a very capable candidate for the next stage of the bid.

To win the Games required a set of individuals to deliver in harmony. Seb Coe and Keith Mills worked powerfully in tandem in the run-up to the bid, so much so that the London 2018 World Cup team has seconded them to the Board of their bid to ensure they capture the learning. Seb brought the political savvy and elite sporting experience, Sir Keith the business and team-leadership experience. Now in delivery phase, LOCOG and the ODA have continued to balance the skill sets needed to deliver the Games very effectively. Chief Executive Paul Deighton acts as a similar foil to Seb now that LOCOG has entered the delivery phase. Similarly the ODA (the public sector organisation responsible for the Games infrastructure) has hired prominently from the private as well as public sector.

The blend of commercial and political skill we see in Deighton and Coe harks back to Burghley and Elvin's blend of political and commercial skills. While Elvin was fundamentally the delivery engine for the Games, the practical reality is that even then political influence and connections were needed to secure the agreement of the IOC to pick London as a host venue. Further back, even Robert Dover had needed the assent of King James to create the Cotswold Olimpick Games!

Winning the bid to host the London 2012 Games was primarily a masterclass in planning. The bid team managed to weave together an acute understanding of the IOC political landscape with a practical understanding of the core priorities necessary to win. No stone was left unturned. Votes from each IOC member were predicted – first choice city, second choice, third choice and so on. London ran models to forecast specific voting scenarios and so understand who they needed to influence to swing the vote.

Sir Keith Mills tells a story of one IOC member who they knew would be likely to vote for Moscow first and then potentially Madrid should Moscow go out. Despite this, they believed that the member's third choice (likely to be between Paris and London) would be critical should Paris and London ever go head-to-head. Sir Keith flew to the country in question to understand the culture and the challenges in which the Member operated, and also what was important in a host City to the domestic Olympic Association. This was done with a modesty and genuine sense of enquiry which created not just a more empathetic bid, but also a better reception for it in the corridors of power.

Critical to putting London in a position to potentially win the bid, then, was a combination of meticulous planning, commercial acumen and astute leadership. That said, the build up to the day of the vote is a little like the semi-final of an Olympic competition. No medals are given out for winning at this stage. All that can be done is to put oneself in the frame to be competitive on the day. The actual process of winning depends on small, seemingly marginal changes of mind (switching a country from third choice to second choice, for example) which often happen on the day. These decisions are based more on emotion and instinct than traffic planning and venue logistics.

In fact, it is believed that up to 10% of voting decisions are either tentative or changed once the formal proceedings begin. When the margin of victory or defeat is regularly one or two votes, every shaken hand or persuasive word makes a difference. Bogdanowicz says, 'What made the difference was us taking a different tack at the final presentation. That does not undermine the work done in the corridors and in advance talking to people and convincing them London was able to deliver. Technically the bid was as strong as all the others so really it was down to the last presentation. London talked about the Games and the legacy and youth. The final film didn't even show London but showed the young African boy and his dream. All other cities showed you their city, their landmarks… what you would expect, but London was different.'

The atmosphere in Singapore and in Britain at large had built during the days preceding the bid. Each breaking piece of news about the British bid, now firmly ensconced as the lead story on British television news channels, seemed to create a sense of building impetus.

As London's plans emerged, from the ultimate decision about the party of delegates London would take to the Games to the sizeable investment of Tony Blair's time, David Beckham's inclusion to the very different tack of the speeches themselves, each piece of news seemed to create even more impetus. From being an outside bet the sense slowly increased that London was capable of upsetting the odds. This reached fever pitch as Britain opened its eyes on the morning of the bid.

Bogdanowicz says, 'I put a bet on London winning at 8-1, nothing major just £20, but I won. I put the bet down when I heard that they were no longer taking any "suits" into the main bidding room but taking children instead. That for me was what changed it, I really believed they could do it then and put down my bet! And I had great pleasure in collecting my winnings. I still have the winning ticket in a frame in the offices of my company b-focused!'

Juliet Slot worked as part of the bid's winning team and then joined the Organising Committee, LOCOG, for two years before becoming MD of Haymarket Network and latterly Pitch Communications where she puts her breadth of experience to work on a broad mix of sporting clients. She concurs with the view that the bid team used an extraordinary focus and detailed planning to deliver a bid victory. 'The bid felt like we were working on a general election,' she says. 'We had a plan – the money we had to raise, the profile we had to establish and the bid we had to put together but most of all the votes we knew we had to win. We therefore had to be nimble and flexible enough to change direction if something wasn't working or to take advantage of opportunities that came up every day.

'Our whole focus was based on putting together a foolproof bid with the right venues, the right transport solutions and to the right budget and then selling it to the 202 IOC members who we needed to vote for us.'

The final piece of that sales process came on 6 July 2005 when the final decision was announced at the Raffles City Convention Centre in Singapore, where the 117th IOC Session was held. London had two aces up its sleeve in the days preceding the vote. Firstly, there is no doubt in hindsight that the arrival in Singapore of Tony Blair to talk personally to key IOC Members had a significant impact. Blair was the only leader of the five candidate cities' countries to lobby personally. This was no one-off time commitment on his part. He had also been the only one of the leaders to attend the 2004 Olympic Games. Many of the bid team has gone on record to pay tribute to his influence in winning Britain the Games. Sir Steve Redgrave, by far Britain's most successful Olympian, said to the media in the immediate aftermath of the victory, 'For Tony Blair to take three days to come out here has made the difference. [Jacques] Chirac didn't have the chance to speak to members and was only here for the presentation. The presentations were important, but it's that meeting and greeting and showing that full support right the way through. If you're the Prime Minister of a country, then you are going to get an audience with a number of people.

'Hats off to the Prime Minister. Seb Coe has done an amazing job, but if you have to pin it down to one person it's Tony Blair coming out here and doing that.' But even with Tony Blair in town the devil was in the detail. The meetings with Blair needed to feel special for each member so the timings were very strict to ensure IOC members did not cross in the corridor on the way to or from his quarters and so have their experience tarnished in any way. Additionally, two years of preparation went into understanding the motivations of each IOC member inside out so that the conversations Blair had would be deeper and more credible than a simple handshake and polite conversation.

As Redgrave and Bogdanowicz have both suggested, Seb Coe's speech on the eve of the voting – presenting the London bid to the IOC – also made a significant impact. London was really the first host city that recognised that the rules of the game had changed. Rather than focus on why the IOC should give its gift to them, it spoke instead of the legacy a London Games could give to Britain, the IOC and the world. This struck an emotive chord. The accompanying video was of children, not prototype Olympic Villages. Coe's speech was recognition of the Games as a social and economic catalyst and the critical role of the IOC members in granting that right. This did not happen by chance – it was a painstakingly-crafted piece of communication which was the product of some brilliant marketing minds – with Sir Keith Mills, Mike Lee and Chris Denny (the Head of Marketing at the Bid Committee) all playing significant roles in the drafting and redrafting which took place.

Coe got the tone absolutely right because his message was both real and credible. The reality is that the IOC's fundamental challenges as it laid them out – that 'today's children live in a world of conflicting messages and competing distractions' are Britain's fundamental challenges. London won because they offered to partner with the IOC towards a solution.

Elvin had taken the initiative with the IOC in advance of 1948. He had taken things beyond the sphere of political influence to demonstrate that a London Games would deliver a quality event with a quality venue at its heart which would add equity to a Hitler-tarnished Olympic movement. In the same way London 2012 won the Games by pushing on the IOC's thinking once again. Every bidder at the voting stage is now capable of putting on a brilliantly executed Games. London was able to broaden the IOC's horizons and be bold enough to suggest they could create a catalyst for change.

While Bogdanowicz might have been early to sense Britain was genuinely in with a chance of winning, the British population as a whole hardly dared to dream. Richard Hughes, B2C Commercial Director at EDF Energy, was in Trafalgar Square in person on 6 July. His memories of that day are very vivid. 'On the morning of the announcement I was in an office near to Trafalgar Square,' he says. 'Along with thousands of others, I headed out at lunchtime to watch the results live on the big screens. Like most things that I really care about, but can't influence, I tried to manage my own expectations – telling myself we didn't really stand a chance and that it didn't really make much difference if we won or lost. The atmosphere when it was announced that London, not favourites Paris, had won the bid to host the 2012 Games was incredible. I don't think I can have been alone in not letting myself believe we could win. The surprise, relief and the sheer extent of unfettered joy shown simultaneously by such a large number and concentration of people was unlike anything I have ever experienced. As an employee of EDF Energy I am immensely proud that we both sponsored the bid to win the Games and are now a sustainability partner of the London 2012 Olympic Games.'

The power of London's bid and proposition on that single day in Singapore changed the marketing strategy for global sporting events forever. 'Legacy' has been a much-used word since in bids for World Cup football, the Winter Olympic Games in Sochi 2014 and the Summer Olympic Games of Rio de Janiero 2018. More important, however, has been the fact that the reality of what these events leave behind in the host nations is now central to the way in which the Games are being delivered.

If winning was against the odds, and successful delivery is now odds on, then the delivery of the legacy component is currently the most at risk for Britain. This is political dynamite at a time of significant public debt. The challenge of delivering London 2012 is in realising that the job is not done when Jacques Rogge hopefully calls London the best Games ever at the closing ceremony. The job is truly done when sporting participation is made possible in 2022 through improved facilities up and down the country; when youth obesity begins to decline and when British business looks back and can demonstrate that that one of the key levers of their escape from deep recession was investment via the Olympic Games. When they won in Singapore, London challenged the model for winning and delivering global sporting events. If they succeed in delivering legacy under a workable business model, they will change the face of global sport forever.

Given this challenge, the focus of LOCOG's senior leaders has been not just to deliver the Games itself, but also to deliver this Olympic legacy into the community. This is something all of LOCOG's leaders genuinely take seriously and Seb Coe's blog hints at the hectic schedule he follows to enable him to achieve this. Ian Barham recounts Seb's visit to a Buckinghamshire 2012 Conference in 2009, saying, 'For most people Seb Coe is the face of London 2012, so we were delighted to welcome him to the first Bucks 2012 Conference at Green Park in 2009. For over 40 minutes he held an audience of 200 community, civic and business leaders absolutely captivated talking about the many opportunities the Games provided to inspire our communities. He spoke passionately about the impact the Games could have in making a positive impact on young people, changing perceptions in relation to sporting participation and in attitudes to disabilities and access. Many of the people I have met since say how their efforts have been galvanised by his words and inspiration from this event. On the day I felt particularly proud when he said how he felt he was following in the footsteps of a Buckinghamshire resident, Lord Desborough, and how significant a role Stoke Mandeville and its historical legacy had been in securing the games for Great Britain.'

Of course the euphoria on the day of 6 July 2005 did not last long. The London bombings of 7 July put events in Singapore into perspective as the capital reeled from the broader international instability intruding on its daily working life. Stories abound of the overnight celebrations meaning individuals were later the next morning in catching the trains into work than they might usually have been. Gill Hicks's excellent book *One Unknown* captures her story in incredible detail. She was one of the unlucky ones, being slightly later than she might have expected. She was sitting in the same carriage as one of the bombers and lost her legs in the blast. One of the central themes of this book is that, rightly or wrongly, it is impossible to separate the Olympic Games from the broader social context of modern Britain. 7 July 2005 remains a tragic reminder of exactly that.

PART FOUR

Going for Gold

'Not a single Olympic cycling title must
leave this country'

Motto of National Cyclists' Union,
responsible for British cycling
team selection in 1948

9

1948: Performance, Athlete Support and the Rise of International Rivalry

As we have already seen, the context for the London 1948 Games was harsh in the extreme. They are frequently referred to as the Austerity Games, principally due to the fact that rationing had not yet ended. Between 1945 and 1948 the level of rationing experienced actually worsened, a situation exacerbated by the fact that, in the post-war period, limited supply of basic food drove up the prices of what was available. Even bread became a rationed commodity in 1948. In some cases, the nutrition situation in the countries which had been invaded, or even defeated, was better than in Britain.

Many teams brought food with them to London for the Games and were content to share with the British athletes with whom they shared sporting interests. Although it did not quite cause the same level of outrage as the ITV ticket scandal at the 2010 FIFA World Cup, it was certainly true that the emerging black market in tickets, as the Games progressed in 1948, was also driven by international visitors – in this case often the athletes. Prevented by British Government regulations from bringing in and exchanging sufficient currency to help them buy food and drink throughout the competition, they were forced to sell tickets purely to be able to sustain the quality of diet they had become used to and depended upon for their training. It speaks volumes that in the French team manager's subsequent report on the Games, which ran to 14 typed pages, 12 of those focused on the quality of the catering!

Providing the infrastructure for an event like London 1948 was always going to be challenging so shortly after the war. Today it is difficult to comprehend how the basic lack of resources might have played out in the reality of individual competitors and teams. The French football team, for example, arrived with all their kit and yet had failed to remember to bring a ball. Sourcing a ball to enable them to start training was not a matter of hours, but days.

Finding sport in the first place in post-war Britain was often a matter of chance. Sylvia Disley (formerly Cheeseman), who ultimately ran in the 200 metres in London 1948, says, 'As a Sixth Form Grammar School student I read in the newspaper that the first post-war athletics championships were going to take place the next weekend. I was told that entries for that competition were closed, but a helpful lady suggested I get in touch with a club called Spartan Ladies near where I lived in Twickenham. Within a year I went to the European Championships and came fifth. I remember both the gold and bronze medallists had very deep voices, so perhaps I deserved more.'

Given the severe rationing which existed at the time among the British population, it is hardly surprising that many athletes' nutritional preparation for the Games was at best basic. Athletes received few useful benefits over the rest of the population and those they did receive were often provided at random. There was little or no understanding among coaches at the time of what diet would support stronger athletic performance, let alone among those who were giving the additional food out. In many cases, this meant that what extra bits and pieces of support could be given ended up being hopeless.

Disley says, 'The problem was that an extra loaf of bread has limited benefit if you are a sprinter. I did receive one parcel from Australia and while most of it was inappropriate for an athlete, there was a bag of dried mixed fruits, apricots or similar, which were delicious and which I ate as sweets. Unfortunately at the bottom of the bag was a collection of wriggling visitors, presumably collected during the months on the ship.'

Medical care was similarly basic and reflected the overall onus on the athlete to prepare themselves for competition. Injury was the athletes' own responsibility to diagnose and cure. Disley injured her ankle badly playing netball before she took up athletics seriously and, as a result of failure to receive appropriate treatment, was later found to have a running stride which is four inches different between her left and right side. Over 200 yards this could mean a difference of five yards. This theme of individual responsibility carried through to athletes being responsible for finding the appropriate sporting kit to be competitive. Disley had to buy her own starting blocks, the first British woman to do so.

Things were particularly tough for the female athletes. While the men were put up in former UK and US military camps, the women were segregated into nurses' homes. Disley shared a room in Victoria outside the bus station. Not only was it hard to sleep at all, it was also close to the red light district so the girls sometimes needed to take evasive action to avoid being accosted.

Disley's experience was fairly typical. British sport stood at the tipping point of committing to elite level performance, but was not even close to understanding what that commitment actually meant. John Parlett was a finalist in the 800 metres, and Dorothy Manley a silver medallist in the 100 metres. Now married, both Parlett and Manley vividly recall their experiences.

Parlett says, 'At that time sport was part of school life and those, like us, who had natural ability beat their peers and progressed from there. Athletics clubs took over in this progression, giving us access to support and experience.' Like many athletes of the day, access to coaching came via a more circuitous route. While representing the RAF, John was fortunate to encounter some high-profile athletes and their coach, Bill Thomas, who had also coached Oxford University. John recalls with affection Thomas's contribution in refining his running style: 'Bill's training schedules were very personal, and geared to you as an individual,' he says. 'As an 800 metre runner, training for me involved a mixture of distance training, including lots of 600 yard time trials to assess progress. At the end of each Bill looked at his stopwatch and either said "that was good" or "do it again." Roger Bannister was also coached by him briefly but they didn't get on. Roger was a bit of an intellectual, he wanted to know what time was shown on Bill's watch.'

Manley was originally a high jumper and sprinter through her school years and for her club, Essex Ladies, a highly competitive club to this day. She was included in the 'possibles list' for the Olympic Games as a high-jumper. Those on the list who did not have a coach were allocated one. She considers herself to have been lucky to be under Sandy Duncan, an international athlete as well as a talented footballer. 'After a couple of sessions my coach said that he felt that my future did not lie in high-jumping but that he had been really impressed with my running in the warm-up sessions. He asked if I would like to try sprinting and I did. I was astounded when I was announced in the team for the Olympic Games.'

London 1948, then, was really a crossroads for the understanding of elite sporting performance. As winning became more important, so did individual athletes' motivation levels. That said, British athletes were still trying to compete despite, rather than because of, the support structures which existed for them. Our London 2012 athletes will be constantly warned against consuming nutrition from unusual sources, for fear of drug contamination, and supported by every kind of medical and coaching expert to help them succeed. Yet as relatively recently as 60 years ago, food parcels of dubious origin were a bonus, the level of medical support a danger to one's stride length, and the availability of quality coaching a matter of luck based on the town an athlete happened to live in.

Many stories behind the British performances in London 1948 follow similar themes of last minute preparation and individual resilience amidst adversity. The British focus was very much on delivering the Games rather than winning them and Britain's performances in general were disappointing. While there certainly was a notion of home nation advantage, crowd support for the British competitors was far less partisan than Team GB might expect to receive in 2012.

While each sport found itself in rather unique circumstances, none of these were straightforward. One of the core themes across many of the sports was the often contradictory ways in which the notion of amateurism was dealt with as a social tension and competitive barrier.

As we have already seen, British sporting history to 1948 is littered with these conflicts and contradictions. Of all events, rowing displayed both the positive and negative side of the system as it had evolved to this point. It also provides an insight into how things were done in the British corridors of power after the War.

Oxbridge connections not only formed the backbone of the team, they also funded it. Preparations for the rowing team were certainly amateurish as we would currently understand the term. The Chancellor of the Exchequer of the day was Sir Stafford Cripps. He had confirmed that no money from the public purse would be forthcoming in support of the Games, neither for infrastructure or supporting the performance of the British team. His predecessor as Chancellor in the Labour Government had been Hugh Dalton, (Edward Hugh John Neale Dalton, later Baron Dalton of Forest and Frith), who had been educated at Eton and Kings College, Cambridge. Dalton recalls in his diaries having been approached by the President of the Cambridge University Boat Club (also a Kings man). He was informed by the President that, due to a lack of funds, the British crews would have to row in old British boats with old British oars. The implication of this was that this would create an almost impossible challenge to overcome for the British crews since the old boats were anything but fast in the water. The great irony of this was that foreign crews would mostly be racing in new, British-built boats with new, British-built oars, since boat-building was a leading trade in Britain at the time.

Former Chancellor Dalton's reaction was to go straight to the top, in the form of both the Admiralty and the Secretary of State for the Air. The latter was not only another old Kings College student, but also a former President of the Cambridge Union and Olympic Captain. He agreed immediately that the Admiralty would provide suitable boats and oars for British crews in the Olympic Games as an exceptional case. It is incredible to think that this was solved as a priority issue for the Secretary of State for the Air. One might imagine the Berlin airlift happening concurrently might have been a slightly higher priority!

The same general sense of chaotic unpreparedness was apparent in the selection and support of the rowing crews themselves. Many were put together in desperation, in a matter of months, after the Henley 'trials' events of 1948 had been won largely by contingents from overseas. New combinations were hurriedly constructed to meet the Olympic challenge on the same course.

The coxless fours was a little-raced event (that is, it didn't feature at Henley). However, it was an Olympic event. Janie Hampton's book *The Austerity Olympics* recalls the comments of one of the crew, Robert Collins. 'We had a coach, but he didn't really know what to do. He believed too much training could make you go stale. Two days before the race we all got gastroenteritis and he prescribed champagne, sulphonamide (an antibiotic) and port. We felt a lot better, but it didn't cure us.'

This level of preparation did not necessarily impede performance in London, given the talent of some of their team. John Wilson and William Laurie were best friends and both rowed in the record-breaking 1934 Cambridge crew before joining the Colonial Service in Sudan. They took first place in the Henley coxless pairs in 1938 as they visited Britain on a holiday visit. Returning on six months' leave early in 1948, they won again at Henley after just six weeks' training. They were invited to represent Great Britain at the Olympic Games on the back of this rare success for Britain at Henley and won an even rarer gold for Britain at the Games themselves. Laurie's son Hugh later followed in his father's footsteps, finishing as a runner-up at Henley and winning a Cambridge blue for rowing. He is, however, better known as an actor on both sides of the Atlantic, having been awarded two Emmy awards for his work.

Also gold medallists for Britain were Richard Barnell and Bertram Bushnell in the double skulls. The backgrounds of the double scullers could not have been more different. Both were steeped in rowing history, although for different reasons. Burnell's father had won gold in the 1908 final, whilst Bushnell's family owned a boatyard nearby. Owning the boatyard was not necessarily an advantage for Bushnell. In fact, if he had worked there he would be deemed professional under the rowing authorities' interpretation of the rules of amateurism. As a result, it was necessary to move away and become apprenticed elsewhere to maintain his eligibility. He worked a 52-hour week and was not paid for the days he took off to compete in the Olympic Games. His company did not altogether approve of his time off. Richard Barnell's eligibility was not questioned as an Old Etonian and Oxonian. This was particularly ironic as he, too, also made a living from the sport as Rowing Correspondent of The Times. The day after the competition itself, Barnell found himself in the unique situation of reporting on his own gold medal performance. He chose to mention the victory as a mere postscript, a bold decision which must surely have come under editorial pressure given that Britain won only three gold medals in the entire Games!

Of course there is a significant irony in the fact it was impossible for Bushnell to work in the boatyard. Let us consider this a little more for a moment. Britain was manifestly short of suitable rowing boats, to the extent it needed to dip into old school connections to source them. Not only this, but it was also impossible for one of Britain's gold medallists to build his own boat. Despite this, somehow it was perfectly possible for his partner to flout the regulations entirely in being paid to report on his own success.

As a final example of the turmoil which surrounded British rowing, the story of the silver medal-winning coxed eights crew is also revealing. Ultimately, the British crew was beaten into second place by a very competent American University crew. This was only half the story. In a way which foresaw the shambolic England football team politics and performance at the 2010 FIFA Football World Cup, the British eight were riven by internal conflict in the run-up to the race because two separate Cambridge crews were initially selected to compete at the Games. It is hard for us now to imagine the administrational circumstances under which this could have been possible. Both crews were beaten at Henley, so a fortnight before the Games a final eight was selected with participants from each boat. Today British boats might spend at least four years identifying and supporting the development of the perfect crew. Two weeks is another thing altogether!

Rowing was not an isolated case. Finding the right boat to compete in was an issue in yachting, too, although more for reasons of disorganisation than austerity. Despite the fact that all of the British team came from a social class which made sailing (or more accurately owning a boat), a normal situation, many of them had never seen, let alone raced in, the class of boat in which they would be racing.

Given that the British team had not seen the boats they would be racing in, it is hardly surprising that selection was also inept. The clear winner of the trials event, Winifred Pritchard, was excluded as late as May 1948 because it was pointed out by the IOC that women were excluded from the yachting event. The Bahamian pairing of Knowles and Farringdon, who held the 1947 World Championship title in the Star Class, were colonial recruits to the Great Britain team at this Olympic Games. Initially performing well, their performances quickly deteriorated. They were disqualified and lost a mast in the final two races of the seven race series, ultimately finishing fourth. They were to medal at a later Olympic Games for their 'first claim' homeland nation.

The yachting itself demonstrated the stark class divide of the times. The cost of participating in the sport meant the competitors were from a high social class, while the support crew was drawn from the lower, manual working class. The menial conditions in which the support crews were expected to live contrasted with the relatively opulent conditions in which the competitors went about their business. Support crews were responsible for looking after the 'rigging, gear and condition' of the boats pre and post sailing. Straw bedding on concrete floors was discovered at their accommodation. Peter Scott, YRA President and team reserve for 1948, later to become Sir Peter Scott, took immediate steps to redress the situation.

If rowing found itself paralysed by its stance on amateurism, athletics was far worse. As we have already seen, the stars of British athletics in 1948 were far from the funded superstars of 2012 and had inherited a questionable 19th Century definition of amateurism which had seduced even de Coubertin. Among all sports the British Amateur Athletics Association set the most absurd standards. For example, after selecting Dennis Watts, the AAA champion, for the Hop Step and Jump, they found he had applied for a job as a Sports Teacher. This meant under their rules he was now classified as a professional. Indeed, the AAA went as far as to decree that professional coaches were not allowed to work directly with Olympic Athletes. This led to the ludicrous situation that the professional coaches had to train amateur coaches in order for those individuals to be able to support Britain's elite. It is inconceivable now, when the likes of Dave Brailsford and Jurgen Grobler are themselves sporting household names, that the role of athletics coach would be sidelined to quite this extent. Each sport was left to its own devices to decide upon the rules that regulated it and therefore the competitors and support staff it selected. Athletics suffered from its particularly rigid interpretations.

Joseph Birrell was an 18-year-old schoolboy who dramatically qualified for the GB team in the 400m Hurdles having won through unexpectedly at the AAA trials. After the trials Birrell continued to be coached by his school physics teacher, who had played rugby but never actually hurdled. The London 2012 Great Britain team outfitters adidas would shudder at the fact that Birrell's shorts, made by his Mum, were too long and used to knock the hurdles down!

Britain's male athletes won only three medals in 1948 – two silvers and a bronze. Perhaps the most remarkable of medallists was Tebbs Lloyd-Johnson, who finished third in the 50km road walk. He was 48 years old and became the oldest ever winner of an Olympic track and field medal. He had represented Great Britain in Berlin, finishing 17th. He had been competing for 28 years, attributing longevity to his healthy lifestyle. He was not perceived as a 'possible' for London 1948 and so received no extra rations at all. This did not phase him – in fact, he thought the food shortage was often used as an excuse for poor preparation and performance on the day.

Although athletics is theoretically the simplest of sports to manage, the competitor experience in London was occasionally very shoddy. In the marathon

Belgian Ettienne Gailly looked set to repeat the experience of Durando Pietri. He entered the stadium first, but despite being passed by the eventual winner Delfo Cabrera of Argentina and Briton Thomas Richards in the stadium, he held on for bronze. The Briton Richards claimed afterwards he thought he was fourth, so was concerned to gain a place rather than attack the lead. Unusually for Britain, sultry weather and a strong wind took its toll, with only 30 out of 41 competitors finishing.

As we have seen, Dorothy Manley (now Parlett) had only concentrated on sprinting that same year, having been urged by her coach to consider switching from her background as a club standard high-jumper. 'I trained four evenings a week after work and also at the weekend,' she recalls. It has been suggested that she and Fanny Blankers-Koen were the only ones who ran the race with fire and lack of inhibition. In his book *The 1948 Olympic Games* Bob Phillips suggests that all the others 'looked far too dainty', although John Parlett was swift to counter this suggestion.

Now in her 80s, Dorothy has a musical background and continues to teach piano. Her experience of the competition itself is very telling. She says, 'I had competed for Essex Ladies and won a couple of county titles, but the first time I ran in front of more than a few hundred people was at Wembley in front of almost 100,000. I was a notoriously bad starter but had the start of my life in the final. If I had a little more composure and experience I could possibly have made it tell but I was absolutely privileged to be there and never really had any regrets.'

Maureen Gardner also took silver behind Fanny Blankers-Koen, this time in the 80m hurdles. Gardner, too, had music in her blood – she was a 19-year-old ballet teacher from Oxford and was relatively unique in terms of the British team in terms of preparation for competion. Blankers-Koen was warming up when Miss Gardener arrived by car with hurdles stacked in the back. There were no hurdles available at the training ground. Despite allegedly feeling intimidated by this show of confident competitive focus, Blankers-Koen asked, and reached agreement, to borrow them for her warm-up. This event provided the only world record set up in the track and field events, both Gardner and Blankers-Koen finishing in the same time, 11.2 seconds. It is perhaps no surprise given the level of her personal preparation that Maureen Gardner's fiancé was Geoff Dyson, recently-appointed National Coach to the AAA and veteran of the British Army

Training Schools in East Africa and Italy. Certainly any equipment advantage nowadays is not shared so readily with the opposition.

Notwithstanding the general belief that the British performance at Wembley was sub-standard for a number of valid reasons, it should be noted that in Berlin 12 years earlier only seven medals were won (two gold and five silver) as against six silver and one bronze at Wembley. Neutral (or occupied) countries were by far the most successful at the Games. The degree of athletic continuity and nutrition they had managed to maintain through the years of conflict made a difference. This was of critical importance for the future since, as we shall see, 'winning' was to become increasingly important for the identity and pride of individual nations. The neutral countries effectively created a kind of scientific control group to help athletes, coaches and governments understand the importance of unrationed and nutritious diet to delivering elite level performance.

In contrast to the likes of yachting and rowing, cycling in Britain post-war was very much a common man's sport. Again the British team was a fractured one, principally because of the presence of Company Director and then-World Champion Reg Harris. Harris represented one of Britain's best chances for a medal. He was initially dropped from the team a few days before the Games for refusing to join the training camp, preferring instead to remain in Manchester. He was reinstated after a public outcry and a 'ride-off' against his tandem partner, a race which took place very close to the competition proper.

The *World Sports Official Report* suggests that 'Britain lost the sprint and the tandem largely because internal dissentions centred on the crack sprinter Reg Harris.' The impact of the face-saving ride-off on the readiness for competition was not mentioned. The cycling was held outdoors at Herne Hill Velodrome, a venue which still exists to this day, with the tandem in particular proving a compelling spectacle. The only problem was that nobody could see the outcome in the fading light. The Italians were judged to be victors by six inches at an arena with no floodlights. It is unsurprising that the ride-off between Harris and his tandem partner was the beginning rather than the end of tensions between them. Harris was quoted in the *Staff Reporter* section of the *Express* as saying, 'We get on the machine and win. I dictate the tactics and Bannister has implicit faith in me.' In the run up to the competition, any faith Bannister ever had was never made explicit to the media!

In addition to the issues caused by Reg Harris's presence, the cycling organisation was poor at best. Tommy Godwin is quoted by Bob Phillips as recalling, 'We had no training camp beforehand and no manager. I wasn't told until the Monday night that I'd be riding in Wednesday's time trial…..eventually we had Harry Ryan come in as manager and he knew nothing about Time Trialling or my other event, Team Pursuit. The four of us had only ridden together once before the race, selection was made only three or four days before the event and really we had no idea what we were doing. The complete lack of organisation for the Olympic Games was typical of what the sport was like in those days. We had no knowledge of technology, scientific research, nutrition or physique. We knew nothing about recovery rates. All you had in your favour was a belief in yourself. At the time, Tommy was working 48 hours a week as an electrician in the BSA Factory.'

One might imagine that Great Britain's preparations for a regularly-played team sport like hockey might have been more straightforward. Certainly, the silver medal they achieved was very much more than was expected at the outset. In fact, British hockey teams had not been sent to previous Olympic Games because, in the words of the Federation at the time, 'We do not play hockey in the summer.' Certainly many of the British team took the long closed seasons as opportunities to pursue their significant talents at other sports. Many British hockey clubs were born out of cricket clubs to give cricketers a game to play on the outfields during the long winter months. Britain's 1948 star player and 30-year-old captain, Norman Borrett, had also represented Eastern Counties at rugby; played first class cricket for Essex; was English Amateur Squash champion 1946-55 and also a four handicap golfer. He also qualified for Wimbledon, but was too busy to play. He became a schoolmaster, which perhaps fuelled the amount of time at his disposal for training and competing.

In reality the fact Olympic hockey was played in the summer was a convenient excuse. The real reason that there had been no hockey representation in the more recent Games before 1948 was probably that there was no representative ruling body. Each of the Home Nations was independently affiliated to the International Hockey Board. Delicate negotiations over an extended period reconciled the situation for the 1948 Games. Perhaps there are echoes here for the football competition in 2012, although the financial and political challenges which surround the London 2012 football question dwarf those of 1948 hockey.

As with other Olympic sports traditionally played during the British winter, team selection was difficult because people were simply not playing hockey at the time. Putting on the event itself was just as difficult. All the prospective grounds for the event were being used for cricket and tennis at the time.

This slightly ramshackle approach to the event continued in the competitor list. Sixteen of the 18 nations entered had confirmed their attendance by mid-June but, 48 hours before the opening ceremony, three had still not arrived. Poland, Hungary, and Czechoslovakia did not take part, but some 25,000 spectators still attended the final at Wembley Stadium. The heavy pitch was not conducive to a good spectacle of hockey. While it suited the British combative style of play, this was insufficient to achieve victory. A British team with an average age of 30 lost 4-0 to India with an average age ten years lower.

It is hard to comprehend now that one of the Olympic disciplines in London 1948 completely restricted entry to military personnel, but that was the reality of the Modern Pentathlon competition. The participants nevertheless demonstrated a wide range of backgrounds, from extreme wartime danger on one extreme, to nominal active military service and participation in the Winter Olympic Games on the other. The event itself was chaotic in the extreme, coupled with some competitors showing courage beyond the call. A Hungarian who fell and broke his collarbone in the riding had it strapped and continued to fence and pistol shoot with his wrong hand. Despite this, he knew he would not be able to swim the next day. Hungary continues to be one of the world's leading nations in Modern Pentathlon.

The competition was won by a Swede, Captain Wille Grut, who was the inspiration for an article written by *Punch* that same year. In it his feats are lauded, to the extent he is compared to the fictional hero Rudolf Rassendyl from Dumas's adventure stories. Part of the feature on Grut written by Antony Pope reads, 'At riding and swimming there was no one to touch him, with the epee he was equal first and at shooting he was fifth, and in the cross country run he was eighth. One gets the impression, reviewing the Captain's achievements, that he would be a useful man to have with one in a tough corner. If I were unlucky enough to be beset in a castle at any time by armed desperadoes I should pick out Captain Grut without hesitation as the man to send off for help. 'Grut', I should say, "I depend on you!" and I should clap him on the shoulder with a valedictory "Good luck" at the same time indicating a secret way out of the castle. He would then swim the moat with contemptuous ease, pistol his way through the beleaguering lines, shooting with deadly effect until his ammunition gave out, and after dispatching with some well-timed thrusts, one or two hulking fellows ill-advised enough to try to bar his progress, he would leap on a handy horse and ride till the gallant beast dropped dead beneath him. There would then be nothing for it but to cover the last 4,000 metres to the police station on foot, which he would do in 15 minutes 28.9 seconds. What, in fact, compels admiration about the Pentathon is that it calls for qualities normally to be found only in heroes in adventurous romance.'

Stories of disappointment for Britain continued beyond these core sports. One medal in the swimming pool was not deemed sufficient for what *The Times* suggested was 'Two years of intensive preparation funded by public donations of around £10,000.' The Americans dominated the pool with the best of their University teams, who were more used to regular competition.

On the basketball court the most successful teams in the British league of the day were comprised primarily of European exiles and US Evangelists, so it was no surprise when the British team finished 20th. A more telling development was the withdrawal of the Hungarian team from games to determine the positions between nine and 16 because they had run out of money. This contrasts with the bravery demonstrated in the Modern Pentathlon. Hungary's gymnasts also remained, chiefly because they still had medal chances.

The football tournament itself was the poor relation of other Olympic sports – arguably it continues to be so to this day. The draw had to be revised because, much as on the hockey pitch, five teams pulled out of the competition before it began, unable to muster a full side. The British football team was managed by Matt Busby, a professional coach who understood the situation he was facing. Previous matches between the England professional team and some of the national teams he was now facing in this competition had resulted in losses, so he was under no illusions about the task in hand. He had no relish for the challenge he faced.

Busby said, 'If amateur football is a yardstick of quality, then the amateur game in Great Britain does not compare with the amateur game in other countries. Some of their big stars, though they may have other jobs for the benefit of the casual enquirer, play football all year round and they are paid money, often big money to attend to the necessities of life. Those nations who continue to act according to the book are faced with two alternatives: they must either refuse to compete against such unfair odds, or enter the Olympic Games knowing they have no earthly chance of success.

'The British policy was to enter', Busby added, 'on the assumption that it was better to have the Union Jack trampled in the turf than not to show the flag at all. Every four years, Britain's football clerks, football grocers, and football pitmen are exposed to something akin to ridicule.'

Maybe it was a sign of the times that when it came to the play-off for the bronze medal, Busby chose to include in the side all those who had been in the squad, but had not yet had a game. This was very much the Corinthian approach as he would have understood it. Britain narrowly lost the game. One wonders how Busby's equivalent would react in similar circumstances in 2012.

Britain's gymnastics team gave a creditable performance in spite of the shortages of training facilities, apparatus and coaches. The British team trained in the basement of a brewery and practised on home-made equipment, and organisers had to borrow equipment from overseas for the Games proper.

The leading male gymnast, George Weedon, was a stunt man by trade, who had to avoid doing somersaults in the course of his work or he would be deemed a professional. Unknown to most, the team were assisted by the adoption of a German prisoner of war, Helmut Bantz, a former Olympic gymnast, who coached them before and throughout the event. At Helsinki, Bantz competed once again for Germany. He was ultimately to win a medal in Melbourne. Against the backdrop of poor, amateur or even non-existent coaching in many sports, it is ironic that the one coach praised the most for his contribution to British performances was not only non-native but originally held in the country against his will. One wonders whether Bantz ever really realised he was starting a trend, since the most successful British team coach in the 90s was also a German – rowing's Jurgen Grobler. Grobler was a similarly controversial appointment initially, having grown his own reputation as part of the East European regime.

The level of British athletics support was inconsistent at best – which should be no surprise given the coaches who made a living from their occupation were not allowed to be involved. It comes almost as poetic justice that the most potent motivational impact of the British Athletics Manager was allegedly to comment on a foreign star that she was 'too old'. The comment was reported to her by her coach at the point where this foreign athlete was suggesting that she wanted to withdraw because she was too tired and nervous. One wonders whether this made the difference between Ms Gardner, our British hopeful who arrived at the training ground with her hurdles in the boot of a car, and a certain Fanny Blankers-Koen. Mrs Blankers-Koen did rather well in the hurdles after that little motivational intervention from the British coach, just after she had borrowed Gardner's hurdles to practise with.

When asked about the standard of coaching at the time, Sylvia Disley is very clear. 'Technical coaching at the time was really non existent,' she says. 'My club became famous for sprinters but my inability to start was a major handicap, which is why I contested the furlong. At the 1946 National Championships a club coach told me to bend my arms more. I did, and I fell flat on my face. That meant I was unable to represent my country that year at 100 metres.'

Things improved markedly for Disley when Geoff Dyson was appointed national coach in 1947. As a schoolgirl National Champion, the Games Master at her co-ed school felt able to set up a training session for her with Dyson, his old Army colleague. 'I was exhausted by the end of the warm-up but it was a fantastic experience. He looked at my start position and told me there was not a single thing I was doing right.' Dyson later married Maureen Gardner, the unfortunate victim of the team manager's motivation of her closest opponent!

Disley says, 'Geoff Dyson's work, and his book *The Mechanics of Athletics* is still valuable today. He liked to take talent and adapt it to wherever he felt it would be most successful. He watched with my husband John Disley in 1948 and turned him into a steeplechaser, where he won bronze in Helsinki. Dyson also went on to set up a network of coaches nationwide which was world regarded and delivered a series of middle distance runners.' John Disley went on to even greater contributions to British athletics, co-founding the London Marathon with Chris Brasher many years later.

Coaching was slowly developing as a discipline and while certain athletes were beginning to benefit enormously, the development was not fast enough for many to realise their potential in 1948.

There was little sense of a co-ordinated approach of any sort to competition among the British team. This contrasted with the American effort, much of which was honed in the fiercely competitive and performance orientated structure of the US university system. American athletes were not necessarily any more talented individually, however they did possess more cohesion in the team environment. It does seem strange that coming so soon after the Second World War there was no real sense of an overall British team spirit and pulling together. Silvia Disley suggests why this was the case, saying 'Our team spirit was not strong with the team scattered all over London.' This is certainly a far cry from the British Olympic team living at close quarters together in the Olympic Village in Beijing, with Union Jacks and good luck messages draped over every balcony and the stands filled for every sport with British athletes who had already concluded their own event.

In 1948 there was a wider frame of support for the British fan. All the Commonwealth athletes were heavily supported where a British athlete was nowhere in contention. Indeed Jamaican Arthur Wint and a couple of his countrymen had appeared in the list of possibles for the GB team, just in case his homeland had not been able to afford to enter a team. These stories were carried by the media, chiefly the BBC, into the workplace and the home. The Commonwealth continued to play a key role at a time when British nationhood and world identity remained under domestic scrutiny.

The British Olympic Association has tried hard to maintain a sense of community between those British Olympians who competed in 1948. Marzena Bogdanowicz ran the 50th anniversary celebrations the BOA hosted for them. 'It was absolutely amazing,' she says, 'like a tea party for people over the age of 60! So many of the Olympians had not seen each other since the Games. In fact there was a canoeing pair where one had thought the other had passed away, so he was stunned to see him. Some hockey players got uppity as they were not all sitting at the same table… the usual pranks… it was brilliant! I loved every single minute of it.'

As one might expect of an international competition coming so soon after the War and with Germany and Russia not present, the spirit of fair play was more prevalent in 1948 than it was at times in London 1908. When the US 4 x 100 metre relay team was disqualified, allowing GB to take the gold, the stadium audience was muted and somewhat embarrassed. A successful US appeal using filmed footage was largely welcomed.

Britain was in no doubt that putting on the Games was the biggest achievement of all, which is reflected in the preparation of some of its athletes for the Games themselves. Certainly it is unlikely that many other nations could have achieved what they managed in 1948. Those that could, such as the United States, would certainly have been too remote for many of the nations to attend in such force. There were plenty of hints that de Coubertin's interest in the taking part over the winning was already under challenge in certain quarters. Ironically this trend was unwittingly started by the biggest star of the London 1948 Olympic Games.

London 1948 was really the first Games where international sporting rivalry came to the fore, as distinct from the political rivalry of Berlin 1936. Despite the odd British and Commonwealth success, actually it was a Dutch housewife and mother of two who became the nation's sweetheart. There is no doubt that Fanny Blankers-Koen's was the stand-out performance of the event, although nobody had expected this to lead to stardom in Britain as well as her native Holland. The importance of this was lost on nobody in power in Great Britain. It was also picked up by those attending from Russia – who came to London 1948 to observe proceedings and then dominated in 1952. Winning became important not just because the Games themselves were becoming more competitive but also because countries began to realise what sporting supremacy could do to levels of morale in their own countries and their standing in the world. This had, of course, been picked up before by Hitler for the 1936 Berlin Games, but figures like Blankers-Koen demonstrated that raising morale and pushing national pride did not necessarily need to have aggressive intent behind it.

It is interesting to review the medal table from the London 1948 Games. Prominent among the successful nations were those who had funding to support their athletes in their preparation and in particular those who were not subject to such aggressive rationing regimes. Finland, Sweden, Switzerland and Denmark all finished above Britain.

The links between financial investment (coaching, diet and infrastructure) and medal performance were becoming increasingly clear. Blankers-Koen, for example, was very explicit about the role that quality coaching had on her performance. This stood in direct contrast to the view of amateurism which the Amateur Athletics Association in Britain had adopted. Certainly the British athletics preparation continued to be slightly haphazard beyond 1948. For example, John Parlett says that he travelled to Auckland for the 1950 Commonwealth Games, which took six weeks by boat. He won the 800m and 'a few days later went to the stadium to watch to find I was on the programme for the one mile. Nobody had told me I was entered! I had no kit with me and I was not able to run! There was no discussion. Who was I to complain? This was after all a free trip to New Zealand – the chance of a lifetime in those days.' The atmosphere in the British camp was not at all one of struggling against the odds. John Parlett says, 'We did not feel underprivileged. We rather appreciated what we had all the more. I try to convince the youngsters today it was all such fun.'

London 1948 provided the first real insight into the conditions which create elite performance. They also demonstrated that, for the cream of the crop, international sporting stardom was likely to follow in an age of sporting news being broadcast into people's homes, cinemas and workplaces. All of this was playing itself out at a time of international instability and a need for morale boosting news in a world still recovering from war. While it took Britain time to catch up, the race for sporting glory across the globe had begun. Helsinki 1952 would see the rules of that particular race change for good.

10

2012: Building Team GB, Competition and the Rise of Sports Science

If London 1948 represented the beginnings of a perception that winning really mattered at an international as well as national level, this view has increased in importance steadily ever since, reaching its height in Beijing.

In Berlin 1936, victory had been abused so as to signpost the supposed supremacy of the Aryan race. After 1948, Eastern European, Russian and now, arguably not just the Chinese regime, but also many Western and Middle Eastern nations have used gold medals to convey international pride and a nationalist agenda. In some instances this verges on the edge of the rules – for example the number of distance runners of African origin competing for Middle Eastern nations, Jamaica's former medallist Merlene Ottey competing for Slovenia and African middle-distance runners competing for Denmark. The plain reality is that it also sometimes goes far beyond them, as we see when the spectre of programmatic or individually-driven drugs abuse looms.

While these regimes have undoubtedly damaged sport in general and the Olympic movement in particular, over the same time period we have also been able to gain a sense of the kind of human performance which is possible without recourse to illegal means, given the right levels of support, coaching and consistent focus.

The current Great Britain system is worth examining in a little more detail. The British government through UK Sport unashamedly prioritises those Olympic sports which deliver medals, while Sport England and other national bodies focus on a broader participation agenda. On one level, this investment in UK Sport might seem confusing. One might argue a Government's priority should be almost exclusively towards supporting a broader participation agenda. However, this would ignore the reality of how and why people, in particular children, take up sport. John Steele, until recently Chief Executive of UK Sport, has been unapologetic about this stance, the dividends of which speak to a large extent for themselves. He explains, 'Our targets for 2012 are ambitious. We simply have to ensure that every penny at our disposal counts. Our sporting system cannot operate in a bubble from the current economic challenges. One thing we can be sure of is that our competitors will be seeking to up their game, so we must ensure we continue to do the same. We take a no-compromise approach in order to maximise medal success, but equally want to ensure all sports can achieve their ambitions in London.' The final part of Steele's statement is critical to the philosophy that underpins UK Sport. Underperformance is not rewarded with ongoing investment, as some Olympic sports (for example women's volleyball and men's handball) have discovered. They are now confronted by ongoing funding shortfalls for London 2012 and the need to fundraise to continue on their journey.

Steele's strategy is supported by the reality of the impact that gold medals have on sporting participation. Gold medals breed national participation as well as national pride. According to Transport for London, the number of journeys taken by bicycle each day rose by 9% in the year post Beijing. Cycling has boomed on the back of British success in 2008. For this very reason, Sport England and UK Sport are both critical parts of delivering sustained gold medal performance on behalf of Great Britain. When these statistics are further supported by infrastructure investment, broader change becomes possible. Boris Johnson, London's Mayor, has said, 'Our aim is to make London a city where two wheeled, pedal-powered transportation is the norm and not the exception.'

Adrian Moorhouse, who won breaststroke gold in Seoul and was world number one for six years in total, started swimming and dreaming of winning a gold medal when he watched David Wilkie do the same. He says, 'As a child of 12 it was my biggest dream to win gold. Ever since seeing David Wilkie win the 200 metres breaststroke in 1976 at the Olympic Games. I spent the next eight years training and competing at various levels from county to district to national, achieving quite rapid success. It all started though with seeing someone else succeed.'

Mark Richardson was the only European ever to beat Michael Johnson. He won a World Championship gold medal for the 400m relay and Olympic silver in the same event. 'My seminal moment came from watching the exploits of the GB team in the Olympic cauldron at the LA Olympic Games in 1984 as an 11 year old,' he says. 'Watching the likes of Daley Thompson and Seb Coe was the most mesmerising and inspiring thing that my young eyes had seen. My inspirational role model from the Games was Carl Lewis who took on larger-than-life proportions for me. I knew with absolute certainty that I wanted to become an international athlete and win an Olympic medal for myself.

'Having such a definitive sense of purpose and underlying galvanising force that spurs your every action is incredibly powerful. It helps you through the inevitable ups and downs that come with any challenging endeavour. It drives you to prepare in the best possible manner so that you can capitalise on the moment when it comes. My favourite proverb is of Chinese origin and it reads, "If you want to be fulfilled you should set goals that command your thoughts, liberate your energy and inspire your hopes."'

For this reason, British sport has a significant focus on the 'podium' end of its programmes. Specific athletes are funded based on their performance levels and future potential. Whole systems are funded and benchmarked with a good amount of scientific zeal, both against their competition but also the other British Olympic sports.

Talent development is taken seriously. Even the smaller Olympic sports work very hard to increase their talent pools – modern pentathlon run Talent ID programmes across swimming and riding, the toughest sports to learn late in life. The entire approach to sporting performance has matured significantly over the last 20 years.

Greg Searle is perfectly placed to observe this in his chosen sport of rowing, having successfully returned to the Great Britain team aiming to compete at London 2012, after winning gold in Barcelona 20 years ago earlier on 2 August 1992. He says, 'The second of August is a day I've celebrated every year like a birthday with Jonny Searle and Garry Herbert, who I won with in Barcelona. We always send each other texts or messages. I thought it would be incredible to be able to row on that day in London, exactly 20 years later. I was only 20 in Barcelona and I'll be 40 in London. It might seem selfish or self-serving but when I look long term this is a chance in a lifetime I have now. When would I be able to try something like this again?'

Greg is able to observe the British rowing system and the ways it has evolved on the back of increased technological and funding support. He brings an older body but wiser mind to the system, something which is extremely valuable in a team sport.

'Getting back for me has involved working with the current system that Britain has in place, not against it,' he says. 'At first I had to work hard on my own to be recognised and brought inside the training squads. Now I hope to be seen as an asset to be nurtured, just like a 19-year-old high-potential athlete.'

'It has been interesting to see the changes to training now as opposed to last time around. Funding, of course, is a big change. The system requires a genuine, full-time commitment from all. This allows for much better recovery. It is quite eye-opening to share a room with someone who is prepared to sleep for more hours than they are awake! The levels of support generally for British athletes are so much better now – for example, we are able to do technique and fitness analysis using technology to download and investigate our own performance data.'

Sarah Winckless is a former British rower. She won a bronze medal in double sculls with her partner Elise Laverick at the 2004 Athens Olympic Games and was twice world champion, in 2005 and 2006. She is now the Chair of the British Olympic Association Athletes' Commission, which has a responsibility to represent the athletes' voice in the decision-making of the British Olympic Association across all summer and winter sports.

Winckless began rowing very late in life while at Fitzwilliam College, Cambridge. Fitzwilliam has a reputation for prizing sporting alongside academic achievement, in particular the extent to which one enables the other, and is consistently the strongest Cambridge College for many sports. It says much for the culture at Fitzwilliam and Winckless's attitude to life that, by the time she stepped into a boat, she had already represented Great Britain at athletics in the discus and won Cambridge blues at athletics, netball and basketball. 'As a teenager I made a conscious choice not to row although my Dad had done so. I really enjoyed a variety of sports, competing mainly in netball, basketball and athletics. I developed an ability to focus on my individual skills in these sports and loved the instant feedback that throwing a ball at a hoop gave me. However on this journey I injured my left knee, meaning I wasn't able to play netball and basketball to the level I wanted to and with the freedom of trusting my body.'

Interestingly, Winckless's impetus for starting rowing was not immediately to become elite. 'I was a left-handed discus thrower and began rowing on the bow side to strengthen my right hand side and balance my body. It was a way to keep fit and strong in the winter without injuring my knee as I attempted to qualify for the Commonwealth Games athletics team in 1994.

'Immediately there was something massively appealing for me to suddenly be in a crew environment and a new learning curve. It was exciting to be embarking on the challenge of turning my sprint-focused physiology into one that could survive a 2000m race or even an 11-minute Cambridge Inter Collegiate course. After years of athletics my improvements in that sport were tiny with huge effort for small gains. It was fun and exciting to be on a new and steep learning curve. When I threw the qualifying distance for the Commonwealth Games, but failed to get the selectors' nod that summer, I decided to spend a year doing this new and different challenge and try to add a rowing Blue to the netball and athletics Blues I had won in my first year. That's where it all started!'

It is important to emphasise that rowing is one of those sports which retains a strong amateur ethos and also attracts some extremely bright people. Winckless's formative rowing career was managed alongside a demanding Cambridge degree. As we shall see, many Olympians to this day continue to balance their training with other working commitments not only because funding demands it, but also because it helps them keep a more balanced approach to their lives.

The way in which Winckless was able to progress quickly in rowing is very revealing. She is a self-starting personality, but the infrastructure of the sport at Cambridge also did an excellent job in supporting and challenging her from a very early stage. The culture of the University as a whole is to create the environment in which individuals can perform and invite them to make the most of it for themselves.

'In my first couple of years on the fringes of the Great Britain rowing squad it didn't feel so different to competing in athletics. I was training in my club environment and got the odd opportunity to row with athletes from different clubs. I was extremely lucky to be able to work with both the women's Blue boat coaches and have the odd session with the men's coaches, using a huge amount of knowledge and talent around me. This was similar to my training group in athletics where we had one coach but there was a great deal of experience in our group and ideas were shared and developed. You could work with the coach of your choice and were completely free to design your training as you saw best.' After Cambridge, the change in culture which Winckless experienced in the elite squad is very interesting. Effectively she became one of a far larger talent pool.

On UK Sport's mandate Jurgen Grobler's British rowing squad has just one purpose – to create boats who can deliver to gold medal level on the global stage. While this involves individuals being given the opportunity to develop to be the best they can be, it also requires coaches to make firm and sometimes life-changing decisions around which individuals make certain boats go faster. The atmosphere is one of competition – mostly healthy.

'Once I got invited to train full time with the squad it was a completely different scenario,' says Winckless. 'All the squad athletes were expected to train at the same place under one coach, every athlete was expected to complete the same training program, we were in constant competition with each other, each training effort seen as an opportunity to prove your place or plot your improvement. I could see the logic behind this, as ultimate success relied on us being able to form crews and row with similar technique, but it was a big learning curve.'

Elite sport is increasingly a numbers game, not just in terms of the performances of elite athletes but also in terms of the talent pools which are required to create the competitive environment. There is a stark reality here that not every athlete will make the grade. Depending on the sport in question, the impact on the lives of the forgotten majority differs significantly. Even those fortunate enough to succeed rarely have a completely smooth path and Winckless was no different.

'I had the huge privilege of trying to be the best I could be on an international stage,' she says. 'To get through the good days and the bad ones took a huge amount of optimism, resilience and support from friends, teammates and support staff.'

Football is often seen as the most competitive and cut-throat of sports at a professional level and to a large extent this is true. Professional clubs might end up with one first team player from every 2–300 who pass through their ranks. However, those who dedicate their formative years and yet fail to make the grade do at least have the option of playing lower league or semi-professional football if they remain uninjured. This gives them the chance to make some money from their apprenticeship even if their initial work prospects have been compromised. Many failed Olympic hopefuls are not as lucky. There is no semi-professional rowing scene and the athletes are often left with the need to rationalise and translate their learning into later life after the event, as Sarah Winckless is now doing.

'The biggest lesson I learned from rowing was the preparation for competitions,' she says. 'Nothing was left to chance and there was a significant shift in training programs from long endurance work to shorter, sharp pieces, each designed to relate to a part of the race. Warm-up was planned and practiced, tweaked and improved. Timings of race day were precise, planned and rehearsed in advance. Instead of competing most weekends for my club and a few times for internationals as had been my athletic summer, rowing races were few, just trials, three World Cups and a World Championship. Each opportunity was taken seriously with goals set and results learned from. This is the kind of approach I am taking into my new role as Chair of the BOA Athletes' Commission'.

This environment creates a pressure cooker environment for elite athletes expected, and funded, to deliver. Their reactions on leaving the systems that have been such pivotal parts of their lives and identities are revealing. Mark Richardson is now a father to a young daughter, Rudi, which gives him an interesting lens on his past and her future. 'I would support her to do whatever she wants in life,' he says, 'including joining an athletics club if that was what she wanted to do. It is not an easy choice though.'

Liz Yelling picks up this same theme. She aims to compete in London having represented Great Britain in the Athens and Beijing Olympic Marathons and won a Commonwealth Games bronze medal in 2006. She says, 'If my young daughter Ruby showed she had the talent and desire to compete in elite athletics then of course I would support her. Ultimately if you are going to make it the drive has to come from deep within you. I have gained so much from a lifetime in running and the benefits have been great. Hopefully my daughter will find something in her life from which to experience similar joy.'

Yelling's career has balanced significant highs and lows which demonstrate the level of desire and resilience which an elite sporting career requires. Every

Commonwealth Games medal typically balances with a disappointing race. For Yelling, one of those was the Olympic Marathon in Beijing. She says, 'Before Beijing I knew I was in great shape. The best shape of my life. I felt if I performed to my best I really could hit a top ten, and if you have the tools to do that then really anything is possible on the day. To get tripped and break a rib after leading for much of the first ten miles was quite hard to get my head around at the time. I struggled for the final 16 miles but still ran a 2.33. My goal for London is to get myself back in that shape and then really go for it on the day! Once you're in the mix in the final six miles it's anyone's race!'

While on one level marathon-running is a very simple sport, the difference between a medal-winning performance and a top ten result can be 1% or less. It is simply impossible to cut corners and also very hard for anyone who lives outside of that elite environment to appreciate just how much hard work and commitment is required to stay at the top. It is all too easy for us to think that an Olympian's life is cosseted, whereas actually it is anything but. As a nation we arguably make the same sweeping judgements on the lives of many others leading lives in the limelight – senior politicians, businesspeople, doctors and the like. For each, the reality is of constant pressure, moments of self doubt and the need for unshakeable belief.

Yelling's challenge is to operate at a world class level at the same time as being a great mum. She says, 'The world's best marathon runners train hard, really hard, and the standards are always rising. It's really important to make sure that I cross the 't's and dot the 'i's each time I train hard for a marathon. Doing more isn't always right, it's more about seeking to walk the knife-edge of elite performance for as long as you can without falling off. That edge gets sharper the closer you get to a race so it becomes even more important to get things right. Different elements such as nutrition, hydration, core stability, listening closely to my body, balancing my other life and family commitments, sleep, recovery and training are all blended together to bring about performance. Marginal gains can often come about through very subtle changes. I like to use trial and retrial to find out what works and then have a plan to follow. The key is also flexibility. It doesn't always go to plan and how you respond can significantly influence performance in the short and long term.'

Another example of the lengths that individual sports go to in order to drive small percentage gains is the innovative work of Chris Boardman, a former

Olympic cycling gold medallist now working at British Cycling. Chris has been a trailblazer for the reinvention cycling has been through in this country. The jerseys Boardman sourced for Beijing featured the combined efforts of several different apparel manufacturers. None of the manufacturers knew who the others were – in fact, not even the Great Britain Performance Director Dave Brailsford knew. Dave jokes now that there is no way he could be treated with such privileged information. After the Games every single uniform was burnt to protect the competitive advantage for London. A far cry from 1948 when athletes were sewing their own uniforms!

Of course, not all of Britain's athletes are in the fortunate position of being able to focus full time. Funding in Paralympic teams in particular remains inconsistent. Many of the Paralympic sports are going through a significant swell in participation and young talent identification. However, blending this quickly into a cohesive performance structure is not easy. Clare Strange is a key member of the Great Britain Wheelchair Basketball team having competed at both Sydney and Athens Paralympic Games. She says, 'We currently have a very young team and one of the biggest challenges for us is the geographical spread of the team and the challenge of athletes still being in full-time education. Also although our funding has significantly improved, it is still a big stretch to get ideal preparation each year for our major championships.'

Hopefully as awareness of the sheer spectacle of Paralympic sport increases during 2012, more of the funding models for these sports will become sustainable in the long term. Certainly the audience which attended the European Women's Wheelchair Basketball Championships in Stoke Mandeville in 2009 was absolutely spellbound by the skill level and spectator experience the Games provided. Having worked for the NBA, author Matt has been lucky enough to attend the NBA All Star Game and a New York Knicks home game at Madison Square Garden, but neither could compete with the 2009 event for the engaging quality of the action.

As with most areas of sporting endeavour – whether Premier League football or British cycling, ultimately there is a very direct correlation between sustained, significant and strategically-focused financial investment and gold medals.

Recognising this, some international federations are now taking strides to limit the competitive advantage that sustained spending can generate. Cycling's governing body, the UCI, is attempting to limit the competitive advantage that Boardman and Brailsford, along with the Australian and German federations, can generate. As it stands its efforts seem as impotent as those it has taken in the war on drugs. Footballing authorities are also trying to even the playing field before it is too late. UEFA is attempting to limit the financial exposure of individual professional football clubs, operating through financial regulation rather than manipulating a free competitive market. Not every club will be as lucky as Chelsea, who were able to swiftly swap debt for equity with their owner Roman Abramovich.

As with Premier League football, it seems likely that sporting domination will become increasingly directly correlated with economic supremacy. Rick Burton is the David B Falk Professor of Sports Management at Syracuse University and former Chief Marketing Officer of the United States Olympic Committee, and served the USOC during Beijing 2008. He wrote in *Sportbusiness International* magazine, 'If we look at the recent (and rapid) rise of Chinese sport in almost every discipline and we factor in that population experts believe India will surpass China as the most populous country on earth by 2030, it's not hard to imagine that once India decides to draw from its nearly 1.2 billion-person talent pool (more than a sixth of the world's population) it will surely find champions in sports other than cricket, field hockey and air rifle. Wealthy Middle Eastern nations and heavily-populated countries such as Brazil and India are starting to build world-class training facilities, hire world class trainers and explore their sporting upside.'

Economic supremacy does not necessarily equate to sporting supremacy, but once that economic supremacy filters through to strategic and well targeted investment in sport, gold medals should theoretically be purely a matter of time.

One sport which has tended to buck this trend in Britain is tennis, where tens of millions of pounds are spent annually by the Lawn Tennis Association. Critics argue that rather than following a long term strategic plan, the LTA's regular changes of leadership and strategic direction have stilted any real chance for investment to equal medals and Wimbledon titles.

The challenge for British tennis is that financial investment is only useful if the culture of the sport itself is genuinely prepared to change and set its sights on world class performance levels. Pockets of excellence do exist, but the cultural shift away from the traditionally elderly, sedate and socially exclusive culture of

British tennis clubs will not happen overnight. One newer model which is working well can be seen at Halton Village Tennis Club which blends elite and mass participation tennis with a unique model more akin to that used in Continental Europe. The club's ethos is a million miles away from the traditional British tennis club, with a vision that is 'to create the complete tennis, fitness and social experience, help the future of British tennis and serve our local community. And in doing so: educate, motivate and inspire people through the power of sport to help them achieve their potential and to be the very best they can be.'

Halton's ethos for its junior players makes no bones about the level of sacrifice required to achieve success. Their marketing literature for prospective players reads, 'Performance sport is, we believe, perfectly captured by Ernest Shackleton in his advert in *The Times* newspaper in 1914 for the expedition to the Antarctic: "Men Wanted: For hazardous journey. Small wages, bitter cold, long months of complete darkness, constant danger, safe return doubtful. Honour and recognition in case of success." It presents a vivid image of the journey that lies ahead for our performance players.'

Sports such as tennis are increasingly truly global, which in turn creates a global market for governing body talent. Perhaps this could be seen as the natural evolution of the insight the British gymnastics team had from their German prisoner of war coach in 1948! Performance Directors from British sports hail from around the world – Netherlands (athletics), Australia (swimming), Czech Republic (modern pentathlon) and rowing (former East Germany) among others. This reflects an increasing understanding of the impact of an organisational as well as individual view of performance to deliver incremental performance gains. Given the tightening of funding for British sports beyond 2012 against a backdrop of public sector debt, one could also imagine a search for commercial talent within these governing bodies to boost revenue streams and help balance the books to 2016.

This organisational lens on performance is certainly an area in which Britain has led the way, including as the subject of academic study. Dr David Fletcher of Loughborough University and Christopher Wagstaff from the Cardiff School of Sport, University of Wales Institute note in their white paper *Organisational Psychology in Elite Sport* that traditionally, elite athlete development has tended to focus on financial and life support for the full-time athlete, an appropriate competition structure for the athlete to develop and individualised coaching and sports science support. They suggest, however, in the current global sporting arms race these are essentially a given in any first world sporting system. Often, they suggest, the very best sports systems also manage the hygiene factors of Olympic village distractions, media intrusion, stress levels among coaching staff and so on. The world's best sporting systems display an attention to detail which many a FTSE business would be proud to demonstrate.

Gold medals require financial investment, world-class coaching and widely available sporting infrastructure. They also require hard work and commitment. While tennis certainly has a way to go on a number of these, the remainder of British Olympic sport has stepped up its game admirably. When the new world global powerhouse economies really decide to really invest, the medals will flow for them, too. At that point Britain will either need to match them, knowing our pockets are unlikely to be as deep as theirs, or back down. Our role in London is to enjoy our place in the sun, however brief it might be.

This is all a far cry in just 60 years from the general lack of acknowledgement of the importance of individual coaching in 1948. It is amazing to contrast this experience with that of Sylvia Disley who was one of a fortunate few to be able to take advantage of a summer school at Loughborough, for just two weeks, in the year preceding the 1948 Games. In 2012 Loughborough will provide the ultimate holding camp for Team GB before athletes travel to compete.

One element which Team GB prides itself on doing better than any other is the cross fertilisation of knowledge, science and ideas between sports. In the run-up to all recent Games, and of course London, the British Olympic Association has invested a significant amount in ensuring that innovation and best practice is shared between the leaders of sports. Dominic Mahony won a bronze medal in the Seoul Games and is now Team Manager for modern pentathlon as well as a Board Director at Lane4. He says, 'The whole ethos of being a member of the British team has changed significantly since I competed. Now, our athletes are members of Team GB first and foremost. At recent Games there has been a real sense of energy and impetus in the British camp from the moment Britain won its first gold medals – with Nicole Cooke a classic example in Beijing. Success breeds success. We would also like to think that we have done a really good job in previous Games of blocking out the distractions which surround our athletes.'

There will in fact be even more areas of challenge in the London 2012 modern pentathlon, because the international authorities have controversially changed the format – running and shooting now happening together in a biathlon-style climax rather than existing as separate events. This has been a difficult challenge for the British team, traditionally strong runners but weaker shooters, to adapt to. Dominic says, 'There are so many things to focus on within the sport itself – for example, controlling a difficult horse, or 32 individual fencing bouts in one day. We now have a new event to focus on as well. The last thing our athletes need to worry about is accreditation, media intrusion, transportation to and from the venue and so on.'

Sarah Winckless certainly found the Team GB ethic to be central at Games time. 'I definitely saw myself as part of Team GB, especially in Sydney. Many of my old athletics teammates were part of the Games and this had an instant impact on me. I had attended the BOA's multisport preparation conference and as a team many of us were at the Gold Coast for a pre-Games camp. It was an incredible opportunity to be part of something bigger than a rowing event and while my focus was on the rowing lake until my competition was over, it was hugely powerful and inspiring to be part of a larger team.'

There are some very promising signs amidst some sports which have been at best stagnant since earlier glory days. Men's hockey, for example, is on the up… England are currently European Champions. Wil James, a consultant at Lane4 where author Matt also works, has been working with the team and its coach Jason Lee with a focus on sports psychology. Wil says, 'The players would say that they have been able to help each other more because they spent time understanding each other's motives and because they worked on the skills to be able to be more open with each other – giving and receiving feedback. Jason has been clear that he was changing his approach and needed players to step up and take more responsibility for their own development rather than waiting to be taught. He has introduced technology to do this which ties in with the new culture in allowing players to review their own performance via video.'

The majority of Wil's ongoing work within sport is with the English cricket team. He draws an interesting distinction between working with Olympic and non-Olympic sports, 'Most Olympic athletes still don't see training and competing as a job, by which I mean a way to earn a living. They are doing it almost with the mindset of a hobby. This doesn't mean they are not professional in their approach – they are meticulous and self-disciplined – sometimes more so than in professional sport.'

The involvement of the British Olympic Association, as the guardian of Team GB, steps up as the Games pressure increases. The BOA is responsible for several areas of preparation towards the Games themselves. It provides a sports science and research programme which specialises in areas of collective interest across Olympic sports, with expert advice around acclimatisation, hydration, jet lag and performance having been high on the agenda for Beijing. It is also involved in operational and logistical management around the Games including kitting out the athletes.

The support structure for athletes is significant, in particular in sports like boxing, another British sport on the rise. Mike Loosemore says, 'As well as my doctor role, the boxers are supported by a physio, psychologist, performance analyst, nutritionist, strength and conditioning coach, a team manager and of course the coaches. The guys are very grateful for the support they get and are often not used to it in boxing whereas in sports like athletics it is more regular. We have a great chance in boxing in London because Rob McCracken the Performance Director really understands the benefits the broader support network can bring. Things have moved so fast. Just ten years ago the coaches would not let us do strength and conditioning work with the athletes because they believed it made them slow. Every one of our medallists in Beijing was having significant medical treatment in the run-up to competing in Beijing.'

Wil James was also the lead Sports Psychologist for Team GB at the Holding Camp for the Athens Games. He says, 'It was a fantastic opportunity and it is not always an easy role. The biggest challenge when working in a holding camp as a member of the BOA team is to know when to intervene and when to resist. Performers are unlikely to come and ask for support, so getting the balance right with regards to intervening is always very important. Performers and coaches should be looking to maintain normal routines in the run up to competition. The key is to help them stay focused on the plans they have set out. In my experience much of the work was with the coaches and performance directors who also want to help but who also probably need to do less rather than more.'

Georgie Harland won a bronze medal for Britain at the Athens Games and was a direct recipient of this level of support. 'While on the day of the Olympic competition in Athens the first discipline of shooting was far from perfect for me, it was through the use of my mental skills training that I was able to regroup and found the focus to move from 31st to third by the end of the day. Psychological skills are like physical skills, they need to be learnt and then trained.' Georgie was able to deliver the turn-around performance and was helped to focus purely on this because she knew Dominic and the rest of the modern pentathlon support crew had taken control of the other potential distractions.

This cross-fertilisation of knowledge and mutual support also extends to sports medicine. Paul Thawley is a current Senior Physiotherapist to the British Olympic Team who has built his own practice, Elite Physical Medicine in Aylesbury, in conjunction with Dr Mike Loosemore. Together they have worked with a who's who of British Olympic talent. The practice works with elite international athletes and members of the public alike aiming to 'treat everyone up to and including international athletes with the same standards and care.'

Paul agrees that cross fertilising knowledge across sports is critical to Team GB's success. 'It's a philosophical thing. My experience in Team GB is that we have worked hard to share our learning across the different sports. For example, Mike and I work closely with boxing but also with Dr Ben Ashworth and the British Judo team. While the mechanics of the sport have differences, there is also a lot we can learn by working together.' Ben adds, 'Ongoing research and sourcing of leading thinking is just critical for us – the mindset has to be of continuous improvement. Standing still as a medical team means our athletes will be falling behind.'

Sports nutrition, too, is an area that has continued to advance since the days of rationing in 1948. Professor Adam Carey is a medically-qualified doctor who has specialised in nutrition. He was in charge of nutrition under Sir Clive Woodward during his tenure at the RFU during two World Cups, including England's victory in 2003. He also held similar roles for England cricket for their Ashes success in 2005, Chelsea for their Premiership titles in 2004-06, as well as working with many Olympic squads and athletes. He says, 'Sports nutrition has changed beyond all recognition over the last 15 years. In 1995 there was just very little sports nutrition practised. Most of the advice that was offered came from work based on research in endurance athletes. As a consequence of this a great deal of emphasis was placed on consuming low fat, high-carbohydrate diets with little concern for other nutrients. While this advice was effective for many endurance athletes to a degree, when it was then proffered to other sports like football and rugby it had disastrous results.

'When I first worked in rugby in 1997, it was common for players to eat vast volumes of starchy carbohydrates like pasta. Since the body has a limited ability to store carbohydrate, excessive consumption above an individual's energy requirement drove them to store excess intake as fat. There were a significant number of fit, fat, players within the England international set-up when I began working for Sir Clive Woodward. Added to this was the doctrine that outside of a requirement for carbohydrate, athletes should be able to get everything they need from a 'well-balanced' diet. This was just not the case even then and now it is clear that while the foundations of health are based on a high quality diet, there are many instances where additional nutritional support will either optimise health or significantly improve performance.'

Alison Mowbray's experience supports Adam's views. After gaining a PhD in genetic engineering in Cambridge in 1997, she joined the British rowing team and won a silver medal in the Quad Scull in Athens. Now working at Lane4, she brings her insight in nutrition into her corporate work. She says, 'I was so careful about what I ate when I was competing, firstly because I really believed it makes a difference and was trying to do everything that would give me an advantage in my sport, and secondly because the training was so tough I had to eat the right kinds of food just to get through it. There didn't seem much point in training all hours to improve my performance and then eating rubbish.' The sum product of all of this investment and collective pooling of knowledge is that Team GB should be the best prepared British team ever. London 2012 will see a team of more than 500 competing. It will also be the largest since a team of 676 at London 1908. This is boosted by the International Olympic Committee relaxing qualification criteria in some sports where Britain does not traditionally excel. It is expected that only the United States, Australia and China will also have teams of 500 or more in London. The size of Australia's team, in particular, is staggering for a country with a fraction of the population of Great Britain. In Beijing 2008, 435 Australian athletes competed, gaining a total of 46 medals.

The British Olympic Association is exerting as much pressure as it can to ensure that qualification criteria are established early on for each sport, to avoid as many controversial selection scenarios as possible. That said, a rowing boat does not always go the fastest with the fastest four individual oarsmen in its seats and there will inevitably be controversy along the way. This will hopefully, but not necessarily, be kept out of the courts. UK Sport has been very explicit in its desire to come fourth in the medal table in London – much will be forgiven if this is achieved.

Not everyone, however, supports such a focus on training and competing. Interviewed in April 2010, well before the FIFA World Cup 2010, John Parlett said, 'I am 85 now and am still active and reasonably fit. Good food, good exercise and not too much of either. We trained hard in our day, but we didn't over-train. This is a big problem today – they train too much and the body does not have time to recover or repair. Look at Wayne Rooney. He is in plaster one minute and the next he is playing again at the top flight in a contact sport. Masking the damage cannot be correct. I fear for him and I fear he may not be the same again.'

Certainly the competitive landscape between 1948 and 2012 has changed completely. As John Parlett says, 'As a nation we are now obsessed with winning gold. That just was not the case when I was competing. In my view it impacts on the way we engage our youngsters in sport.' While this is undoubtedly true, Adrian Moorhouse was inspired by David Wilkie's gold medal and in turn has inspired countless children to start swimming competitively, or perhaps even just learn to swim.

Whether we like it or not, everything that becomes high profile in the 21st Century becomes a serious matter – whether a connecting technology like Facebook, a tasty smoothie like Innocent or even a mass participation sport like running marathons. Ultimately, we need to remember that John and Dorothy Parlett, Sarah Winckless, Sylvia Disley and Adrian Moorhouse all succeeded because they loved what they did. Each of these remains active to this day. Some, like Greg Searle, even go back for more. Greg says unapologetically, 'I realise now how much I loved it first time around!'

PART FIVE

Driving Social Change

'Amateurism…was devised by the aristocracy
of the 1860s who were determined to exclude
"undesirables" from competitions they were
organising.'

Harold Abrahams

11

1948: The Myth of Amateurism and the Emergence of the Health Agenda

The use of sport as a means of preserving the social status quo has been a constant theme in British history. Amateurism itself was never really a genuine intent to preserve any 'spirit of sport', but only really took off as a concept after the Reform Act stopped any other means of preserving sport for those rich enough to be able to play just for fun. As we have shown, the British performance at the 1948 Games was haunted by the spectre of amateurism.

Britain in 1948 offered anything but egalitarian access to sport for all. The rules of amateurism were written in such a way as to exclude rather than ensure inclusivity. The context in 20th Century Britain was very much of a dominant amateur ethic. Journalist and author of *All-Round Genius, the Woosnam Story* Mick Collins recounts the story of Max Woosnam, an all-round sportsman who was a shining example of the amateur ethos in the early years of the 20th century. His achievements are almost overwhelming in today's terms. Woosnam became an Olympic gold medallist, Wimbledon champion and Davis Cup captain at tennis. He was a Cambridge Blue at five different sports. He also toured Brazil with the all-amateur Corinthian Casuals football team. The second tour of Brazil was interrupted by the outbreak of war, and he returned immediately, signed up and survived Gallipoli.

After the Great War, the constraints imposed on the Corinthians in terms of who they were allowed to play presented a major frustration for Woosnam the footballer. In any event it was necessary to find paid employment as he now had a family and none of the private money associated with many in his class. He had played briefly as an amateur with Chelsea before the War, which proved an asset when a job opportunity occurred in Manchester. Chelsea recommended Woosnam to Manchester City and readily transferred his registration in 1919. He agreed, playing strictly as an amateur, on the understanding that he could only play home matches in order to effectively meet his working obligations. Certainly this was an altogether different process and context to the transfers of multi-millionaires Wayne Bridge and Shaun Wright-Phillips who left Chelsea for the same team.

Woosnam was soon one of the stars of the side. He was appointed captain by unanimous consent despite playing alongside professional colleagues. However, problems arose when the team's poor away performances without him caused rumours to start among City's followers that his employers, the engineering firm Crossley Brothers, had refused him permission to play. Sensing total disaster for their own reputation, the company insisted Woosnam played for Manchester City whenever requested to, whatever his work commitments, or risk censure. In this manner, they recognised the opportunity and were able to use Woosnam's celebrity as an aid rather than as a threat to the business.

Before his career was cut short by injury in 1922, Woosnam added to his international amateur cap by captaining the professional side in a 1-0 victory over Wales. His business career also flourished, and he ultimately topped an extraordinary life by joining the board of ICI.

Back inside the Olympic movement, the definition of amateur was also a constant cause of friction. In 1964, Harold Abrahams, a gold medalist from 1924 and respected BBC journalist with over 40 years' experience of administration in national and international sport, wistfully reflected 'amateurism did not originate in some high-minded ethical desire to establish a supreme principle. It was devised by the aristocracy of the 1860s who were determined to exclude "undesirables" from competitions they were organising. Undesirables such as labourers, mechanics and artisans.' He went on to suggest the IOC's stance on amateurism would fail, 'not because it is not clear, but because nobody believes it is being complied with.' This assessment was not well received at the time, but now it is easy to see that he was very close to the truth.

It is also interesting to see the way in which the words 'amateur' and 'professional' have changed in meaning over the intervening period. The word 'amateur' has come to mean 'less than competent', whilst 'professional' now means 'well carried out', rather than its former meaning of 'tainted by money'. Many sports only reluctantly accepted professionalism in the Games towards the end of the 20th Century, admitting only that it was necessary in order to prevent the Olympic Games becoming a festival of second class sport, no longer marketable and hence no longer economically viable. As we shall see, things have changed significantly in that regard and in Britain at least most Olympic sports are embracing the newer commercial realities.

For the athlete, the Olympic Games remain the pinnacle of his or her achievement. While the rules regarding amateur eligibility in 1948 were clearly stated, the reality as we have seen is that each sport within its own national environment determined the eligibility of their athletes and some were stricter than others. A British athlete could not even have applied for a post as a PE teacher without being declared ineligible.

A sizeable proportion of the British athletes were still in the forces, at university or medical students, but each sport served up its stories of factory workers having difficulty in getting time off from their employers even just to compete. Not all were blessed with the talent of Woosnam or the benefit of a populist support like that found in football to sway his or her employers. From the stunt man gymnast, prevented from doing somersaults in his work for fear this activity would damage his amateur status, to the yachting fraternity where cash prizes were commonplace, each had to live by the competing standards set by those who governed their sport. Certain British sporting federations, athletics to the fore, followed the laws to a ridiculous extent. There is no doubt in hindsight that the principal reason for doing this was to reinforce the social prejudices of the British class system.

Of course these constraints ultimately impacted on the performance of the athletes. Sylvia Disley's experience was commonplace. She remembers, 'I travelled abroad quite a lot with the British team but had to take it as holiday, so weekends were focused on travel and competing. Commuting and travelling for work also took its toll, so as the season went on you became quite run down. When I was chosen for the Empire Games in Auckland I left my job because the total travel time was around four months!'

There was, of course, the odd blind eye turned – in particular when medals were on the cards. Some of the examples from the rowing team we have recounted were testament to this – it is hard to understand how one could suggest that the Rowing Correspondent of *The Times* was not making money from rowing! In certain cases (in particular cycling) the breakdown of the notion of amateurism was beginning and to this day cycling has continued to be one of the most explicitly commercial of sports, with professional teams formed and disbanded on the whim of a corporate sponsor. There are some sports where the amateur principles remain, for example boxing. Jurisdiction for this largely remains an individual sport's prerogative.

While London 1948 was the catalyst for change throughout the Olympic movement, the paradoxes of amateurism remained an inconvenient truth for a good deal longer in many Olympic sports. In 1958, ten years after the London Games, Matt Busby, who had shepherded the GB football team through their Olympic challenge, was again appointed to international management as Scotland's manager for the World Cup in Sweden. Severe injury in the Munich air tragedy prevented him from carrying out his duties, but it is the response of the Scottish FA which is of interest. They opted not to replace him, but instead to appoint a 'trainer' with no playing experience to fill the role. The team was picked by the Committee, who did not attend the training ground and on more than one occasion included players who were not fully fit. The politics of the various clubs whose chairmen made up the Committee loomed large in the selections. The starkest contrast of all is that the players were paid no per-diem expenses and had to repay any temporary loans provided to sustain them while away. They did of course receive match fees, but those not selected for a game received no match fee. Tommy Docherty was not alone in owing a significant sum to the Scottish FA on his return. Not being paid to play an international sporting fixture is one thing, paying to do so another thing entirely.

At home and abroad during the Second World War, promises had been made of a brave new world once the War was ended. The Beveridge Report was intended to reinforce the ideals of what was being fought for by the British nation. It is a mark of the age that when the Labour Government was somewhat surprisingly voted to power, they believed they had an obligation to deliver on their manifesto promises. As we have seen, in many instances these promises were not met despite the best of intentions.

On 5 July 1948, a matter of weeks before the opening of the XIV Olympic Games in London, the National Health Service was launched. Tensions regarding whether it was actually viable were compounded by the problems of those projects vying for the same finite resources. Amongst those desperately in need of labour and materials of course were the Olympic venues and it took all the skills of resourceful entrepreneurs to pick a path through the morass. There were some stark choices along the way. The scaffolding for the essential Wembley scoreboard for the Games was also needed for the completion of the new wing of St Mary's Hospital. Funds and labour were needed desperately to refurbish access to Wembley Stadium for the spectators and contestants and yet at the same time those needs were certainly less pressing than housing for those displaced by the Blitz.

Clearly in this environment the Olympic Games were not going to be the top priority and Elvin sought a solution any which way. Loans were mortgaged against future ticket sales, material supply bureaucracy was massaged through the Ministry and labour supply was obtained by utilising German prisoners of war still resident in camps in the UK.

Despite these early tensions in the relationship between the NHS and sport it was clear from the Beveridge Report that the nation's health was at the forefront of the Government's ambitions and that sport might ultimately be an enabler to that end. The introduction of the NHS, free at the point of use, meant that participation sport would no longer be a luxury in which only those with medical insurance could partake. Sporting injury slowly became an inconvenience rather than something that threatened one's livelihood. This was critical because it meant that participation in sport, as well as simply watching it, was now an option for the working classes.

Time and affordability remained issues but the groundswell of support for all things sporting that was evident during the 1948 Games carried through to a marked increase in participation once the NHS was operational. Without the ability of the NHS to make sporting participation less of a risk for regular families, the opportunity for a participation legacy from 1948 would have been missed. In the 1950s and 1960s participating in sport, as much as watching it, became a key part of the British way of life. Even royalty was getting the message, with sporting figures featuring in the 1949 New Year's Honours List for the very first time.

Given the early days of healthcare provision for all, it is unsurprising that the standard of medical care was still low in general. There were also no special favours available to athletes despite their role in re-energising the British population through the Games. Sylvia Disley says, 'There was no medical support for the team. If you were ill or injured you just went to the doctor and sorted it out yourself. That was it. In my case undiagnosed ankle damage resulted in a stretched ligament and I was always vulnerable to injury after that, particularly hamstring trouble, which required careful nursing.'

Actually the Disley family's role in the sporting participation and health agenda does not by any means end there. Disley's husband John was also a world class athlete who ran in Helsinki where he won a bronze. As we have already seen, John's legacy also includes launching the London Marathon to Britain with his one time rival Chris Brasher. He also pioneered the introduction of orienteering to Britain, contributed towards setting up the Duke of Edinburgh Award scheme and became a mountain climbing author and tutor of some renown. Although a world record holder at two miles, John's own Olympic ambition was thwarted when he caught pneumonia just a couple of weeks before the Melbourne Games, and was forced to look on as his friend and rival Chris Brasher won gold.

There are two elements of symmetry to this story. Firstly, just as the NHS drove sporting participation in Great Britain and so eventually enabled events like Disley's London Marathon to become the phenomenon they are today, so those same sporting events have given so much back to our understanding of health and disease. The London Marathon has raised half a billion pounds for charity since its creation in 1981, much of it ploughed into charities supporting healthcare-related issues. Secondly, the organisers of London 2012 have announced that the London Marathon organisation founded by Messrs Disley and Brasher will be responsible for delivering both Olympic and Paralympic Marathons in 2012.

12

1948: The Dawn of the Paralympic Games and the Idea of Legacy

If there is one innovation from British soil which has looked to use sport to drive social change on a global level then it must surely be the advent of the Paralympic movement. In just 60 years, its vision of empowering disabled athletes, inspiring personal achievement at any level and, most critically, engaging the rest of our population in a more enlightened view of disability has changed our planet's concept of what disability means. As with Dover and Brookes, the movement started with one individual who believed passionately in the capacity of sport to change individuals' lives and ultimately society as a whole. This man was Dr Ludwig Guttmann.

Dr, later Sir, Ludwig Guttmann was born into an Orthodox Jewish family on 3 July 1899 in the small township of Tost in Upper Silesia – formerly Germany, now part of Poland. Guttmann's school career was chequered, his interest often being more in sport than his studies. Nevertheless, he took exams early in order to enlist in the National Emergency Services pending call-up for the First World War. Here, as a medical orderly, he worked with the paraplegic victims from the coalmines. Returning then to study, he eventually qualified as a doctor in 1923. His preferred medical specialisation was paediatrics, but on being advised this was impossible (he suggested in an interview that 'they already had almost one doctor for every baby') he was forced to opt for the sole available job which was in the Department of Neurology and Neurosurgery. Rising quickly through the ranks, he was at the top of his profession by his early thirties. However, the dictates of the Nazi regime against all Jewish doctors left him unable to practise. Travel papers for him and his family were facilitated by grateful former patients. Despite the scarcity of medical resource in the country at the time, the only immediately available role for a German doctor in Britain, his destination of choice, was a research post at Oxford.

During the war years, one of Guttmann's clinical papers was read by Dr George Riddoch, the leading Neurologist at the London Hospital. Riddoch was then a Brigadier General, although he had also been a former serving doctor at the front in the First World War. He appointed Guttmann to head up a new spinal unit at Stoke Mandeville, Aylesbury, in Buckinghamshire which was being set up in preparation for expected casualties from the imminent second front. Taking into account Guttmann's radical views on treatment and rehabilitation, this was a risky appointment. Given Guttmann's nationality, it was probably also on the borderline of legality.

When Guttmann first arrived at Stoke Mandeville, those with spinal cord injuries were still thought of as hopeless cripples. He could not accept this defeatist attitude. He believed the discomforts which came with major injuries were complications which could not only be controlled but altogether avoided. He also recognised another problem. 'Paralysed individuals lose self-confidence, activity of mind and personal dignity. They become encapsulated and anti-social,' he observed. His innovative treatment programme made work an everyday and mandatory part of each patient's activities. He wanted them to resume normal life as quickly as possible.

Given that most of his patients were young, formerly active individuals, sport was also part of that 'normal' life. It was a critical aid to regaining their strength and their future depended on being able to lift themselves into wheelchairs. It also encouraged them to make the most of their remaining physical capabilities, provide much-needed exercise and restored a mental equilibrium. Viewed from a modern perspective, it would be easy to underestimate quite how inspired and inspiring Guttmann and his staff's efforts were in a very different time. Early archive film of him at work suggests he pulled no punches. Arguably his unusual background afforded him some permission to be very different not just in terms of how he spoke, but the ways in which he engaged with staff and patients alike.

Guttmann was just 44 years old but his prior experiences equipped him with the necessary skills to set about building a team to achieve his mission –

to become the 'bearer of hope for the incurably dependant'. Diaries and books published by those in Guttmann's inner circle suggest that at the outset some sensed they were being punished for some sort of misdemeanour or prejudice in being posted to his team. Physiotherapists, nurses and doctors had traditionally thought of the appropriate treatment for paraplegics as pain mitigation until an inevitable early death. Paraplegics were usually isolated from other patients because of the detrimental affect on ward morale.

Given this context, it is easy to see how medical professionals felt in their early days of working with Guttmann. The immediate starting premise was one of recovery, rather than pain relief. He immediately outlawed a number of treatments, such as massage, and replaced them with a regimen of 24/7 'assisted movement', to reintroduce some flexibility back into his charges.

Charlie Atkinson, who became the lead physiotherapist on his team after joining straight from the army, found himself swiftly becoming a pioneer in sport for the disabled. Susan Goodman in *The Spirit of Stoke Mandeville* quotes him as saying, 'At the start it was a hit or miss affair, but after a while we were able to pick out a pattern and it became easier.'

Guttmann saw sport was a normal part of life and understood how it assisted the route to self respect no matter how tough the regime he set seemed at the time. There were no easy routes. One of his gifts was described by a medical colleague as the ability to 'cajole or bully patients in whatever ratio he felt necessary.' Atkinson allegedly heard a patient complain, 'There's no bloody time to be ill in this bloody place.' A patient's first steps never took place in the physiotherapy department, but in the middle of the ward where the other patients could see. Hope, Guttmann believed, was life-giving.

Guttmann also introduced games – darts, archery, snooker and table tennis – and soon followed up with team sports like wheelchair polo and basketball. Hospital life was certainly no longer as restricted and boring as it had been and word started to get out about some of the initiatives Guttmann was leading.

A milestone event took place on 28 July 1948, the same day as the Opening Ceremony for the 1948 Olympic Games at Wembley. On this day 16 paralysed British ex-servicemen and women engaged in an archery competition on the fields of Stoke Mandeville. This was the first of the Stoke Mandeville Games, now an annual event. Guttmann later said, 'The coincidence gave me an idea which I voiced at the 1949 Stoke Mandeville Games. Looking into the future, I prophesied that the time would come when this, The Mandeville Games, would achieve world fame as the disabled person's equivalent of the Olympic Games.'

The Stoke Mandeville Games were held annually after 1948 and became international in 1952 with the addition of a Dutch team of competitors. That same year the International Stoke Mandeville Games Federation, or ISMGF (later the International Stoke Mandeville Wheelchair Sports Federation, or ISMWSF) was created, and it was decided the Games should be held in the country hosting the actual Olympic Games from this point onwards.

As the annual Games increased in stature, Guttmann invited celebrity sportsmen to attend and then encouraged them to compete, but insisted they do so from a wheelchair. One of the disabled athletes involved described the buzz obtained from beating the British javelin and shot champions in these events and the mutual respect this afforded the athletes.

With some echoes of the London Games of 1908, when the British essentially wrote many of the rules for the Olympic sports, Guttmann, with the assistance of his faithful head of physiotherapy, went on to create the *Handbook of Rules of the Stoke Mandeville Games*. Time and techniques have demanded change, but it has remained a starting point for those concerned with sport for the paralysed. The next significant step forward after 1952 came in 1960 in Rome, immediately after the Olympic Games. Sir Ludwig watched from the Stands as 400 athletes entered the Olympic Stadium. This was a key stage on the road to the Paralympic Games. These Games are now second in size only to the Olympic Games as a global sporting event, the subject of television rights bidding wars and 400,000 British pre-registrations for tickets in the first four months after applications for 2012 opened.

Guttmann's shrewdness was not restricted to sporting innovation. In 1951, with a keen eye for the potential impact of the proposed transfer of his unit back to the control of the local authorities, he somehow managed to have Stoke Mandeville declared the National Spinal Injury Unit. He did not see his role as limited to his wartime patients, but at every opportunity expanded his scope to focus on the 'incurably dependant', whatever the cause.

It was at Guttmann's retirement in 1967 that the concept of the Stoke Mandeville Stadium was born. He set about the task with his usual single-mindedness and it took an extended struggle to gain agreement from the Ministry of Health to build a stadium in their grounds. He identified a consulting engineer and, with echoes of Elvin's entrepreneurial zeal, convinced him to take on the project on the basis that, 'it won't make you a rich man, but you will have done something fine for humanity.' The Stadium opened in 1969, just in time to host the annual International Stoke Mandeville Games.

The progress of the Paralympic Games towards the event we know today has been anything but linear and straightforward. In fact, there have been challenges along the way and at times the Paralympic Games have been seen as an 'optional extra' until very recently.

In 1979 Guttmann commenced his last great project – to create an Olympic Village for his Stadium. He died in 1980 so never saw completion, but the village was opened in time for the 1981 International Stoke Mandeville Games. It perfectly complemented the Stadium and was dedicated to Guttmann's memory, but what is uncanny is his prescient dedication back in the days of the initial stadium construction. 'We will build a sports stadium and an Olympic Village so that disabled athletes of the world will have their own Olympic facilities here in Stoke Mandeville, when other doors are closed to them.' Little did he know how true this would be. Moscow declined to host the Games in 1980, but fortunately Arnhem had taken up the challenge to step in in their place. Another set of challenges followed directly afterwards in 1984. The United States was scheduled to hold the 1984 Paralympic Games with some disability groups being hosted in New York, while those with spinal cord injuries and so in wheelchairs were holding their events at the University of Illinois in July. As late as April 1984 it was announced that the funds to hold the Illinois Games could not, after all, be raised.

Just as De Coubertin experienced in his early efforts to create an institution from his innovation, the fledgling Games were let down at the last minute. And as with the Olympic movement in both 1908 and 1948, Britain came to the rescue. A hasty meeting was convened of the International Stoke Mandeville Games Federation and with a decisiveness which put even Elvin's achievement of delivering the 1948 Olympic Games in three years to shame, the decision was announced to hold the Seventh Paralympic Games for those with spinal cord injuries at Stoke Mandeville.

With just three months of preparation, July saw the Stadium and Village hosting 1,100 athletes from 41 countries. The 'inner team' delivered a stunning event at very short notice. Beyond the venue itself, support from the local area was plentiful. Some 98 athletes completed the first Paralympic Wheelchair Marathon starting from Chalfont St Peter, finishing in the stadium. Canadian Rick Hanson won the event in a staggering time of one hour and 49 minutes. Rick was the athlete responsible for carrying the torch into the opening ceremony of the 2010 Winter Olympic Games in Vancouver.

There were two important legacies of Stoke Mandeville's short notice rescue of the Paralympic Games. Firstly, the most successful of these competitors would take part in demonstration events in Los Angeles which brought the Olympic and Paralympic Games back together in a meaningful way despite the bungled attempts of the United States to do so initially. Secondly, and more importantly, the disparate disability sport bodies merged to ensure every effort would be made to avoid such a split in the future. The road to 2012 for the disability groups has not been without discord, but the experience of 1984 made it clear to all that effective dealing with the Olympic movement could only be achieved by a unified body. The International Paralympic Committee was founded in 1989.

There have been several challenging Games to navigate on the path to general acceptance but that is what positive growth is all about. The path has not been smooth for Stoke Mandeville itself as a facility. In 1983, non-violent demonstrations prevented the closure of the Spinal Injuries Unit and a £10m refurbishment was achieved from voluntary funding. However 'Stoke' now has its future and place in history secured. Sir Philip Craven, President of the International Paralympic Association, recognises the unique legacy of Sir Ludwig Guttman and Stoke Mandeville.

'Sir Ludwig's legacy', he says, 'was in developing and disseminating Paralympic sport to the world. In doing this, he created the first energy centre for the Paralympic spirit which is still changing negative perceptions to the positive all over the world today. The staff at LOCOG were imbued with the Paralympic spirit at both the 2008 Paralympic Games in Beijing and the 2010 Paralympic Winter Games in Vancouver. The legacy of the Games in London for the very first time will be to transform best intentions into actualities. LOCOG has, right from the start, put equal emphasis into the organization of both Games.'

Final word from Guttmann's team goes to Charlie Atkinson, Guttmann's longtime collaborator, who together with Joan Scruton and Guttmann were known as the 'Three Musketeers'. When asked by Goodman in her book for his abiding memory, and bearing in mind all the trials and triumphs he was party to, he selects the following reminiscence.

'It was in the De Coubertin stadium in Paris, on one of our first trips abroad. A French paraplegic team and ours were to play a match, following a display and competition of top class able-bodied basketball players. To have to follow such a brilliant display filled us with misgivings as to the public reception of our match, so it was with mixed feelings the French referee and I filed into the arena to start the game. There was a deathly hush during the first few minutes and then a tremendous roar filled the stadium as the crowd cheered their French team, with the other referee and me being called all the usual names when we decided a foul against the local team. It was amazing. The crowd had forgotten that these people were in wheelchairs and were just watching two teams of basketball players.'

Guttmann was not a conventional medical innovator or an easy colleague. Nobody with his background ever would have been. Many of his relationships could be fractious. One NHS administrator summed it up perfectly in reflecting, 'No man with his drive and purpose could, or should, be a comfortable colleague for an administrator.' However, just like Dover, Brookes, Kilralfy, Elvin and even Coe, he was convinced of the broader role sport could play in social change and prepared to make that change happen. The London 2012 mascot may be called Mandeville, but the legacy is Guttmann's.

London 1948 sowed the seed for the Paralympic Games through the passion and drive of Ludwig Guttmann. As Sir Philip Craven emphasises, it is highly appropriate that the London 2012 Olympic and Paralympic Games will be the first summer Paralympic Games to be delivered from the outset by the same Organising Committee. This should cement the future of the Paralympic Games after a rocky time in the same way that London 1948 cemented the future of the Olympic Games.

While Stoke Mandeville stands today as a legacy of the Paralympic sporting innovation of 1948, in many ways the concept of an infrastructure legacy from the London 1948 Olympic Games is initially harder to discern. London was in a terrible state post-war as we have seen, crippled by national debt and unable to fund the significant capital expenditure needed to return to its pre-war state.

As a result, many of the infrastructure legacies of London 1948 were less around new buildings than the innovative use of current ones. For example, Elvin's use of the Wembley complex was masterful and cemented what was really little more than a greyhound track in the hearts of the British nation for the long term. The Empire Pool, now Wembley Arena, was used for both swimming and boxing – the boxing ring suspended above a partially-covered pool once the swimming had concluded. This entrepreneurial use of the arena continues for London 2012, with badminton and rhythmic gymnastics having agreed to move there from a temporary venue, in a bid to save cost from the overall organising budget for the Games. Elvin did whatever he could to shave cost from the operating bill and improve his facilities at the same time – for example, replacing the floor of his Empire Pool with wood imported from and gifted by Finland. Ever the entrepreneur, he also managed to negotiate the personal purchase of the remainder of the wood at a considerable discount!

In a similar vein, the BBC Yearbook for 1949 notes that 'a coaxial cable for television had been installed by the GPO during the early part of the year, between Wembley and Broadcasting House. This cable is terminated in the Stadium and remains as a permanent installation for future television broadcasts.' The BBC outside broadcast vans were retained and later sold to private companies. In fact, author Martin Rogan purchased them on behalf of EMI some 25 years later for refurbishment and use again for outside broadcasts in nations still using the same monochrome technology!

Herne Hill Velodrome, too, remains as a legacy of London 1948. The Cycling Union had spent up to early 1948 still angling for another venue and Herne Hill was finished at the very last minute. For example, hot water was only installed a matter of weeks before the start of the Games. Budgets were so tight that the slightest extra expenses were haggled over long after the Games were held. The British Olympic Association billed the Cycling Union with the cost of moving the rubble to build up the banks for spectators. The Cycling Union refused to pay because they said that not only was it an unnecessary move, but also that if they had wanted it they could have secured volunteers to do the work for nothing. The matter in debate was the share of a bill of about £150.

Perhaps the biggest infrastructure legacy impact of the London 1948 Games happened outside of the facilities themselves. It is hard to believe now that London authorities in 1948 were very anxious that the extra traffic created by the Olympic Games would bring London to a standstill. As a result they tested and implemented the very first series of one way streets in London as a direct legacy of London 1948. One can only wonder what they would make of the current investment in Stratford and its environs to support the traffic flow in 2012, or the IOC's stipulation of an Olympic lane on major streets for Olympic traffic only!

13

2012: Reversing Amateurism and New Attitudes to Health

While the concept of legacy existed far more in Guttmann's thoughts than those of the London 1948 Olympic Organising Committee, social change and legacy has been the premise on which London built the bid to host the Olympic and Paralympic Games in 2012. Legacy is a fundamental part of the definition of a successful Games in 2012 as opposed to a hoped-for by-product.

The notion of amateurism is effectively dead in Britain in 2012 against the backdrop of increased funding levels and expectations from Governing Bodies. Despite this, the practical financial realities of a football-obsessed market ensure that just like in 1948 only a small proportion of the British team will earn enough to support themselves for more than a few years after retirement.

The impact of this is significant. While Olympic athletes have the benefit of being able to train full time to deliver their best performance in 2012, in a total reversal of the traditional amateur ethos they are also required to think about how to make the most of their skill base during their sporting career in order to allow them to develop their marketability and employment options beyond 2012. For example Coca-Cola, a Global Olympic Partner, runs a programme in the UK with Lane4 which recruits athletes on the journey to London 2012 for work experience placements. As part of the bargain, they are supported in learning how they can apply their experiences as elite athletes back into the workplace both on the journey to London 2012 but also beyond it. Adecco (a London 2012 partner) has launched a scheme which supports Paralympic athletes with locating work placements in the run up to London

2012. Many athletes tend to find an additional focus and mental stimulus helps them get some downtime from their very physical primary occupation.

The reality is that while funding for Olympic athletes remains relatively strong during their elite competitive years, public coffers can only cover so many athletes. The majority of Olympic athletes who reach London will have been able to focus on their training without working but this is not necessarily true of Paralympic athletes or those just beneath the standard of elite level performance. It is also by no means true of those families who look to support aspiring athletes between the ages of 12 and 16. Sporting charity SportsAid's research suggests that the average athlete in this age range spends nearly £5,000 per year on equipment, training, travelling and all of the other essentials required for competing at the top level. In each of the last three Olympic Games the charity has supported more than 50% of the medallists in their formative years. Adrian Moorhouse was one of those who benefitted and he says, 'It was the very first time that somebody really said to me, "We believe you can succeed".'

In many cases, the natural link for athletes is to stay in sport after they have stopped competing themselves. Tim Benjamin, a British 400-metre runner who won Commonwealth and European medals and retired in 2009, was certainly in that camp. 'Even when I was an athlete I knew I wanted to coach. I'd had some tough times in the lead up to my retirement but I've always loved the sport and particularly sprinting. As an athlete I took a lot of ownership of my training schedule, strength and conditioning and racing plans so I really, really learnt about my event – how to break it down, understanding the technical elements. I'd also mentored a young athlete and his coach so knew that I had a passion for coaching and facilitating the performance of others as well as being the performer myself.

'One of the values I can bring to my coaching is that I really know what it feels like to have done all the training and stand in a call room with seven other athletes preparing to race at the World Championships and Olympic Games – the nerves you feel and the preparation that's needed off the track. That's the real test, the mental test, and I was pretty good at it. I've had years where training's gone wrong, injuries have persisted but my mental approach brought me through. My background also helps me appreciate my athletes' concerns and challenges on a slightly different level. As a sprinter I was also very technically and anatomically aware because of my family background (my

Dad's a Professor of Anatomy) so I'm not just a typical athlete transitioning into coaching.' Tim has recently acquired a gym as a base for his personal training and coaching.

There is an interesting contrast here to some of the more lucrative British sports, in particular football. Many of the very best players who would make fabulous coaches simply do not have the financial need or drive to give something back to their sport which is needed for a second career in coaching. One of the athletes that Tim has worked with is Joel Ramsbottom, a 100 metre sprinter who at the age of 17 is already running well under 11 seconds. 'I am now nearly 18 and am focused on 100 and 200 metres,' says Joel. 'I have always run but in the past I have also done gymnastics, tae kwon do, football and rugby. I have competed independently, for clubs and my schools.

'My mum comes from a very sporty family, was a sprinter herself and has always encouraged both me and my brother to get involved in sport. When I was about 13 she took me to the athletics club she used to run for when she was young and showed me the track. Up until this point I had only run on school grass tracks. It's hard to explain but when I stood on the tartan track that day I knew I wanted to be a sprinter. It felt so exciting to be on a proper track, standing on the start line. It was as if the lane in front of me was lit up and all I wanted to do was run.

'I've had a couple of coaches and have got on well with all of them and they've all helped me make good progress in my athletics career. While I have trained with other Olympians and world class athletes, meeting Tim and being given the opportunity to train with him couldn't have been better timed. These next few years are going to be really important for me. Of course it is great to get input from someone who has been there and done it, not just because of their experience of performing on the world stage, but also in Tim's case it is his knowledge of the sport, biomechanics and effective training methods and techniques which he has picked up throughout his own sporting career and now applies to his coaching.

'The most challenging thing for me is to balance my school studies with my training schedule as I'm in the final year of A-levels. I also need to make sure I have enough time to rest and hopefully also stay injury free.'

Another athlete who battled with injury throughout her career was Georgie Harland, a bronze medal-winning modern pentathlete from the Athens Games.

Georgie made a similar decision to stay in Olympic sport – but not in her own sport. She has since worked in canoeing and cycling from a sports psychology perspective. She says, 'I have found the cultures in each sport I have worked in very different. Some hold strong to their traditions, for example in the way their coaches coach athletes, while others are always evolving and sitting right on the edge of the next new piece of technology or equivalent.'

Of course the ultimate example of sportsman turned world class sports administrator is Jacques Rogge himself. Rogge, who has been IOC President since 2001 and was re-elected for another four years in Copenhagen in 2009, was himself a former yachting Olympian as well as being a former Belgian rugby union international! There is a certain symmetry in this given rugby sevens has just been elected to the status of Olympic sport for the very first time.

It is not just the athletes themselves who have turned their initial passions into careers. Many of the British support team also fit into this category. Dr Mike Loosemore is the same. He says, 'I was a decent but not elite rugby player. I became a GP and used to support sporting events as my unpaid hobby at the weekend. Now that there is funding available I have been lucky enough to re-train to make it my career. I was one of a couple of hundred people walking out representing Great Britain at the Opening Ceremony in Beijing. You can't buy that kind of experience, it was just incredible.'

Many athletes, too, find that they need need to think creatively in order to follow their aspirations. Liz Yelling and her husband Martin are building a successful sports coaching business on the back of their respective sporting success. Martin has represented England at road and cross country running, won the national elite duathlon championship twice and also competed in the Ironman World Championship in Hawaii. As he says, 'Standards for funding are very high and rightly so. When you still feel like you can personally achieve more but haven't currently got sufficient funding from UK Sport to continue, you have to find ways to generate income that fit with your performance aspirations. We choose to try to create roles and jobs that we are passionate about and enable us share our skills and experiences to help others improve.'

The Yellings have capitalised on the boom of the individual tendency to train and compete alone to offer high end services to keen amateur athletes and also provide health and fitness support to corporate clients. Martin says, 'Our coaching style is based on an understanding not only of elite coaching knowledge and skills but also motivation, education, health behaviour change, professional development and performance effectiveness. We also aim to work with organisations and agencies to broaden the impact we can have through developing other coaches, groups of individuals, corporate teams and health and sport participation strategy. We hope that in some small way we can bring positive change and healthy impact to individual lives. Certainly the Olympic Games can bring a juggernaut of enthusiasm and participation to Britain. It would be great to be part of this.'

The Yellings' business has grown quickly because, as Martin points out, not only are Britain's Olympic team now preparing like professionals, so increasingly are those that want to be competitive as a hobby. 'The last five years has almost seen an era of professionalisation for the amateur athlete. You'd pay for a driving instructor or a golf pro, and now the field has moved on into other sports and coaching arenas. A personal target for an amateur athlete represents their own Olympic gold medal and the goal of the coaching we offer is to provide some scaffolding, support, motivation and guidance to help them realise this target. The landscape of a traditional 'club' style coaching often doesn't fit comfortably with schedules and lifestyles.'

In 2010 Martin launched a free podcast, *Marathon Talk*, with Tom Williams which aims to improve the quality of freely available training information for the amateur athlete and to do so in an accessible way. Martin says, 'We decided to create a community for runners to engage with and be a part of. We felt that runners needed somewhere trusted to turn to for advice when there is a great deal out there to take in. *Marathon Talk* tries to give opinion, thoughts, strategies and methods to enable runners to begin to make their own choices about how to train in a way best suited for their personal goals and contexts. We wanted to be able to reach more people than a relatively small number of personal coaching clients and create a community that respects each other, takes the lead in helping and supporting each other and most importantly has fun.' *Marathon Talk* had 7,000 people a week tuning in within six months of its creation.

Developing a business proposition on the back of sporting experience is not a new phenomenon. The business that author Matt is part of, Lane4, is an organisation that has grown for the last 15 years by bringing insight and learning from the world of elite level performance sport into business. Founded in 1995 by Seoul gold medal winning swimmer Adrian Moorhouse and Professor Graham Jones, an internationally renowned sports psychologist, the business has grown to 67 people and operates in 23 countries across the globe. Adrian picks up the story.

'In 1995 Graham Jones and I started Lane4 with the express aim of bringing some of the tools and skills that I had learnt in the sporting environment into the business world. Over the last 15 years we have developed into a fully-fledged consulting business. As Managing Director I have discovered that there are many similar challenges in running a business to those I experienced as an athlete. For example, having the ability to stay focused on the overall strategy and goals of the business despite the external pressures of our marketplace and our competitive set. There are many things which I have been able to transfer from what I learnt as an athlete, in particular the way I set my goals, built my belief, my experience of being coached at a high level and understanding of how to stay resilient in changing times.'

The business retains many links with the Olympic and Paralympic Games and many employees remain connected with it in a working capacity through team management, sport psychology support, media work, athlete coaching and so on. Two employees even continue to compete at Olympic level – Greg Searle and Clare Strange, a leading member of the Great Britain wheelchair basketball team. Both Searle and Strange are able to balance working with senior business leaders and also their sporting commitments. Searle says, 'It's great to be in a position to work with the elite every day. Now I am doing it in rowing again as well as in business. I get a similar feeling working alongside other consultants and senior leaders in our client businesses as I do in my rowing squad. It's not hard to balance this when you really care about both worlds and there is a sensible challenge to be met.'

Clare Strange's perspective as an elite level athlete is that for her the choice of career and employer has been critical. 'I have the benefit of working for a company that understands the time challenge and need for flexibility,' she says. 'This has been invaluable in managing any tension between my sport and my work. It is still a challenge to fit in both the quality and quantity of training needed and the appropriate rest time. Rest days are often work days which can work well but can also be tiring with the demands of travel in both my sport and work life.' Searle and Strange's working lives are demanding, supporting senior teams in British blue-chip businesses through their own changes. Their ability to manage their time and their own focus – from FTSE board meeting to gym – is extraordinary.

Moorhouse's ethos has been to try to create a business which provided 'everything I thrived on in my time as an elite athlete – which felt like a Great Britain Olympic Training Camp.' Lane4 and its Board regularly appear in the respective Top Tens of the '*Sunday Times* Best Companies to Work For' lists. Moorhouse has twice been voted Best Leader in this list and also Director of the Year by the Institute of Directors.

Searle and Strange are by no means the only ones who balance their sport with working at an elite, high-pressured level. Tim Brabants, for example, who won flatwater canoeing gold in Beijing, returned to his role as a doctor soon afterwards and has only recently switched back to full-time preparation in time for the build-up to London.

There is a clear reversal here from London 1948. At that time, the imperative was to ensure that none of the British athletes were profiting financially from their sporting talents, principally as a means of reinforcing social class structure. As we move towards London 2012 in a less fixed social system, athletes are being actively encouraged to think through how they can monetise their experience, whether directly through coaching the next generation or less directly through organisations like Lane4.

While the concept of amateurism from London 1948 has mostly been left behind, there remains a sense of injustice in the wealth distribution of British sport. Football has retained its 'sport of the people' appeal from London 1948 and in doing so has made millionaires of many, in particular in the Premier League. Individual Olympic sports will need to ride the wave of London 2012 effectively to ensure that this divide is not a permanent one. Even today, in the run up to London 2012, some athletes likely to take part are mostly unfunded. One example of this is Bobby White, the goalkeeper of the Great Britain handball team. White and the team aspire to compete in London in two years' time.

White did not grow up dreaming of being a handball goalkeeper. He started his senior sporting life as the semi-professional goalkeeper for Newport Pagnell FC and has actually only been playing handball since January 2008. White, along with seven of his teammates, was selected from over 2,500 athletes that applied for the 2007 Sporting Giants Talent Identification Programme (TID) which was led by UK Sport and the English Institute for Sport. After a series of fitness and skill-based trials he was eventually offered a full-time contract starting in January 2008 at a sports academy in Denmark where he joined the existing GB squad members in preparing to go from learning the rules to playing in the Olympic Games in just four years. White says, 'I saw Sir Steve Redgrave on the BBC promoting the talent search. As he listed off the criteria (sporting background, over 6'3'' and under 25) I thought "well, I tick those boxes". I decided I'd apply for handball given my background as a goalkeeper.

'I wasn't optimistic but received a letter inviting me to a trial. UK Sport had shortlisted 120 athletes from an estimated 2,500 applicants. We had several trials and 18 of us were invited to the third trial, a week's training in Denmark with the GB Squad. It was eye-opening. We met some "average" Danish players who looked amazing at the time and also got to see a first division match. Finally 15 of us were asked to come on a 10-week full-time training programme at the English Institute of Sport in Sheffield. This was the most intense training I'd ever done, three sessions a day involving strength, cardio and speed training as well as handball. It was a tough period but enjoyable at the same time. As you'd expect a lot of banter was flying around but we worked very hard through this period as we could see that we were nearly there. Nine trialists were offered places in the end.'

The aim of the programme is to create a competitive handball team to compete in the 2012 London Olympic Games, targeting a top eight finish. It has not been an easy path for White and the team, principally because news of a significant reduction in funding has meant immediate changes to the set up of the programme. UK Sport funding is focused on delivering podium athletes and this, coupled with a squeeze in broader Government funding, means that handball effectively needs to be self-sufficient at a time when it is still investing heavily. This creates an even deeper tension for White than it did for our penniless athletes of 1948. Then, at least, it was sufficient to train in evenings and weekends to stand a chance of making the team. White needs to eat, sleep, drink and think handball between now and London 2012 in order to stand a chance of hitting the necessary standard and yet effectively this means going into debt.

The impact of the financial austerity is now being felt. White says, 'Of the nine that started, only four remain in the squad. Some of the boys didn't take to the sport and a few others quit for financial reasons. It has been very tough since the funding dried up. We lost our "wages" back in March 2009. We were receiving £330 a month from UK Sport as well as our living costs but that was also cut. Somehow most of us have managed to find part-time work, or beg, borrow and steal to get ourselves through last season. Last summer I worked as a fitness instructor to secure some money and we have been lucky enough for SportsAid to give us a small amount of cash, but that works on an individual basis. Next season will be tough, but it looks like the British Handball Association will start to provide some money for us again to help cover our living costs. I have actually been lucky enough to secure a modest pro contract in the Greek League. Unfortunately there isn't a great amount of money involved and I'll probably still have to get a part-time job as I have debts from my uni days of around £100 per month. This needs to be covered somewere along the line! But I am doing something I love and it will make all the hard work seem all the more worth it when we walk out at 2012!'

Britain might have created the platform for White via Sporting Giants, but that does not change the rigorous nature of the funding strategy which his team has yet to match up against. On one level it seems harsh to be taking away funding so early in his journey in the new sport, in particular when Buckingham Group are currently delivering a world class £27m venue to host the competition and reduced funding means Britain will not perform as they might within it. On the other side of the coin, UK Sport has a finite pot and more than ever must prioritise its investment. Gold medals today drive participation tomorrow.

One athlete who is certainly a gold medal hope in London is World Triathlon Champion Alistair Brownlee. Triathlon is an increasingly professional sport in terms of the training required and level of financial rewards available for the very best. Participation is booming in Britain which fuels the potential of the sport as a commercial opportunity for the absolute world elite level. Despite this, Brownlee keeps his feet resolutely on the ground, living and studying in Leeds. He explains, 'The mixture of elite level care and training support I receive at Leeds, balanced with the possibility of keeping a balanced, normal life as just one of thousands of students, works really well for me personally. While triathlon is booming and the demands on my time outside training are significant, I am far happier training and preparing in an environment I know well. Training and racing well is my total priority – everything else will follow if I get those bits right.'

Of course developing sporting participation in Britain is about far more than just discovering the next Alistair Brownlee. Since 1948 our understanding of the importance of cardiovascular exercise as a means of maintaining psychological and mental health and preventing illness has increased exponentially. Corporate sponsorship and government investment have driven a significant extension of the coaching infrastructure to support this participation agenda – for example, through the successful McDonald's-driven football coaching development scheme. Recent corporate schemes such as the British Gas Free Swim Programme have focussed on delivering access to facilities which is the critical other side of the coin. There is no point developing swimming coaches if the pools themselves are closing.

An increasing percentage of the population has a deeper understanding of our health than ever before. Many of us now understand our individual allergies, read in detail the make-up of the foods we eat and search for low-fat, vitamin-rich, organic produce in our staple diet. It is easy to make over-simplistic assumptions that this is the same segment of the population who use private gym facilities and can afford to look after their health by paying for monthly gym membership or home deliveries of organic food. In fact there is little if any evidence of this – it is more a case of a broad cross section of the population making lifestyle choices. There is no evidence that the average disposable income of a marathon runner is any higher than that of the general population.

While an increasing number of the British population take these areas seriously, they remain in the minority, as Professor Adam Carey explains. 'Nutrition in the general public remains a long way from optimal. We see that, like athletes, 10% of individuals believe they eat well and on investigation do; 10% of individuals recognise they eat very poorly and they are never mistaken! But 80% of the population believe they eat well but don't.

'Obesity is now starting to overtake smoking as the single most important health issue for the public. Many aspects of health have gone backwards rather than moved forward over the last 30 years. We are tending to live longer but with more ill-health and a poorer quality of life; with an entirely avoidable epidemic of non-insulin dependant diabetes that is set to overwhelm the NHS in the UK in the next 20 years; where one in three children born today are predicted to become diabetic. There has never been a more important time to reflect the learning we have identified in sport back into the general public.

'We will all be expected to work for longer as the age of retirement inevitably increases and to do this organisations are now beginning to recognise that they need to invest into the wellbeing and health of their staff, to improve their performance, reduce absence and stress and contribute to a workplace where individuals want to stay and actively contribute. My business, Corperformance, has been running coaching programmes for the last five years for a number of large businesses to help them educate and support their staff to improve not only their individual wellbeing and performance, but also the health culture overall within the organisation.

'Most of us know something about the food we eat, but notwithstanding this we are obviously still getting something wrong. There is a vast amount of confused information in the public domain and a lack of clear, effective advice. Like the athletes we see, most individuals over-consume refined processed foods and do not eat enough vegetables, fibre and protein. The translation of five portions of fruit and vegetables a day into four portions of fruit and an orange juice is, I believe, an example of one of the nutritional nightmares that exist in the backdrop of a typical UK diet. Since fruits are just vegetables with added sugar, a more appropriate interpretation of this common policy might be to consume four to five portions of vegetables (this does not include potatoes and grains) a day with possibly one piece of fruit in season. Like our elite athletes, individuals need to learn how to change their long term behaviours to deliver personal outcomes that are meaningful to them.'

Alison Mowbray's experience supports this view. She has built on her experience as an Olympic rower to support corporate teams with their own diet and nutrition strategies, however has also had to manage her own diet now she is outside of full time training. She says, 'Even though I trained extremely hard and was tired pretty much all the time for the seven years I was on the squad, I was rarely ill and never injured. I suppose some of that was down to luck but I think most of it was down to the care I took to eat what I needed. Now in my life at Lane4 I am always on the go and on the road and eating in hotels and so on. People often say to me now "So, can you eat anything you like now you're not an athlete?" The answer is a resounding "No". I was much closer to being able to eat what I liked when I was an athlete, because I was consuming 4-5000 calories a day. Now, I know I can only eat maybe 2,500 a day before I start to put on weight (even with some exercise) so I have to think very carefully about my food choices. I actually think my diet is better now than it was when I was an athlete because I have more knowledge. Some of the advice we were given as athletes I now know is just wrong.'

Alison, too, decries the convenient 'five a day' target. 'Firstly, the science doesn't say five portions of fruit and veg a day, that's a government target not a scientific one. Scientific studies on people who live long, healthy, active lives shows that they have been eating eight to ten portions of fruit and vegetables a day throughout their lives. This is the government recommendation in most Scandinavian countries. I follow this and believe it has the biggest beneficial effect of any diet measure. When I recommend it to friends and clients and they try it, within a week they'll report back that they feel better and feel like they have more energy. Fruit and vegetables have become the main source of carbohydrate in my diet and I think this is the other myth about an athlete's diet that needs busting. We were recommended to eat pasta, bread, cereals, rice and potatoes because they are good complex sources of carbohydrate. As a result, I ate loads of them. I've since found out that they all have a very high glycaemia index which means the glucose molecules are released almost immediately and they will cause a blood sugar spike and cause your body to release a lot of insulin to bring it down again. This sugar yo-yoing causes you to feel alternatively 'high' and then dead tired. It is the same effect that leads to the development of type II diabetes in overweight people with a poor diet. I read around to find out what was going on and switched to mainly low GI sources of carbohydrate, the really good carbs that I should have been eating for training all along. Fruit and vegetables are the best sources of carbs (not including white potatoes) also oats (so porridge and muesli rather than processed cereals) rye breads rather than wheat breads (all wheat products including pasta and couscous are high GI) and the high protein grain quinoa.'

If healthcare experts paint a worrying picture, at least Sport England data would suggest that sporting participation is now on the rise overall. During the 12 months to January 2010, seven million adults aged 16 and over participated in sport three times a week for 30 minutes at moderate intensity (16.6% of the adult population in England). This is an increase of 186,000 adult participants from 2007 when 6.815 million adults (aged 16 and over) participated at that same level. We can see underneath this overall increase some of the reasons that the Yellings' business is booming. Participation in cycling and athletics (road running) are both increasing significantly. These are sports which can be fitted flexibly into a busy schedule. Martin Yelling finds that 'a good amount of the value I can add as a coach for keen amateur athletes is helping them fit their training into a busy schedule in the rest of their lives, to help them get value from the time they do have available. For most people, the danger is training too hard without any real plan behind all that hard work.' On the flip side, more club-based sports including rugby, bowls and golf are declining across all demographics. These reductions seem to be particularly pronounced in the 16-18-year-old age gap – the critical age for ensuring that sporting participation carries through to adulthood.

From London 2012's perspective it has been critical to ensure that the Games energise all of the population who might want to re-engage with sport, on whatever terms they wish. This requires the provision of facilities for all, and builds on some recent strong progress made by the likes of the Football Foundation as well as investment driven through the National Lottery. Since 1997 the Heritage Lottery fund has donated some £4.4bn across the UK. Although that is less than half of the entire budget for the Olympic Games, it has been focused on local delivery and started to quell on some level the damage done by systematic selling-off of playing fields and sports facilities in the UK by successive governments. A good example of this is the clubhouse of the last football club author Matt played for (Watlington Town, in the Oxfordshire Senior League) which was funded by the Football Foundation. This facility, built in the mid-1990s, hosts adult and junior football and cricket teams as well as various community events, sporting and otherwise.

Certainly most of the current British Olympic governing bodies are booming. As Peter Hart, Chief Executive of Pentathlon GB, says, 'The best thing about running modern pentathlon at the moment is that we have more opportunities to make people aware of the sport and give them the chance to participate and experience the sport(s). If they wish, we can help them fulfil their full potential. I know how rewarding it is when we organise a major event such as the World Cup and how much satisfaction all of us experience when we deliver a well-organised event, a large happy crowd and Britain ending up on the podium.'

Certainly the grass roots of British sport are healthier than for a very long time. One of the most interesting developments of the last year has been a new running phenomenon which takes up the challenge of delivering sporting experience for the masses, without cost. This is called Parkrun. The concept is simple. A central website and brand is essentially licensed, with no charge, to local individuals who wish to organise a five kilometre run in their local park. Costs are funded centrally by core sponsors – including Nike and Lucozade Sport – who are attracted by the opportunity to engage with grass roots runners in a cost effective and scaleable way.

Author Matt's experience demonstrates the ease of access. After a two-minute registration process online, he is now able to simply turn up and run a race any Saturday at one of 30 sporting locations across the UK by simply bringing along a personalised bar code. His first Parkrun event was very low key – some 130 attended, from elite club runners to those for whom this was a very first race. The bar code was read at the end to record a finish time and Matt received a personalised e-mail by the end of the day of the race registering his finish time, finish position and pointing him back towards the Parkrun website for free available photos from the event and a race report provided by the race organiser.

The following Thursday a chatty, friendly Parkrun newsletter arrived – updating on the growth of the phenomenon, promoting some of the newer races, gently emphasising the need for volunteers to make the runs happen and thanking the sponsors whose funding made the events possible in the first place.

These two final elements of the jigsaw are critical to the Parkrun model. Firstly, volunteers are the lifeblood of the event in order that participation can remain free of charge. An ongoing points-based competition between athletes rewards volunteering as well as competing. Secondly, sponsorship funds ensure that investment in the technology platform which delivers such a compelling experience can continue.

This type of sponsorship is a world away from £80m Olympic sponsorship deals. While securing formal rights is critical for organisations like Lucozade Sport (who are linked with UK Athletics and the FA Premier League among many other organisations), it is at the grass roots that these deals come alive.

This is the point of influence of purchase. In today's fragmented marketing and tight economic environment, making a tangible contribution to the opportunity for new and elite runners to compete for free on a weekly basis is a very potent message. This is not something the brands need to hard sell to participants – the message is clear.

Attending one of these Parkrun events is an interesting experience. One would tend to assume that the web-based focus might threaten the traditional club feel of the Saturday morning run. In fact the reality is very different. There is a buzz of conversation between the regulars as you arrive and those who are able wander over after the event for a coffee at the Park Café. The event feels surprisingly communal. It might be a different structure to the traditional running club but it is no less valid as a facilitator of mass participation sport.

This tallies with the experience of a Parkrun event organiser. Parkrun Leeds was started by Tom Williams from *Marathon Talk*. Having never previously run more than a couple of miles, Williams trained for, and ran, his first marathon in 1999. Since then Williams has run a further ten marathons with a personal best of 2:49 achieved in London 2008. In 2006 Williams completed his first triathlon and has now finished seven Ironman races. He explains how he came across Parkrun.

'About three years ago I saw Bushy Parkrun mentioned in *Runner's World* and was instantly sold on this amazing new concept. I couldn't wait to start something similar in Leeds but, aware of the need for others to commit and also my own weekend athletic commitments, I needed to wait for the right moment. Sometime around the summer of 2007 I was invited to a meeting with the Sport Development office at work (I'm a lecturer in Sports Science at the University of Leeds) where the agenda surrounded ideas for providing volunteering opportunities for our students while promoting physical activity and exercise. Within a couple of months we'd contacted the founder of Parkrun, been down to London for a training session, written the volunteering duties into the Sport and Exercise Science degree programme and created paid roles for four second-year students to act as race directors during term time, with us providing a guiding hand and taking over during the vacation periods.'

This is a fantastic example of the agility and entrepreneurialism which is now driving British sport at the grass roots level. Arguably Parkrun thrives despite rather than because of any formal public sector infrastructure. Williams continues, 'As we were the first Parkrun event outside of the M25 (Brighton arrived a week later), not many people were aware of the concept. But word quickly spread and we broke 100 runners for the first time at event number seven. Since then we've held 147 events with 3,646 different people completing 19,768 runs. We've also achieved our first 100 club member in Aamir Murtaza – which means he has competed 100 times – and now have an event committee consisting of both members of the community and students from the University who work in partnership to deliver Leeds Parkrun 52 weeks of the year, extreme weather permitting.'

In this sense not only is Parkrun contributing to the participants' lives, it is also living out the increasing Government mandate to Universities to actively engage with the communities in which they operate.

'I think the key to Parkrun's success is largely due to its inclusive and accessible nature,' says Williams. 'Almost all barriers to participation are removed and people of all abilities are made to feel welcome. We also work hard to foster communities around each event. For example, one of the conditions of staging a Parkrun event is that you have a designated coffee shop where runners can get together straight after the run and the organisers attend every week. We often find ourselves at 10am on a Saturday morning sharing stories with more than 30 different people from all walks of life, most of whom would never normally find themselves in the same social space. In my experience at the end of a more typical running event people go their separate ways.'

The future seems rosy for this model of participation sport. Parkrun has already expanded internationally and is at the tipping point. They say, 'We have had approaches from Australia, New Zealand, North America, Canada, South Africa, Italy, France and most recently Sweden. It's often quite tricky starting a new event overseas and these can take longer to get off the ground but the Parkrun family, and all we stand for, seems to have legs everywhere. We remain firm and steadfast in the protection of our core principles while we manage the challenging growth opportunities.'

This is not to suggest that all local authorities are under-delivering on their responsibilities to deliver grass roots support. Like Parkrun, some recent, more progressive, intiatives are intended to reflect rather than fight against the sports participation trends we are seeing. For example, South Bucks District Council has recently launched a Cultural and Community Programme to drive further sporting participation. The list of activities provided is very telling. Alongside free swimming for under-16s, programmes include Advanced Brazilian Soccer (skills-based rather than team competition), Junction2Dance workshops, the Local 2012 Programme which includes talks from Olympians, health and nutritional advice, rowing on the Olympic venue at Dorney Lake and events in local schools, and MEND workshops (Mind, Exercise, Nutrition, Do It) targeted at 7-13 year olds above their ideal weight.

Certainly the participation agenda should make a meaningful difference to ease the short term pressures which Andy McGrath described the NHS as facing. However, going forward it is also likely to change the nature of provision required. He explains, 'I imagine broader sporting participation would hopefully mean less cancer and chronic pulmonary disease (breathlessness in old people). Today these make up about 60% of our admissions. Healthier people would also mean people live longer, so I imagine going forward we will see different types of illnesses making up our daily work. I would expect we will also see more need for care in the community as people will become fitter, but also older.'

Overall, a combination of events like Parkrun and targeted investment happening at a local authority level suggests that Britain is making strides to drive the health message through sporting participation. The messages both convey are not to fight against social change, but to consider how one might embrace them to deliver sporting experience. Too often the growth of the internet is given as an excuse for dwindling numbers at sports clubs and sports leagues across the country. In reality, this is just an excuse.

As Adam Carey says, 'The UK's current health issues are because of a combination of a poor quality diet and inactivity. And while it is not possible for most people to exercise their way out of obesity, being physically active is hugely important in supporting a healthy mind, body and probably soul too.'

Lord Sebastian Coe – Chairman of the London Organising Committee of the Olympic and Paralympic Games 2012. (© *Bucks 2012 Partnership*)

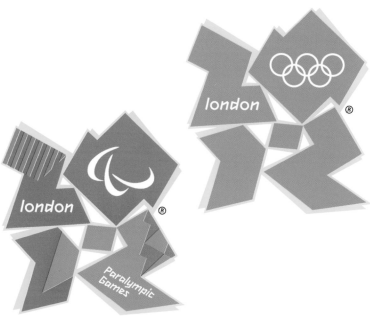

The multi-media logos for the London 2012 Olympic Games and Paralympic Games – organised together for the very first time.
(© *London Organising Committee of the Olympic and Paralympic Games*)

Sunset at Dorney Lake, Rowing and Sprint Canoeing Venue for the London 2012 Games. (© *Bucks 2012 Partnership*)

The Great Britain K4 Canoe Squad gathered at the 1000 metre point, their start line, to mark the 1000 day countdown to the London 2012 Olympic Games in October 2009. (© *Bucks 2012 Partnership*)

Sam Weale, Great Britain's 2010 European Silver Medallist Modern Pentathlete, in action at the World Championships at Crystal Palace in London in 2009. (© *Phil Searle, digiscape*)

Weale in action on the same day in both fencing (left) and the new final run / shoot discipline (exiting the shoot area). Modern Pentathlon itself was actually De Coubertin's own innovation and contested for the first time at the Olympic Games in 1912. Its International Federation, the UIPM, was created as a legacy of the London 1948 Games. The sport continues to identify the most rounded of all Olympic athletes at each Games, and celebrates its one hundred year anniversary in London in 2012. (© *Phil Searle, digiscape*)

From athletics and basketball to rowing – Sarah Winckless, now Chair of the British Olympic Association Athletes' Commission (right) pictured with Elise Laverick (left) in Sydney in 2000. (© *Empacher*)

Uxbridge Lido – a popular destination in 1938.
(© *Hillingdon Local Studies, Archives and Museum Service*)

The same venue recreated for the 21st Century.
(© *Hillingdon Local Studies, Archives and Museum Service*)

Greg Searle – preparing age 38 for the 2010 World Championships. (© *Lane4*)

Liz Yelling coaching Poole Runners. (© *Helen Turton*)

Clare Strange in action for Britain at the World Wheelchair Basketball Championships in Birmingham in 2010. (© *SA Images.com*)

Former Olympic Minister Tessa Jowell and Clare Strange visiting Cressex School, High Wycombe in December 2009. (© *Bucks 2012 Partnership*)

From football to handball – Bobby White in action for Britain against Bulgaria in a Euro 2012 Qualification match.

An International Athletics Competition at Stoke Mandeville in August 2009
demonstrates athletes pushing the boundaries of their disability
(© *WheelPower*)

Bucks 2012 Conference, February 2009, left to right: Paul Mainds, River & Rowing Museum, Henley; Ian Barham, Bucks 2012 Manager; Adrian Moorhouse, Chair, Bucks 2012 Partnership and Sebastian Coe, Chair of LOCOG. The placard reads, 'I have been inspired by'… Coe has written 'self exploration'.
(© *Bucks 2012 Partnership*)

Tribes-people of the Omo Valley in Ethiopia building a London 2012 Olympic Stadium with artist Rachel Gadsden. (© *Bucks 2012 Partnership* / *Rachel Gadsden*)

Parkrun Leeds – a great example of 21st Century participation sport.
(*both © Helen Turton*)

14

2012: Paralympism Comes of Age and the Application of Legacy

As Sir Philip Craven identified earlier in the book, it is very apt that the first full integration of Paralympic and Olympic Games by an Organising Committee from the outset of delivery is to happen in Britain in 2012. Certainly there was a notion even as recently as Beijing that the Paralympic Games were not delivered in an integrated fashion. While the travel network in Central Beijing catered admirably for disability, this was not always the case for those willing to travel beyond the core Paralympic Games area.

Britain has continued to lead the way in terms of awareness of and support for Paralympic sport. Events such as the London Marathon, for example, have driven a wider awareness of Paralympic sporting opportunity. Arguably the breakthrough moment in this regard was Dame Tanni Grey Thompson's second-placed finish in the BBC Sports Personality of the Year Awards, an award which is decided by public vote. Corporate support in recent years behind Paralympic sport has been significant, with the likes of VISA, BT, Adecco and Sainsbury's proactively engaging with it and driving its profile in the media. In the run-up to London 2012, Britain has supported a Paralympic World Cup in Manchester at an elite level which has created another televised showcase. Slowly things are changing.

Clare Strange, nominated for *Sunday Times* Paralympic Sportswoman of the Year in 2010, has seen this transition first hand as an elite wheelchair basketball athlete. She says, 'I think that in Britain we were already progressing in our support and knowledge of the Paralympic Games due in part to the ever-increasing coverage on the BBC initially. However since winning London 2012 the publicity of the Paralympic Games has definitely increased. It is now recognised as an elite event and the athletes competing in the Games are held in high esteem. A significant change for us since London won the Games has been the increase in funding, taking the stress out of needing to continually raise funds to pay for foreign trips and so on.'

This is a telling statement. It is a sign of how egalitarian British sporting bodies have become that Britain's wheelchair basketball team remain relatively well-funded when the able-bodied female volleyball and male handball team have had funding taken away. The reason lies in the current performance of Clare's team, European bronze medallists and improving quickly on the road to 2012.

Of course sponsors rely on television exposure for their investment. Intriguingly, domestic TV rights for the Paralympic Games were sold separately to the Olympic Games rights for London 2012 – with Channel Four paying £5m in total for the rights to 160 hours coverage. It has also committed to a higher marketing support spend than for the Ashes cricket and its racing coverage plus the support of a broader range of Paralympic sport going forward. Lord Coe's comment at the announcement of the deal speaks volumes for the opportunity this represents: 'Channel 4 shares our vision for the Paralympic Games, has a very strong appeal to young people and will play a hugely important role in increasing public engagement and involvement in Paralympic sport in this country.'

Signs of some of the strides being made in Paralympic sport are evident in Stoke Mandeville itself. A significant programme of activity is underway to ensure that the local area makes the most of the London 2012 Olympic and Paralympic Games. This includes making accessible the archive collections connected with the story of the development of the Paralympic movement at Stoke Mandeville and creating a documentary film to capture its story to date and aspirations for the future.

Martin McElhatton is Chief Executive of WheelPower, which is the national organisation for Wheelchair Sport in the United Kingdom and exists to provide, promote and develop opportunities for men, women and children with disabilities to participate in recreational and competitive wheelchair sport. Annually WheelPower introduces many young and newly-disabled people to the tremendous benefits of participating and competing in sport. This is a particularly challenging brief, working from the grass roots to the absolute elite. McElhatton says, 'We have to focus our efforts on the most important projects, the reality is that there just aren't enough hours in the day or people in the team to do more.'

Stoke Mandeville Stadium itself has boomed as a Centre of Excellence for Disability sport since reopening in 2003 after a £10.2 million redevelopment. It is an extraordinary place to visit, watch and play sport and hosted Clare Strange's bronze medal-winning performance in 2009 at the Women's European Wheelchair Basketball Championships. The journey started in 1968 when work started on Stoke Mandeville Stadium, built at a cost of £350,000 on hospital land leased from the Ministry of Health. Opened in 1969 by HM Queen Elizabeth, it has gone from strength to strength despite ongoing funding pressures. Beyond the Sports Centre itself, facilities now include a 400-metre high quality athletics track, state of the art inclusive fitness centre, tennis courts, an indoor bowls centre and an on-site 100 bed hotel to add to the existing athlete accommodation.

Sir Ludwig Guttmann died aged 80 in 1980, however the Centre's progress is a barometer of the steadily improving provision for disabled people in Britain. Clare Strange's hope for a Paralympic legacy is that these kinds of facilities become a more mainstream part of our lives across the country. 'I would like to see the Games changing the attitude to disability both in UK and worldwide,' she says, 'in particular to see physical access improved in London. It should be possible to use innovative and practical solutions, not over the top expensive adaptations. These, coupled with excessive red tape, can cause resentment from both sides and create a negative connotation with the principle of accessibility.'

With every opportunity comes a cost, however. Sadly British Paralympic sport is now experiencing somewhat of a participation boom on the back of recent combat in Iraq and Afghanistan. There is certainly poignancy in the way this takes us back to the initial participants in Guttmann's Games. Guttmann himself said when interviewed by the BBC, 'If I ever did one good thing in my career, it was to introduce sport into the treatment and rehabilitation of disabled people.' Certainly the experience of recent war veterans is now to be introduced to sport as a critical part of their physical but critically also mental rehabilitation.

Sir Philip Craven's concerns for the future of the Paralympic movement itself relate to building on an inevitable success in London. He says, 'The vision of the International Paralympic Committee is to enable Paralympic athletes to achieve sporting excellence and inspire and excite the world. I believe that from what I have observed and felt over the past five years, the success of the 2012 Paralympic Games in London is all but assured. Great teams of people coming together will ensure this happens.'

As a result of his confidence around the delivery of the London 2012 Paralympic Games, Sir Philip's aspirations for the future of his movement are spread much further afield. He says, 'The biggest challenge facing the Paralympic movement from May 2010 onwards is securing sufficient resources (both human and financial) to ensure that the maximum number of new Paralympic athletes is generated in all IPC member nations and at all levels of competence.'

In many ways the London 2012 Paralympic Games does risk preaching to a British nation that is already converted. That said, as Clare Strange suggests, there is certainly an extent to which our access and infrastructure for disabled people needs to be as even-handed as the increasingly positive mindset which prevails in British sporting circles. The hope is that British infrastructure built around London 2012 will provide the model for what this should look like to Britain and the world.

Stoke Mandeville Stadium is certainly one of the shining lights of British sporting facilities. This is obviously important at an elite performance level, although, as Tim Benjamin suggests, there is a flip side to the provision of fantastic facilities in that they risk creating athletes who are overly comfortable. 'Usain Bolt trains with some of the most basic facilities in world sprinting and it hasn't dampened his drive and motivation,' says Benjamin. 'For sprinters in the UK, the cold weather can be a problem when it comes to fast block sessions, so indoor facilities are excellent and all of the high performance centres are set-up with physios and masseurs on hand to prevent injury. That has to be a good thing, but for me facilities and motivation levels are not related – or at least they shouldn't be. If an athlete doesn't want to train because it's cold – you've got a problem. If an athlete won't travel to find the right weight training facility – you've got a problem. In 2001 I moved my life from Cardiff to London to work with the UK's top 400 metre runner at the time and his coach because I knew I would not be a world class 400 metre runner without them.' Certainly the argument made about British tennis is that our elite players have been too comfortable for too long, a sentiment a visit to the National Tennis Centre in Roehampton does little to dispel.

This level of support cannot be provided straightforwardly. WheelPower, who are responsible for the Stadium at Stoke Mandeville, as well as boosting individual wheelchair sports at a mass participation and elite level, are consistently required to fundraise to make ends meet. Funded through donations and contributions from charitable trusts, groups and individuals, the charity annually tries to raise around £1 million to fund its work in providing sporting opportunities for disabled people.

This is the practical reality of maintaining quality sporting infrastructure in the United Kingdom, in that there is ongoing dependence on a positive relationship between local government, private sector and end consumer. Even Stoke Mandeville itself has outsourced a commercial provider of fitness facilities to run a gym within the facility. Many local authorities have outsourced the provision of their leisure facilities to third-party commercial operators who operate as social enterprises and are finding the recession a challenging time. We currently have an over-supply of gym facilities (which are relatively cheap to supply and use minimal square footage) and not enough astro-turf football pitches, tennis courts, swimming pools and the like which are far more costly assets to run and monetise. The best of these relationships are extremely successful, although often there are tensions between the commercial mindset of the tenants and the public sector landlords.

Richard Lewis, Chairman of Sport England, has pointed out on several occasions that actually having the facilities is just part of the jigsaw. He understands that one of the more fundamental challenges can be ensuring relatively exclusive access for clubs to what facilities already exist, to enable them to train at an elite level. This is not a petty complaint, but a real challenge which arises from opening facilities for more exclusive usage. Providing good quality lane swimming for competitive athletes is a good example – opening a pool from 6 to 8am to ensure that athletes can train adequately will incur extra costs in terms of utilities, lifeguarding, caretaking and the like. Against the backdrop of public sector debt, these are not easy for either cash-strapped local authorities or a social enterprise to take on without question. Neither are they easy for the athletes themselves (directly through their clubs or independently) to cover.

Of course, the biggest challenge to an infrastructure legacy in and around the Olympic Park is not building the venues, but ensuring they do not become white elephants once the Games have left town. Let us tell the story of one such venue from the 1988 Alberta Winter Olympic Games, to see what we might learn.

As you drive to Banff from Calgary Airport you pass a town called Canmore. It is not a big place – its total population (permanent and non permanent) being around 18,000. Canmore grew up steadily from the late 19th Century onwards – benefitting from being on the Canadian Pacific Railway route and the discovery of coal in the town. This combination guaranteed success until 1979, when dwindling demand for coal meant that Canmore Mines Ltd ceased operations. Canmore's economic future seemed dismal until the announcement in the early 1980s that Alberta would host the 1988 Winter Olympic Games and that Canmore would play host to the Nordic events (cross-country skiing, biathlon, Nordic combined and blind cross-country skiing).

Ultimately this provided the impetus for the regeneration of Canmore to the tourism and recreation destination it is today. However, if one looks more closely at Canmore's story, the journey has not been linear and successful transformation of the town is still not guaranteed. There seem to have been three mistakes in Canmore's regeneration which offer some lessons for London.

The Canmore Nordic Centre was built with the specific purpose of hosting the Olympic Games in 1988. This it did very successfully, however the investment stopped the moment the Games left town. Over time elite events stopped coming – and with them the quality of the facilities dwindled. It was only in 2005 that the authorities reinvested in the facilities to bring them up to the standard required to host World Cup events once again. The venue now hosts Canadian teams training in these disciplines as well as World Cup races – and as a result remains a magnet for enthusiastic amateurs who pay the bills on a daily basis. Financial investment for long term sustainability must not finish with writing the final cheque for the Olympic Games themselves.

Given the reality of this first lesson, there is a need to balance the books after the Games. While ongoing World Cup events help, they do not do this on their own. Even in Canada, Nordic skiing is a minority sport which means that corporate and television support does not straightforwardly balance the books.

During the summer months, the Centre converts to include mountain biking facilities and plays host to several national and international mountain bike events every year, as well as orienteering. It even hosts an 18-hole disk golf course during the summer months. The Nordic Centre offers full-time services such as a cafeteria, meeting rooms, equipment rentals and lessons. The ongoing sustainability of the venue needs to be considered at the time of construction, not as an after-thought.

Sadly, despite learning these initial lessons, Canmore has one further challenge to overcome. The town itself has yet to move into becoming a fully-viable concern for the 21st Century and sustainability remains elusive in economically challenging times. Concerns over urban growth adjacent to Banff National Park have led to a limit on future development. The town was initially expected to reach its maximum 'build out' following the completion of the Silver Tip and Three Sisters Mountain Village developments sometime around 2015–2020. Recession has hit Canmore hard, however. Three Sisters went into receivership and burnt down during later stages of completion in the spring of 2009. So as we see public deficits in the UK too, we are warned that sporting infrastructure cannot survive independent of the broader economic picture. Ongoing salvation remains frustratingly at a distance for Canmore, but it continues to try very hard indeed.

Many of the lessons of Canmore are apparent in the story of one of the London 2012 Olympic venues. Happily, it is a case of lessons learned. Dorney Lake – the venue for canoeing and rowing in London 2012 – is in fact already providing a legacy return to its local area. There are tremendous examples of creativity and innovation throughout the project.

The venue was actually conceived as an idea by Eton College rowing teachers in the 1960s. They felt a still-water rowing course offered greater safety than the River Thames. The Thames has unpredictable, fast currents, varying widths and increasing traffic. They believed that having a year-round safe facility was important for the growth of rowing as a discipline within the school. Serious planning took several years in the 1980s and 1990s and a ten-year construction period began in 1996. Completion was achieved on target in 2006 and the World Rowing Championships held just a few years later.

It would be all too easy to suggest that Dorney is an example of Eton College's largesse and finances, however the venue was financially viable from the outset. While Eton did own the tract of land, the digging of gravel, which occurred to build the lake, largely funded the creation of the facilities in what was effectively a green-field site. This was not an easy construction process. Issues such as flood and environmental protection were absolutely fundamental to the success of the project. While the planning permission for the project stipulated that the gravel was permitted to be extracted, this was the only change permitted to the landscaping of the area.

After constructing the venue, Eton College set up the Dorney Lake Trust (a charitable organisation) to run the site. This has three objectives:

- To provide safe rowing for Eton College pupils;
- To offer the highest level facilities for major rowing events;
- To welcome all community sectors for sporting and other activities.

The legacy component provided for the community is particularly interesting and certainly points to the future of such venues. Residents of the local area can often be found walking, running, cycling or dog walking on the closed roads which surround the lake itself. More than one hundred schools and clubs also access the lake for rowing and canoeing.

The corporate sector is fundamental to the ongoing success of Dorney as a venue. Hospitality is provided for corporate functions and events, the proceeds from which aim to keep rowing and canoeing charges as low as possible, in particular for younger aspirant athletes. As a result of London 2012, the Dorney venue will not only remain as the best in the world in the eyes of elite competitors, but be improved still further for all users.

Most interestingly, Dorney has been built with additional types of sports in mind. A closed road five-kilometre trail around the lake enables the venue to be used for countless running, cycling and even triathlon races all year round. Swimming in what is a very clean lake is a tremendous experience to start the triathlons which dominate the summer. The construction of the lake ensures that this is possible and the water is practically drinkable. Access to this facility has meant that a host of sports event companies have sprung up in and around the local area, which cater for vast numbers of athletes, travelling from across the country and in particular Central London, most weekends.

Ivor Lloyd is Managing Director of Dorney Lake Services, which manages the business of the venue on behalf of the Trust. He was appointed to ensure that ongoing maintenance costs of the venue were covered as quickly as possible, so that the Trust could continue to deliver on its objectives for the long term. Ivor has a blue chip career behind him, including 32 years at Marks & Spencer and senior change roles at WH Smith, GlaxoSmithKline and also as Managing Director of a cosmetics business. He has also rowed competitively for Britain and is Chair of Leander Rowing Club, which hosts the majority of the Great Britain rowing team for the vast majority of their training.

The blend of business and elite performance sport background was fundamental to Ivor's appointment and the continued growth of Dorney Lake. As he says, 'You can't make money out of sweat alone. We have the benefit of a tremendous space here which, subject to planning permission of course, we can continue to evolve in a sympathetic way. We aim to continue to create a high performance ethic in everything we do. We can only really be curtailed by a lack of imagination.'

So far, the story is of success. Lloyd says, 'While the recession had an impact on every conference space, our diversification into team building, other sports and so on has given us a real breadth. Everybody who comes here gets the wow factor the minute they turn into the drive. It is an awe-inspiring space. We hope the Games will broaden the message from Dorney Lake so that more people will be attracted to visiting and using our facility – whether as athletes or as corporates.'

Ultimately the Games are also ensuring that a world class venue is maintained. 'In many ways we have already had our test event,' says Lloyd, 'in the shape of the 2006 World Championships. We welcomed 1,270 competitors to those, whereas the Olympic Games will consist of 550 Olympian rowers, 270 flat water canoeists and a total of 130 Paralympians. Despite this, we are absolutely not resting on our laurels. Our responsibility to the Organising Committee and the IOC is to create the ultimate experience for every athlete.

'Of course the Olympic Games constitute a much bigger logistical challenge than the World Championships. For example, we will have 30,000 people a day attending the Olympic Games, whereas our limit at the World Championships was 10,000. That has big implications. For example, we cannot look to ferry people over to the venue from Windsor Racecourse as we did in 2006 – currently we are looking at other solutions to get such a volume of people in and out of Dorney quickly. It should be a fantastic visitor experience – we have 3,500 volunteers allocated to the venue to make sure everything is taken care of. We had a delegation of 45 from Beijing share their experiences with us around challenges like this and we will ultimately support Rio in the same way.'

Certainly the future looks rosy for Dorney Lake. As Lloyd says, 'All the research from Sydney in particular is that while there is an appreciable halo effect of commercial opportunity for venues like ours before the Games, the real corporate opportunity comes afterwards. We need to make sure this effect remains with the venues after the flame has moved on. Currently I feel optimistic about this – interest in our venue is increasing in all areas already, well before the Games. I would like to hope our job will be to appropriately and sensitively manage our destiny as a centre for high performance of all types, rather than have to actively generate it ourselves.'

Many venues have tried to follow the model of an additional partner to support the investment and development behind a new construction project in the same way Dorney has Eton College. This does not always mean new buildings. For example, the National Volleyball Centre made its home in a space that was constructed in Kettering some 20 years ago as part of a leisure and conferencing facility. The Conference Centre owners were co-investors in the construction process, along with local councils and Development Agencies.

Just down the road from Dorney Lake in Uxbridge is another example of a world class facility, which has been built with the future in mind. As you leave London on the A40, just before it becomes the M40 and heads towards Birmingham, it has been possible for years to see an artificial ski slope on the left hand side. This has been part of a sports complex which has stood since well before the 1948 Olympic Games, which began with the building of an open air swimming pool in 1935.

The Uxbridge pool was built at Hillingdon House Farm and operated for 63 years in its first incarnation. In 1935, lidos were a very popular family activity and photographic evidence indicates the open air pool was very heavily used for decades until the quality of the facilities began to decline when alternative leisure options became available. The pool itself was actually used as a swim training venue for the American team in the 1948 Olympic Games and also as a training base for some of the water polo competitors. Up to the mid-1980s, it formed part of a broader sports complex with Uxbridge Tennis and Squash

Clubs; the Cricket Club, which regularly hosts Middlesex first class fixtures; a significant number of football and rugby pitches and of course the cinder athletics track. Additionally, a ski slope was added to broaden out the potential uses of one of the first big green spaces in Metropolitan West London.

Towards the end of the twentieth century, the venue did not manage to move with the times. Outdoor swimming became increasingly unpopular, with the growth of indoor facilities available just down the road, despite the beauty of the listed swimming pool construction. The outdoor ski slope suffered as access to mainland Europe became cheaper and less extravagant an option for weekend breaks and was long perished before indoor ski domes became part of the domestic leisure scene. The cinder athletics track became overgrown without the benefit of regular competition and the challenge of irregular upkeep from the local council.

The facility found itself at a crossroads. Rumours were rife that the valuable land so close to London was being offered as an option for theme park operators. Finally, after heated debate and many a front page of the local papers, and on the back of the funding and political impetus London 2012 provided, commitment was gained to reinvest in the whole venue with a focus on the athletics and swimming facilities. Boris Johnson came to open the facility.

Many of the changes which have been made again point to the changing nature of our sporting participation in the UK. While the principal aim of the project has been to bring the athletics and pool facilities back into use for the benefit of local people and the wider community of the London Borough of Hillingdon, there has been realism about how this might be achieved. In the case of the swimming pool, in the words of Hillingdon Council, 'As with the restoration of all listed buildings there is a desire that they should be preserved, but it is also recognised that to secure the long term future of these buildings it is best to establish a viable beneficial use for the facility.'

As with Dorney Lake, viability means mixed sporting usage – a broader mix of sports and also attracting a broader demographic of Hillingdon residents than a freezing outdoor pool and a cinder athletics track were able to generate. This is a sizeable investment, £31m in total. A private operator, Fusion, which acts as a charitable trust, is responsible for running the location on behalf of the council and, ultimately, the Borough of Hillingdon residents.

The new pool caters both for elite and serious swimmers, with a 50 metre provision which remains outdoors but is matched indoors, the indoor version with a leisure pool at one end. A children's pool has geysers, bubbles and jets and is also heated. The warm water flows to the outdoor 50 metre pool and enables an extension to its operating season. In addition, a sports hall, a café and a dedicated health and fitness block have been built. The athletics track has a similar forward-looking view, with a café provided for those who have finished their training and access to five-a-side astro-turf facilities and even a petanque area next door to the athletics arena.

Of course, there is no guarantee that Hillingdon will not become a white elephant. Our example of Dorney Lake and the 5km of closed road paths demonstrate that often it is the smallest detail in design that can make the biggest difference to ongoing viability of a venue. In the case of Hillingdon this is likely to be the variability of water depths via the use of a floating floor. While this might seem like an unnecessary luxury, it shows how detail in planning can provide for many different uses, and, ultimately, more customers. The floor provides:

- 150mm depth for parents and toddlers or splash dance;
- 300-800mm depths for learning to swim programmes;
- 600-900mm depths for swimming development training and school use;
- 800-1500mm depths for general recreational swimming;
- 1500mm-2000mm depths for race diving practice, life saving, synchronised swimming and competitive swimming;
- Easy pool access for wheelchair users.

Both Hillingdon and Dorney have been built with ultimate legacy in mind. Of course not all facilities are as lucky and have not been created with such a far-sighted approach to sporting participation. Another world class facility at the other end of the spectrum is the Manchester Velodrome. Used for the Commonwealth Games in Manchester and still the home of the all-conquering British Cycling team, the centre itself struggles to be economically viable without the ongoing support of Manchester City Council, which covers an annual shortfall. While the broader benefit of the renaissance of cycling in Britain is undoubted, the centre itself is struggling.

Manchester Velodrome has several disadvantages to Dorney. Of course, it does not have a benefactor like Eton behind it, but also it does not have the capacity to offer so many different sports. Situated within the broader SportCity environment created for the Manchester Commonwealth Games, many of the potential routes for a venue of this type to offer additional facilities (for example, gym facilities, tennis, squash and athletics) are offered by other parts of the complex. As a result, it really only offers minority participation sports to the Manchester public. Track cycling, badminton and netball will realistically see limited demand. The venue desperately needs to capitalise on the commercial potential of its key tenant, although as yet has failed to do so.

The stories of Stoke Mandeville, Canmore, Dorney Lake, Uxbridge and Manchester all point to the challenges and opportunities of creating a sporting infrastructure legacy from London 2012 beyond Central London. Within the Olympic Park itself the reality is just as challenging. It is easy to dismiss as 'disgraceful' the prospect that the Olympic Stadium might not ultimately become a flagship venue for British Athletics. However, the lessons of those venues we have already mentioned would suggest that at very least a broader mix of sports might be considered. In particular when we think (much like Manchester SportCity) that many of the obvious multi-use facilities, which could fit around an athletics track, will exist within other areas of the Village. Arguably, a Manchester City football stadium, full to the rafters every other Saturday and bringing investment into the local area, with a more modest and well-used athletics facility alongside, it is a better testament to the broader social legacy of the Manchester Commonwealth Games than an under-supported velodrome not more than 400 yards away.

London, of course, would be fighting a losing battle to try to compete with Beijing in terms of the grandeur of its venues and arenas. Seb Coe told the BBC in Beijing, 'The International Olympic Committee themselves recognise that this is the last edition of an Olympic Games which is going to look and feel like this.' As with the objectives which underpin Dorney Lake Trust, a sporting infrastructure legacy is critical – but it is only one part of the infrastructure legacy for the Olympic Games.

Transport represents a good example of this broader East London infrastructure legacy. Living in a particularly populous small island, the British do tend to be very critical of what they perceive to be a creaking transport infrastructure. As with policing, the sheer complexity of delivering the Olympic transport plan is staggering. This is particularly true as the full benefits will only be realised with a confluence of projects which are both directly related to the Olympic Games themselves and those (such as Crossrail) which will ultimately benefit the East London region, despite not specifically being part of the Olympic plan. Of course, these projects are not part of any ring-fenced investment and relate to other broader agendas. For example, there is still conjecture as to whether there will ultimately be a fully operational Eurostar station at Stratford, something the Westfield Shopping Centre operators are obviously vehemently in favour of!

It is worth considering the sheer amount of footfall which Transport for London manages on a daily basis. Some 340,000 people a day travel into the City of London, in order to generate 2% of the GDP of the entire country. 285,000 a day work in and around the West End and a similar number shop there every day. Already 100,000 a day travel to Canary Wharf for work (of which an ever increasing number are at the offices of LOCOG and the ODA). While these numbers seem vast, they pale in comparison with the additional infrastructure requirement for London 2012. The Olympic Games will likely issue some 8 million tickets, the Paralympic Games another 1.5 million. Within the Olympic Games alone, 3.4 million will be for events in the Olympic Park, with an additional 850,000 at the Excel Centre. It is clear that Stratford Station will need the 240,000 people per hour capacity it is building.

Managing the transport flows on the day does not simply require the transport of spectators to be taken into account. Olympic Lanes for athletes and officials will clog up the roads and are bound to create a good deal of controversy, even without domestic politicians stoking the fires in order to curry favour with Londoners. Contracts guaranteeing this level of access were signed long ago. Events such as cycling, the marathon and triathlon on the open roads are likely to create road blockages and the timings of these blockages are already a source of healthy debate. Live sites in Central London and the Festival planned for Hyde Park will create more complexity. As a result, a Transport Co-ordination Centre (TCC) is being created to manage things proactively.

The legacy of this planning process should exist on several levels, but principally around the ongoing connectivity of our public transport. The Javelin system will open up access to East London from St Pancras. The capacity of the DLR will be greatly increased. Three Olympic Park gateway stations are being created – Stratford Regional, Stratford International and West Ham.

London Overground routes are being transformed from a 'snowflake' type design, with travel opportunities radiating from Central London main stations, to an orbital network which will directly link 22 of London's 33 boroughs. Transport maps plotting this are already being used across the network. Investment in the river network also continues as a fundamental part of this network, which will offer the ultimate way to travel to the Olympic and Paralympic Games come 2012.

Sean Collins is Managing Director of Thames Clippers, probably the flagship provider on the Thames. Sean is a river man through and through, and rowed in the Great Britain lightweight squad. He has also won the traditional Doggett's Coat & Badge, the oldest contested rowing race, which up to six apprentice Watermen of the River Thames in England have competed for every year since 1715. Sean recognised the opportunity to build a consistent high-speed commuter and passenger river service and has grown the business from a one boat operation to a fleet of 13 vessels, carrying over 8,000 passengers per day. The business has grown quickly, to the extent that it is now majority owned by AEG, who also own the Olympic gymnastics and basketball venue the O2 Arena. Sean says, 'I captained the Storm Clipper on her first journey from Greenwich to Savoy Pier at 06.48 on May 24, 1999, with a grand total of two passengers onboard. I remember, as I drove the vessel down the river that morning, wondering if there would be any more on the next run.

'There were. In fact, by close of business on the first day we had welcomed a further 79 customers, and by the end of that week over 100 commuters had committed to travelling regularly with Thames Clippers. It was a good start, but if someone had told me then that ten years later we would own 13 boats, be carrying nearly 3,000,000 commuters and tourists a year and be considered an integral part of the London transport system, alongside the tubes and buses, I think I would have been a little taken aback. The Olympic Games will put the River Thames squarely back on the London transport map – this time, we hope, for good.'

These investments, of course, will only have significant ongoing legacy value if they help to transform a forgotten part of London into a big part of its future. Latterly, London has a good record of achieving this through transport – with Canary Wharf and more recently the Kings Cross/St Pancras areas being good examples.

Perhaps the best recent example of ongoing infrastructure investment and return after an Olympic Games is the Sydney Olympic Park. More than $1.1 billion of new development has been secured at Sydney Olympic Park since the Sydney 2000 Olympic and Paralympic Games. Over the past three years alone, a five and a two-star hotel have been built, in addition to serviced offices, residential buildings, a sports hospital and extensions to the Olympic Tennis Centre. Ongoing investment in sports events and the arts has helped to sustain a sense of culture and community. Some 38 different sports are played at Sydney Olympic Park, from community to elite levels, attracting 1.5 million visitors each year. While the sporting venues in particular are not without their critics, the community survives and, in places, thrives.

Back in London, the relative ring-fencing of the Olympic budget should ensure that the legacy commitments are delivered in and around the Olympic Park, even if the broader impact around Britain remains a matter of some conjecture. The Organising Committee named a budget, including a contingency, of £9bn for the full project and while the press likes to quote this figure at every turn, the reality is that this number includes all the regeneration and legacy work in addition to delivering a world class Games.

Despite the amount of work to be done, the project is ahead of schedule. Given the size of the public debt in the UK, perhaps the bigger challenge to the impact of the Games is delivery of an infrastructure legacy outside the ring-fenced funding of London. It is doubtful, for example, whether the Hillingdon complex would have been initiated if construction was beginning, rather than finishing, in 2010. A critical component here are the training camps for national teams in the run-up to 2012, against which binding commitments for the creation or maintenance of sporting infrastructure have had to be made. Major pre-Games sporting events and training and preparation camps are a significant part of the opportunity to broaden the infrastructure and economic legacy beyond the London region.

Of course, the additional sizeable opportunity for London is from tourism. Indeed, Tourism South East expects that an additional £1bn or so will be spent on the back of the Games. Not all of this happens above the radar and in many cases the tourism effort is a good example of the kind of activity that is needed years in advance of generating any concrete return. At the Beijing Olympic Games, Tourism South East, SEEDA and other regional partners met with hundreds of tour operators, journalists and representatives from National Olympic Committees to pre-promote the region in advance of London 2012 and secure significant up-front reservations. VisitBritain has developed a new, more focused marketing strategy to attract more visitors to the UK in the run up to London 2012. This includes using the Games as a springboard to win more sporting and business events and a particular focus on encouraging more visitors from emerging markets. To that end, the intensive series of promotional meetings held in Beijing were repeated in Delhi at the 2010 Commonwealth Games. VisitBritain also hosted a Discovery Workshop, bringing 125 international buyers as well as 80 domestic ones to view venues in the local area.

Some of the strands of tourism trade activity relate specifically to providing a world class welcome to disabled athletes. The aim has been to motivate the tourism industry to create a lasting legacy of improved facilities, service and welcome for disabled visitors. As well as face-to-face training, video masterclasses have been created working with Ade Adepitan, Britain's iconic wheelchair basketball star, and Peter Norfolk, one of the world's top wheelchair tennis players. These actively encourage tourism businesses to improve accessibility.

With successful delivery of the Games all but guaranteed, the likelihood is that press attention will turn to legacy far earlier than might originally have been expected. Most of the stories will inevitably surround the areas that are still up for debate, whereas in fact the vast majority of legacy planning is on track. Without the Games coming to town, Bobby White would still be playing football; Hillingdon Borough would arguably have its very own theme park and there would be no scheme to coordinate disabled access up and down the country. Most importantly, a decrepid area of East London would be waiting another 30 years for regeneration.

PART SIX

Delivering the Numbers

'The IOC now understands its brand equity better than most.'

Professor Francis Farrelly

15

1948: The Roots of Mass Media Coverage

The world in 1948 was still a relatively big place. Information took far longer to reach its destination and travelling in person longer still. Despite this, the power of the Olympic Games was already such that teams were prepared to travel for weeks to compete in the event. While the flow of information lacked the immediacy we now take for granted, the excitement and scope of the Games demanded extensive facilities to meet the demands of the 59 countries competing. Thanks to the major sponsorship of Lord Rothermere, a newspaper proprietor of the day, Wembley Civic Hall was converted to provide a press centre with quiet writing room, canteen and, just as importantly for journalists then, a bar licensed beyond the stringent opening hours of the day. Elvin understood that managing the reactions of journalists to events as they unfolded was extremely important in influencing the public perception of the Games and alcohol had its role to play in that.

The General Post Office installed a complete telephone exchange at Wembley, manned with military personnel. In addition, ten telephone operators moved about in the arena fitted with breastplate transmitters and double headgear receivers. Extraordinary as this might sound, they were in constant demand. There was always a queue for the four phones dedicated to international calls, which had to be booked the previous day. There were also 57 'press button A' telephones which were available for local calls, with attendants hovering with a supply of pennies so that they could be easily operated.

By today's standards, the amount of time which it took to perform even the simplest of communications tasks was extraordinary. The constant queues for services like these, despite the time it took to make even a simple local call, were testament to the amount of interest across the globe in hearing the latest news as it unfolded. To send an international report the process was both complex and lengthy. A pile of forms were to be found at the press bar, the first stage in sending a telegram. After composing his or her message, the journalist put the form in a tin canister and dropped it from the window down a length of gutter pipe. From this point, a team of Boy Scouts waited beneath for a tin canister to drop down to them. They were ready with their bicycles and when they heard the clang of the tin can, one of the Scouts caught it, extracted the message and cycled away to the teleprinter, leaving the can to be pulled back up the pipe on a string. Once the furiously-pedalling Scout had arrived at the teleprinter, its operator typed the message on an electric keyboard. This went by landline from Wembley to Electra House on the Embankment and from there by morse code to the various countries. This was a rather lengthy process, which took roughly the same amount of time to complete as the 10000 metres mens' athletics final. The Scouts did an awful lot of pedalling over the course of the Games.

Longer events posed still greater challenges. During the marathon, an official waited at each public telephone kiosk along the way. As the runners arrived, the official's job was to telephone the press office with the positions of the runners. Although the British silver medallist was not clear what position he was in as he reached the stadium, the media were.

Live television of any sort was in its infancy and the BBC was initially sceptical that the Olympic Games would prove compelling viewing at all. Certainly its Olympic build-up was anything but engaging. It attempted to use the same basic techniques it had used elsewhere in its post-war output, which made the coverage rather stilted and inappropriate. 'I remember the BBC invited a group of us athletes to Alexandra Palace to give interviews before the Games,' Silvia Disley recounts. 'We were told to look at the camera when answering, not at the person asking the question. It was most unnatural and off-putting.'

Indication that live Olympic coverage might take off could have been gleaned from German experiments with live broadcasts from the 1936 Berlin Olympic Games. There pictures were transmitted to TV stations in Berlin and

Leipzig. But the BBC, perhaps understandably, was in no mood to look to Britain's defeated wartime enemy for inspiration. In Britain, there was simply no precedent for what the reaction to screening the action live might be.

However, the BBC quickly recognised that it was far from correct in its initial assumption that live sport would have no take-up among the British public. It extended its Olympic coverage swiftly as the Games progressed, making the decision to break into planned programme schedules for key Olympic events. It is no exaggeration to state that the 1948 Olympic Games was a key driver of the uptake of television in British homes. It was claimed that the number of receivers in the London area increased from 14,550 in 1946 to 66,000 by 1948, principally because of excitement around the coverage of the Olympic Games.

Two elements were critical in changing the face of British television through the Olympic Games. Firstly, the British appetite for sport at the time was significant, and as we have seen this could not all be met through live sport. Secondly, the BBC's pictures looked stunning and very different from the stilted Alexandra Palace previews. Under blazing sunshine and the watchful eye of 82,000 stadium spectators and the BBC television cameras, the 14th Olympiad opened at 2.45pm on Thursday 29 July 1948. One camera overlooked Olympic Way to catch pictures of the crowds as well as events in the Stadium. Two mobile units (those same ones later sold to EMI!) were controlled from the Palace of Arts: one in Wembley Stadium itself, the other at the Empire Stadium Pool. Each commanded three cameras, with producers watching events on monitors and drawing on the stories of a dozen commentators. We take this style of coverage for granted today, but at the time it was revolutionary.

The ever-entrepreneurial Elvin was at the centre of this innovation, believing it was critical to create great television in order to drive broader awareness of the Games, and so the development of sport as a source of entertainment. His Wembley Stadium effectively became a showcase of what was possible for broadcasting live sport. Elvin himself had lent the BBC the old Palace of Arts, constructed for the British Empire Exhibition of 1924, to serve as a Broadcasting Centre with eight radio studios and 32 channels. A total of 15 commentary boxes were installed with 16 open positions in the stadium and 16 commentary points at the Empire Pool. To lay cabling between Wembley and Broadcasting House was a significant task, which required a labour force from the BBC's regional as well as central operations teams. Live coverage would not have been possible without this cabling. Without Elvin's earlier instigation, it is doubtful the management of the BBC would have been able to react as effectively during the Games to the demand they witnessed in the British population.

The BBC's investment of time and money paid dividends. By the time the Games finished on 14 August, it had shown 68 hours and 29 minutes of coverage, an average of almost five hours of television a day. It is no exaggeration to suggest that the Olympic Games changed the face of the BBC and hard to believe that this transformation happened as the Games were actually in progress. An equivalent to this in today's media landscape might perhaps be for the BBC to have decided to launch a new sports channel midway through the Opening Ceremony of the London 2012 Games, and to have launched it by the beginning of the second week!

Internationally, the BBC offer was more minimal. Radio offered some live commentary through the BBC's World Service connections which had developed during the war years. Even this level of live coverage still enabled more up-to-date means of communication than the gutter pipe relay used in the media centre. In this sense television had stolen a march on the more pedestrian print media in terms of its Olympic coverage, a state of play which has certainly continued to this day as the British newspaper industry struggles to find a genuine role to play in live sport in a 24-7 media landscape.

If ever there was a confluence of talent and opportunity coming together to drive a big innovation, here in 1948 was a classic example. Consider the position of the BBC at that time. It was held in the highest esteem throughout the world for the scope and professionalism of its radio broadcasts during the war years and acknowledged as a world leader. Despite this it was under constant scrutiny and criticism for the manner in which license payers' money was spent. Its senior executive team all had more traditional print journalism backgrounds and considered television as entertainment fodder only, not as a serious news vehicle.

Despite this, the experience of the Corporation's operating and engineering staff was forged during the war years – and they were anything but risk averse. Problem-solving under pressure was second nature to many of the staff who missed the excitement of their lives during wartime. This created an interesting tension within the BBC as the Games progressed, with the energy and can-do experience of the engineers winning the day. Outside the senior ranks, live television was seen as a heaven-sent opportunity to demonstrate the talent within the BBC. With Elvin's help, the front-line staff forced their way into the living room and created the way forward for the role of live television in Britain.

This was a critical legacy not just for the BBC and British society, but also for the Olympic Games and the business of sport in general. The industry has grown by being able to command ever higher rights fees from broadcasters precisely because the content is compelling enough to persuade consumers to trade up their technology – from radio to television; black-and-white to colour; free-to-air to pay television; analogue to digital and more recently into the 21st Century brave new world of High Definition broadcasting. For example, the BBC initially used Wimbledon tennis to drive awareness of its 'red button' interactive service and ultimately fade out the analogue signal. Just as Sky used Premier League football as the principal lever to encourage their customers to trade up to their High Definition channels, so they are now using it in pubs as a gradual means of broadening awareness of the migration of 3D technology from the cinema into the home. Sport has played a major role in driving each of these phases of transition. This unique ability is the reason why sport has continued to get richer despite an increasingly challenging macro economy. BBC Olympic coverage in 1948 was the very first event to hint at this hidden talent, the legacy of which we continue to feel today.

16

1948: The Birth of Branding and Commercialism

Despite having fought long and hard to win the Games, then persuade the British authorities to honour their commitment to host them, Elvin's greatest achievement with regards to London 1948 might well have been to balance the books. At a commercial level, the BBC inadvertently set a precedent which enabled the Olympic movement to solve a problem which had dogged its progress from the outset. The BBC not only proved the market existed for dynamic sport delivered to the home, but agreed to pay for this commodity by agreeing a fee of 1,000 guineas with the Organising Committee for the privilege. Today television rights have become the principal source of revenue for the International Olympic Committee, although interestingly there is some conjecture over whether the BBC's cheque was ever cashed in 1948. This was an absolutely critical part of the legacy of the London 1948 Games because it started to create the economic virtuous circle from which the IOC built the biggest sports property in the world.

Elvin's entrepreneurial zeal was always in play. Not only did he ensure live coverage via his relationship with the BBC, he also ensured a permanent record of the Games in film. To enhance revenues, exclusivity was awarded to the major British film-maker of the day, J Arthur Rank, for the princely sum of £25,000. This was a completely unproven media proposition and £25,000 was a very significant amount of money to convince someone to part with based on absolutely no precedent of success. This fee not only helped to swell the coffers, but also broadened access to the Games to the British population. This was certainly a profitable deal for the Rank business too, which still exists as the Rank Group today.

Consider just how significant the £25,000 Elvin managed to secure from Rank was. To put it in context, the receipts of the London 1948 Olympic Games as a whole were £761,688. J Arthur Rank's entrepreneurial investment equated to more than 3% of the total revenue for the London 1948 Games. If we consider the Operating Budget for the London 2012 Olympic and Paralympic Games is likely to be in the region of £9bn, an identical percentage of that budget would equate to £270m!

Although television rights generated a fee for the first time in 1948, the critical element of revenue was ticket sales. However, the sales process was not straightforward. Elvin was faced with a major challenge when the American team arrived in London and promptly returned 80% of the tickets they had ordered (worth £80,000, or more than 10% of the total budget of the Games). Elvin had already extended a major loan secured against ticket sales to refurbish the route to Wembley Stadium. Fortunately the appetite of the British public to see the Games in person was significant and receipts from ticket sales were above expectation. To be fair to Elvin, he had always recognised this pent-up demand in his role as proprietor of Wembley.

From a cost-saving perspective, equipment was borrowed from competing nations and donations of raw materials were accepted and used to build the necessary competition infrastructure. British athletes were provided with the bare essentials only. Even the style of the individual uniforms worn by Great British athletes owed much to their own families' skills with the needle.

It was not all a question of revenue and costs, however. Elvin was an entrepreneur with an understanding of people and politics at his core. When the pre-Games plan to have the Navy deliver the Olympic Torch across the Channel was declined with the suggestion that a simple steamer be used, Elvin tentatively accepted the decision. However, he also suggested the possibility of one of the European competing nations' naval vessels handling the honour instead. The torch duly arrived in Dover aboard the destroyer HMS Bicester. As with the British rowing team boats, the British establishment managed to avert any potential embarrassment. Budgets were tight but risking international ridicule was clearly not the done thing.

Elvin had made his fortune in demolition and had started his business journey selling off the remnants of the London Empire Games. As a result, the sale of all that could be marketable or salvageable after the Games had finished came as second nature to him. It contributed a handsome profit in some cases. For example, the Games were run from the British Olympic Committee offices at the Army and Navy stores, for which a short-term rental agreement was in place. When they vacated the building, they sold the linoleum back to Army and Navy for £150. It had originally cost just £281.

Sponsorship was also a key part of the 1948 jigsaw, not only in terms of financing but also driving innovation. OMEGA photo-finish equipment was used for the first time to resolve the close athletic finishes at Wembley including, critically, the men's 100 metre final. What is less well known is that an electronic timing system was also installed to record all eight finishers. However, the level of reliability had not reached the required standard, so conventional hand-held timing was used as the real means for making decisions on placings and medal winners. When the original records were recovered in an archive almost 30 years later, there actually were some anomalies in the detail between medals awarded from the hand timings and those which would have been awarded had the electronic system been relied on. The system was further modified before being adopted as standard practice at later events, however without OMEGA's contribution the organisers would not have been able to combine innovation with the need to deliver an Olympic Games on a shoestring.

The first domestic sponsor of the London 2012 Games, Lloyds TSB (now Lloyds Banking Group) was a sponsor in 1948 as Lloyds Bank. Their relationship with the Olympic movement in Britain had been longstanding, having also handled British Olympic Committee finances for the London 1908 Games. Lloyds still holds one of the London 1948 torches, which is on display at its headquarters in Gresham Street when not being shown around the country. In 1948 Lloyds Bank had approximately 2,100 branches, employing around 16,800 employees. An excerpt from Lloyds Banking Group's archive picks up the story: 'When London last hosted the XIV Olympic Games, back in 1948, a makeshift Lloyds Bank was opened in Wembley Stadium. The temporary office was open for just over a fortnight and invited all visitors to London to "Let Lloyds look after your interests."

'Staff included a linguist and adverts offered full banking services, including the encashment of travellers' cheques and letters of credit. An article in the September 1948 *Dark Horse*, the Lloyds Bank staff magazine, described the scene: "During the last week of the Olympic events at Wembley we visited the Bank's temporary office there and wedged ourselves snugly into the diminutive manager's room for a word with Mr J.W. Briant.

'A linguist with a staff of linguists, he told us (in English obviously) that the office was doing brisk business. His first customer had been a lady who hopped in with a sprained ankle, wanting nothing more than a chair, first aid and a kindly word; later came a spate of requests in all languages to borrow pencils for marking scorecards, but after that plenty of orthodox business began to roll in.

'The branch kept open and busy until 5pm every day and at the time of our visit only one member of the staff, Mr A.R. Smith, had managed to get his nose inside the stadium two hundred yards away; he went to watch a nephew of his compete for France (where Mr Smith himself was born) in the 400 metres hurdles."

'The article also tells how Mr J.H. Warham, manager of Teddington branch, was responsible for giving instructions to the torch bearers on the route from Westerham, Kent, to Wembley – during which time there were 40 changes of runner. He not only had to give them instructions but also had to follow them with the hurricane lamp – the "authentic flame" – which had been burning since it left Greece on 17 July. If any torch failed it had to be relit from the hurricane lamp.

'Other Lloyds Bank staff with links to the 1948 Olympic Games were E.J. Holt who was Director of Organisation for the Games – he was retired but had been manager at Belgravia branch. And D.G. Caswell, of Lloyds Bank Treasurer's Office, was Assistant Arena Manager for the Games.'

Elvin's efforts held the act together for London 1948 with the significant contribution of organisations such as the BBC, Rank, OMEGA and Lloyds who were prepared to back his entrepreneurialism and creativity. Just as importantly, Elvin's innovations raised awareness of some of the channels from which the Olympic Games movement could benefit in the longer term. He was responsible for juggling ticket sales, enabling a compelling broadcast spectacle, providing or obtaining capital investment, generating sponsorship and forging a path through all the red tape to commandeer scarce resources. The key to Elvin's success was a clear vision of what was needed, and years of experience of dealing with and through others to achieve his goals. Ultimately London 1948 turned a profit of £29,420 – extraordinary given the circumstances in which they operated and just slightly more than the fee paid by Rank.

It took some time for the IOC to really benefit from this commercial learning. Ironically, it was the paranoia about amateurism which prevented the movement joining the commercial real world until 1952, when Lord Killanin took over the Presidency. He recognised the need for independent financing and despite learning most of the business lessons the hard way, the base was set for the next President, Juan Antonio Samaranch, to build the brand to support the Olympic infrastructure we take for granted today.

Professor Francis Farrelly of the School of Economics, Finance and Marketing at RMIT University Melbourne is one of the world's leading experts on sports and branding. He says, 'The IOC now understands its brand equity better than most – particularly their history, their universal values, for example unity, and of course the quality of a product represented by the best athletes across sports in the world. Collectively this is a truly unique point of difference to consumers, sponsors and media.' He also puts forward the view that, when old certainties are being challenged by global terrorism, the financial crisis and other such events, this identification with competition and the pull of the Olympic brand will continue to help to bring a fragmenting world back together.

17

2012: A New Media Age

The victorious London bid team made some big promises in Singapore and wasted little time coming out of the blocks quickly. Seb Coe announced a First One Hundred Days plan. One of the most important initial moves was the separation of the body responsible for building the infrastructure for the Games – the Olympic Delivery Authority – from the one responsible for the commercial and operational side of making the Games happen – the London Organising Committee of the Olympic and Paralympic Games. Effectively this separated the day-to-day public purse commitments to regenerate East London from the revenue generation and Games delivery private sector responsibilities.

This has proven to be a significant and successful move. While both organisations are joined at the level of the Olympic Board, each is free to develop the culture and approach that match their very different immediate priorities. LOCOG operates in a commercial world of sponsorship sales, ticket allocation and world class event management. Daily agenda items for the ODA are regeneration, planning regulations and environmental sustainability. While each organisation has its own priorities, its leaders are clear that the collective intent is to be greater than the sum of their respective parts.

Juliet Slot was part of the team during this early period having stayed on after the bid and she played a key role in the initial sponsor recruitment effort. She says, 'Once we won, the new organisation was put in place incredibly quickly. We had a strong team from the get-go which meant new recruits added value rather than starting from the beginning. Commercially our team were always clear that we need to ride along the wave of euphoria of winning.

'The IOC said that the transition from bid to organising committee was likely to be a painful process – however most of us working there did not feel it was. They were really hugely helpful to us.'

As we saw earlier, Seb Coe recognised a long time before winning the bid that China was really the only country with the financial muscle necessary to deliver an event with the scale and impact of Beijing 2008. The approximate budget of the Chinese is believed to have been somewhere between three and five times that of London. London's challenge has been to reinvent what an Olympic and Paralympic Games might be expected to deliver for a smaller nation in more prudent financial times. This has re-framed the challenge as building a model for the Olympic Games for the 21st Century – a century in which second world nations might follow and be able to access the unique social and economic catalyst that is the modern Olympic Games. Rio have made no bones about the fact that they intend to follow the model that London create. Brazil's President is believed to have joked to Seb Coe on winning the right to host the Olympic Games that 'we will copy everything that you do!'

One of the central challenges for London 2012 organisers has been to build a plan for the Games against a staggering technological pace of change. Coe and his team had no idea in 2005 when the bid was won what technologies would be mainstream by 2012 and which would still be a figment of fanciful imaginations. The technology challenge for London 2012 represents both an opportunity and a threat for the Organising Committee and its partners. On one level the challenge to deliver information around the world in real time is terrifying for firms such as BT, Atos Origin and Cisco Systems. Internet development is changing and evolving at such a pace that even short time frame comparisons offer little guidance. The 1998 Winter Games in Nagano generated one Terabit of Data, or five times as much as the preceding Lillehammer Games. This amount of data storage can now be purchased for £60 on eBay! On the other hand, the lure for sponsors to grasp the opportunity to showcase their technology on the world's biggest stage makes it worth the risk in order to create the ultimate corporate case study. It is a game of high stakes.

BT has embraced the challenge of delivering for London 2012. Its aim is to use the Olympic Games as the biggest possible global platform to emphasise its ability to scale and secure communications infrastructure, deliver a world class customer service experience and critically also do so in a sustainable way.

Olivia Garfield, Group Director, Strategy, Policy and Regulation at BT, explains the size of that challenge, saying, 'In 2012, every image, every sports report, every visit to the London 2012 website and millions of calls, e-mails and texts will be delivered over a BT network. That means that when it comes to Games time there will be no second chances – the customer experience must be right first time. Projects of this scale and scope come along once in a lifetime and we have the chance to be part of an event that will have a place in British history forever. It all adds up to BT installing a whole new town's-worth of telecommunications infrastructure in just over three years!'

The scale of the media scrutiny is vast and failure is not an option. If BT's communications lines go down in the middle of yet another World Record for Usain Bolt in the Men's 100 metre Final, or in the final strokes of Greg Searle's gold medal 20 years on from his first, BT will be culpable in the eyes of the global public. However, this is not the only challenge. They have also been asked to support the delivery of the greenest Olympic Games ever. Garfield says, 'We are working with the ODA to maximise the reuse of BT's communications services after the Games have finished. We also want to deliver a more sustainable Games – for example real time intelligent information around transport, smart buildings, understanding the carbon footprint of the Games and so on.'

London clearly signalled its desire to embrace new media in all its forms with the early launch of its contemporary logo. The early message that this would be a 'new media' Games was initially greeted with scepticism. However organisers insisted that they could not be sure how the action would be distributed come 2012, that alternative methods of distribution to the TV screen or internet would be necessary and that the logo would need to work in all new media environments. How right they were – in reality, this world is already with us. The BBC Trust has recently approved plans to distribute BBC News via mobile phone applications, a controversial move as it puts the BBC in direct competition with commercial broadcasters in the new media market. Sky already distributes Sky Sports News via similar means, and the strong likelihood is that Olympic coverage will follow onto the BBC's schedule of mobile applications by 2012.

The internet potentially offers a completely different Games experience come London 2012. The Winter Olympic Games in Vancouver have already offered us a taste of this, with countless sports available on television and the internet on a live, delayed live and highlights basis. Broadcasters themselves are already noticing the impact of this multi-channel reality.

Adrian Moorhouse commentates on swimming for the BBC as a holiday job alongside his role at Lane4. He jokes, 'In previous Games as recently as Sydney we used to commentate live for small pockets of the day and then record the highlights. With the advent of the red button we are live on air an awful lot more of the day. It's much harder work – but fortunately we really enjoy it. There is also a different type of commentary required in this. Those who watch swimming when it is on the main feed might have a basic understanding of the sport, but when it is purely on the red button during the heats we have more hardcore fans of the sport watching. We try to adapt our style to reflect that.'

The significant opportunity for London 2012 is to embrace new media to cut some of the traditional costs associated with delivering the Games. For example, we already take it for granted that Oyster cards offer a cash-free journey through London which could save on transport staff costs for Transport for London in 2012. Additionally, e-ticketing for the events themselves could potentially cut a significant cost line from London's financials and increase security at the same time. Ticketmaster's partnership with LOCOG has already started with requests for online pre-registrations of interest in tickets already generating a valuable database of more than one million people at a fraction of the cost of what would traditionally have been a paper application process. Of course technology brings potential problems as well as solutions. The grey market for tickets becomes a larger part of the jigsaw as a result. For example, eBay did a roaring trade for sale of tickets secured via the lottery in Vancouver.

TV broadcasters, too, are broadening their scope towards the internet. This is shaping up to be the big battleground of London 2012. Rumours are rife that web companies such as Google are not far from launching their own TV channels – effectively a 'live' version of the YouTube platform they already own. Rights owners have been keen not to miss the party. The US Olympic Committee unwittingly contributed to Chicago's downfall in the eyes of the IOC by announcing plans to launch its own broadcast network (following the model of sports leagues such as the NBA) in 2009. The IOC criticised this heavily when the plans were announced, citing the complex legal issues this would cause in addition to the difficulties it would create for NBC, the IOC's longstanding conventional broadcast partner in the United States. This is certainly not a discussion that will disappear from view as 2012 approaches.

Another frequent criticism of the many deeply personalised multimedia viewing options available to the British public is that we become a nation which watches sport alone rather than together. Critics of technological progress argue we run the risk of losing the excitement and social benefit which watching sport together can bring. In reality, the likelihood is that the planned live sites across the country will be a tremendous success no matter how widespread the BBC London 2012 phone app becomes. The collective sport experience has become increasingly popular in recent years – from big screens showing football matches at Glastonbury to the model of the fan site in major German cities during the 2006 FIFA World Cup and then worldwide FanFest in 2010, which was universally judged a success for sponsors, fans, broadcasters and organisers alike.

Marzena Bogdanowicz, who is pulling much of the planning together for these London 2012 live sites with her own organisation b-focused, suggests that: 'The most important thing for London to get right is the experience for the public, both the spectators attending the Games and others. I have been to over ten Olympic Games now, seen great ones and good ones all from different perspectives. I have experienced them with an accreditation around my neck and without, just as a member of the public. The latter is what matters to the overall success of the Games. The public will make the Games as much as the success of Team GB.'

The likelihood is that new forms of media will not necessarily cut down on the collective experience of the British public during the Games, but they will increase the amount of sport watched. If anyone should be concerned, arguably it should be the employers of the British sports fan who may struggle to cope with a month of minimal productivity in an economic climate which is likely to remain fragile until Games-time.

18

2012: New Commercial Realities

The altogether more modest scale of London 2012's Olympic infrastructure ambition relative to Beijing has inevitably involved slaughtering some sacred cows. The Olympic Stadium, for example, is half temporary structure which will be peeled back after Games-time. Existing London venues which originally missed the chance to host events – for example the newly-refurbished Wembley Arena – have now been drafted in, in lieu of temporary arenas. There is certainly a touch of poignancy in the use of this former Elvin venue for the badminton and rhythmic gymnastics in 2012, 64 years on from its role doubling up as the home of both swimming and boxing.

Each decision of this nature takes LOCOG still closer to balancing its books. Despite this, things remain tight in this regard, and every decision counts. The overall economic climate in the UK seems to have created the situation where cost focused decisions like these can be made with minimal controversy and fuss.

A Parliamentary Committee report published in March 2010 warned that the £9.325 billion ($14.069 billion) budget for the London 2012 Olympic Games and Paralympic Games is 'tight' with only £194 million ($293 million) available to cover any new risks in the build-up to the Games. It also cast doubt over whether £400 million ($603 million) could be raised in ticket sales. This would equate to recouping £50 per ticket if the anticipated 8 million tickets are issued.

The Olympic Delivery Authority, which is in charge of Olympic build and infrastructure, has £1,270 million ($1,916 million) left from its original £2,747 million ($4,145 million) contingency. Much of this is earmarked to meet predicted risks, leaving only £194 million ($293 million) headroom.

This financial reality creates a culture of austerity which permeates the whole of LOCOG and the ODA's operation. Very often corporate sponsorship negotiations are returning to the world of barter in lieu of cash. For example, LOCOG has opted to second some talented staff from partners such as Deloitte to save on salary cost. This can even be positioned as a benefit to LOCOG partners anxious to demonstrate broader opportunities to their highest performers. Deloitte, for example, have already had more than 1,000 applications from within their business to be seconded in the run-up to the Games.

Just as OMEGA brought significant value to London 1948, so part of the Organising Committee's model is that sponsorship partners continue to bring marketing as well as financial investment to the LOCOG table. For example, John Lewis was 'granted the rights' to open a London 2012 shop, as opposed to the organisers having to 'ask' them to do so. Just as Elvin persuaded Rank and the BBC to pay to market his London Games in 1948, so LOCOG has persuaded John Lewis to pay for the rights to sell London 2012's wares. This type of deal would be inconceivable under any 'normal' terms of business, but such is the power of the Olympic brand that this may yet turn out to be excellent business for John Lewis as well as the Organising Committee.

Intriguingly, the organisers of London 2012 do not actually possess a marketing budget for the Games. Creative partnerships with broadcasters, sponsors and other media platforms are instead used to broaden the key messaging of the Games. In Beijing and Vancouver, for example, every billboard and press advert was Olympic Games-themed and yet all were paid for by the sponsors of the event rather than the organisers themselves. This, of course, is the natural extension of the principles that Elvin established in London through his breakthrough deal with the BBC.

As we have already seen, procurement processes are taken extremely seriously within London 2012 to minimise costs wherever possible and also drive legacy benefits to a broader cross-section of British businesses. For example, LOCOG still has hundreds of millions of pounds worth of goods and services to procure towards London 2012 in areas such as artists, performance and events; security; services; soft facilities management and catering; sports; technology; transport and logistics; venues and hard facilities management. The reality is that world class businesses from across Britain are applying for contracts such as these. This ensures quality is almost given and so costs can be minimised as far as is possible. Rigorous checks ensure that there is little or no danger of default on contractual obligations.

There is a very unique breadth of skills which are required in an organisation such as LOCOG to deliver the Olympic Games. Effectively it is part sports body, part business, part political entity and part project management organisation. Certainly it is light years away from the traditional sporting organisation. Juliet Slot joined LOCOG from Fulham Football Club. She says, 'I went to London 2012 as more of a vocational move than a career move. Football is quite an insular world whereas London 2012 exposed me to a broad range of contacts from the IOC, to sporting bodies, government and of course the world of electioneering.' She touches here on the biggest challenge remaining for LOCOG in the run-up to the Games – the extent to which they are able to maintain 'business as usual' under coalition Government and deepening financial austerity in the rest of the country.

LOCOG's entrepreneurship has already been significantly challenged by the economic environment. On the face of it, selling an eight or even nine figure domestic sponsorship for London 2012 should have been extremely difficult, almost impossible. This is about more than recessionary challenges, it relates far more to the role of sponsorship in the modern world.

Sponsorship as a discipline has traditionally been rather unsophisticated. Rights holders such as LOCOG have a long tradition of selling attachment to their sporting event based on market value of their assets – advertising hoardings, tickets, television billboards, corporate hospitality and so on. These are the unit currencies under which Formula One, FIFA World Cup projects and so on have traditionally been bought and sold. Therein lay the issue for London 2012 organisers – with 20 years of sponsorship under their belts, the big brands had seen it all before. There was also a particular challenge for London 2012, in that (unlike, for example, Champions League football or NBA basketball) there was no advertising inventory to bundle into their sponsorship deals since the Games would unusually be shown on non-commercial terrestrial television in the domestic UK market. Additionally, part of the equity in the Olympic Games brand is that the Games remain the only global sports property to continue to avoid any commercial messaging within the venues themselves. While this is part of the appeal and difference of the Olympic Games, and arguably the only valuable legacy of the obsession with amateur ideals, it makes life far harder for Organising Committees desperate to try to balance their books.

Of course some of LOCOG's revenue generation is already secured since they receive a share of the IOC's global sponsorship deals (with global organisations such as Coca-Cola, a partner of the Olympic movement since 1928) and also their television rights. The IOC's 'TOP' global partners are a phenomenon, a who's who of some of the biggest brands in the world.

Coca-Cola has a long-standing heritage with the Games. Daryl Jelinek is responsible for the leadership of the Coca-Cola 2012 programme. The organisation has recently extended its agreement with the IOC through to 2020. Daryl has a long track record of sporting participation himself, having represented England Under-23s at rugby and captained England Colts. He now coaches his son Joe's rugby team, Cobham Under-12s, and captains a high-level cycling team, Liphook Racing, which puts him in a fantastic position to truly understand the Olympic property on a number of levels. He says, 'Our partnership with the International Olympic Committee dates back as far as 1928 in Amsterdam. Our goal in London is very simple – to make this the most successful Olympic and Paralympic Games ever for Coca-Cola, not just in terms of activation at London 2012, but critically also its legacy for our customers, consumers and staff.'

Certainly there is a strong precedent of investments like Coca-Cola's being shrewd. There is no doubt that the Olympic Games drive sales. While Westfield Stratford City is set fair to launch at the end of 2011, prospects for the remainder of the country are less clear. Keith Evans is in an excellent position to understand what benefit the Olympic Games might bring to the British retail scene, not just given his current role as Chief Executive of the British Retail Consortium's Trading operation and a twenty-five year commercial career at various bastions of the British High Street including Marks and Spencer, J Sainsbury, Currys and B&Q, but also as a keen sailor, cyclist and runner. Keith says, 'Current forecasts are that London 2012 will generate an extra £1bn plus in retail spend in this country. That is probably very much on the conservative side, and should be generated by official licensed merchandise alone. Just as one example, during the Beijing Games in 2008, energy drinks sales in Britain rose by more than 150% versus a more traditional week. Research agency Mintel believe energy drinks alone are already more than a £1bn market in the UK. If that's the impact an Olympic Games can have many thousands of miles away, it is mind boggling to think what the impact of a London Games might be. Retailers who sense the mood of their customers and innovate in a creative way really have the opportunity to trade "two Christmases" in one year, which equates to retail bliss!'

At a global level there are certainly some significant success stories in the sponsorship of the Olympic Games in the retail space. VISA is an example of a long-standing sponsor which contributed to delivering these critical additional revenue streams. Much of the increased tourist investment which will be made as a result of the Games will be made on VISA cards, including payments for £400m worth of Olympic tickets. VISA became involved with the Olympic Games not only because it helps them deepen relationships with their member banks and core retailer partners, but also because it drives payments away from their major competitors, Mastercard and American Express. So happy were VISA with their Olympic relationship that they recently stole the FIFA World Cup partnership from under Mastercard's nose. VISA UK Managing Director Marc O'Brien expands, 'We have sponsored the Olympic Games since 1986 and the Paralympic Games since 2002. This sponsorship has become the cornerstone of Visa's business growth in the past two decades and provides us with an unparalleled opportunity to promote our brand, to drive revenue and to reinforce preference for our products and services at an international and local level. All Visa Europe's members can and do benefit from a direct association with the Games which delivers tangible business value for our members, their cardholders and merchants. As part of Visa's commitment, I am also very proud that we are helping to support Team 2012, a group of 1,200 elite athletes competing to become part of Team GB through providing marketing support and funds which will be allocated across all sports and will go towards coaching, medical support and research.'

Not all sponsorship categories are as 'obvious' a sales proposition as credit cards and soft drinks. Given the context for domestic sponsorship we describe above, and an increasingly challenging economy, LOCOG has been smart enough to know that a traditional inventory based sporting rights holder approach would never generate the £700m corporate sponsorship required from those categories where the IOC has not already signed a global partner. Of course the Olympic rings can prompt a top-level conversation with any corporate organisation, but it does not necessarily guarantee sufficient value. In this sense the negotiation is a little like buying a house – there is an obvious value to what is being sold, but it is only worth the price being asked to a small percentage of buyers, and the more flexible the accommodation, the better. LOCOG understood this and went back to the drawing board. Rather than selling based on the value of tangible assets such as tickets or hospitality, they sold based on valuation of the association to the partner in question.

Juliet Slot says, 'The work that we did in understanding the business case for each potential partner was extremely important in helping us hit the ground running and being able to sign partners quickly.' LOCOG created a valuation model for each category partnership and encouraged prospective partners to consider how they could truly use the sponsorship across their business.

LOCOG understood that to sell a sponsorship for London 2012 required a more sophisticated approach to partnership with the corporate sector than simply selling an inventory of rights. Partner organisations have taken the investment very seriously and are approaching it much like a private equity type investment. They understand the potential sources of value which they can release over the life-span of their relationship, and then build a plan to release that value. As Sally Hancock, Director of Olympic Marketing for Lloyds Banking Group says, 'This is not a sponsorship for us, this is not even a marketing partnership, we view our Olympic investment as a catalyst for the change we are looking to achieve in our business.'

Sally points to a fundamental change in the way companies view sponsorship. Traditionally it has been valued, bought and sold on some fairly basic pillars – opportunities to entertain key clients, increased brand logo awareness, buying the rights to use a sporting logo for on-pack promotions and so on. Lloyds Banking Group is one of many organisations which have thought far harder, deeper and more strategically about their partnership. While not moving away completely from these traditional pillars of a sponsorship, it is also looking in a more fundamental way at how it uses the relationship externally with customers and internally with staff to create the 'change' Sally refers to.

In particular, many organisations have deliberately identified employee performance uplift as a significant source of business return. They have matched their cultural values to those of the Olympic Games in a very deliberate and strategic way and have created plans to create hard business return of tens of millions of dollars against this by releasing people performance through the Olympic connection. BT, for example, can demonstrate how the Games partnership is driving customer service measures through the behaviour of their people. Claire Blakeway, Head of Internal Engagement and Communications for London 2012 at BP, suggests that her organisation is taking a similar approach to drive change. 'Our Olympic partnership offers us a chance to emphasise some of the key leadership behaviours that we are looking to inspire in our people,' she says. 'We know that increasing the incidence of these behaviours will help us drive change more effectively through the organisation. The Olympic sponsorship offers us a chance to amplify leadership at BP.' This is gold dust to organisations like BP in a British employee base which is often disengaged, demotivated and has traditionally held a view that sponsorship really just offers tickets and hospitality for the high flying senior executives.

Thinking about sponsorship in these terms has required a change of mindset in British corporations, in particular when some of the UK's big brands were under fire for the perceived lack of strategic thinking in some of their sponsorship dealings before the recession hit. Olivia Garfield at BT describes an altogether different approach in her organisation. 'Our employees are so excited about the chance to be directly involved in the delivery programme, and in the volunteering programmes,' she says. 'But we also hope that there will be sustainable change within BT as a result of our 2012 partnership.'

Karen Earl is Chair of the European Sponsorship Association and sponsorship agency Synergy, and was named *Sunday Times* Sports Businesswoman of the Year in 2009. She acknowledges that the role of sponsorship is changing for the better. 'The discipline of sponsorship has matured and London 2012 provides a testament of this,' she says. 'Sponsorship is most definitely now considered a central piece within corporate and brand communication strategies. It is now seen as a core solution to business challenges, not just marketing ones. Properties such as the Olympic Games really challenge businesses to think in an active way about how they genuinely want to realise value right across their business. This has to be a good thing for the long-term future of our industry.'

Beyond sponsorship revenue, ticketing too offers an opportunity for incremental income, although LOCOG recognises that it is running the gauntlet in hiking prices too high in a Games which is expected to broaden participation and therefore support access for all. As Beijing showed, while the assumption is that Olympic Games tickets are expected to be over-subscribed in general, this does not ensure that the early stages of the water polo which start at 9am will necessarily be a sell-out. Even with the Olympic Games, the reality is that total ticketing revenue is a function of total tickets sold multiplied by the average sale price. It is likely that organisers will adopt a ticketing method more similar to that of the Beijing organisers or equally the US sports leagues where prices vary significantly between events and quality of seating.

This is not usual practice in Britain. Traditionally UK sports pricing strategy has been relatively undifferentiated, as exemplified by Premier League tickets which regularly only vary between £20 to £75 per game, depending upon the club and the significance of the fixture. London 2012 is expected to price depending on the event in question. Certainly they have been swift to add a hospitality provider to their list of partners to maximise the value of the lucrative international tourist and corporate markets.

There is some good experience in exploiting tourist dollars and euros to be gained from football's Premier League, a very experienced exponent of sports tourism into the UK, something Games organisers are also very hopeful of capitalising on. Craig Edmondson is Head of Marketing at the Premier League and was responsible for pulling together a partnership with Visit Britain to help maximise this tourist traffic. He says, 'We know from our research that 39% of all inbound visitors to Britain state that they are interested in attending or watching a football match during their visit, and each season over 1.2m inbound tourists attend top flight matches. Our international reach is a key strength of the Premier League brand, just like the Olympic Games.'

A short visit to the adidas store in Oxford Street demonstrates that merchandising, too, has started quickly. Aisles are often full with the very tourists Britain aims to lure come Games-time. This is an area which the Beijing Games failed to maximise, probably because the implications of a scale merchandising operation were too explicitly commercial in a communist country. Certainly the sponsor village was hidden away in the outskirts of the Olympic Park in Beijing. In contrast products can already be found on the shelves two years out from London 2012.

Beyond adidas, other early licensees have seen significant initial successes.

Pin badges – a product which has traditionally passed all but the keenest British sporting collector by – are already proving very popular and trading at significant mark-ups on ebay. Model maker Hornby launched the first official toy for the London 2012 Olympic Games, a five-inch miniature replica of the now infamous red London bus vehicle featured in the handover ceremony at the 2008 Beijing Olympic Games. Leona Lewis and Jimmy Page replicas fortunately do not come as part of the set, however it is presented with a certificate of authenticity… and a £30 price tag. Ultimately Hornby will be releasing an Airfix kit of the Olympic stadium in Stratford, a Scalextric velodrome set and a scale version of the high-speed Olympic Javelin shuttle train. LOCOG has also announced its mascots – named Wenlock and Mandeville after the British Olympic legacy this book describes – in plenty of time to generate a hoped for £15m of revenue to swell the Olympic coffers. Limited first editions of soft toy Wenlocks and Mandevilles are already sold out.

LOCOG now has the vast majority of its revenue commitments filled. This puts it in the enviable position of being able to consider supplier deals which shave cost from the accounts as well as drive revenue. Traditionally Olympic Organising Committees have been criticised for fire sales at the end of their tenure, while the general view is that 'all money is good money' just before the Games. Vancouver's final sponsor signed up a matter of weeks before the event. This is far less likely with regards to London 2012. Instead we should expect to see some very creative supplier barter deals which minimise significant remaining cost liabilities for the organisers and maximise the impact of the Games.

One early example of this kind of creativity which will be required to close off the remaining revenue gap is the Lakshmi Mittal funded 'Orbit' tower which will sit above the Olympic Park in the same way the 'Bird's Nest' did in Beijing. It would be easy to write this off as a victory for naked ego over financial common sense. In fact, the £19.1m costs of the tower have been covered by Mr Mittal (to the tune of £16m) and the GLA (the remaining £3.1m). Additionally, and most critically, the tower is also expected to generate a minimum of £5m towards the Organising Committee's budget (equivalent to another supplier relationship) from sponsors keen to wine and dine clients in a totally unique environment. In this way, LOCOG is ensuring it delivers its numbers through business acumen and creativity as opposed to a fire sale and in a way which adds to rather than detracts from the uniqueness of London's Games.

As it stands, LOCOG looks well positioned to hit its ambitious revenue targets. Certainly there is some good fortune tied into this. The economy held up just long enough to secure the majority of domestic sponsors, but began to deteriorate early enough to enable suppliers to be pushed further in terms of potential cost savings. Just as Elvin did in London 1948, however, organisers have needed to reinvent the rules of the game in order to guarantee success.

These subtle changes in the landscape of sponsorship and major event management have not gone unnoticed in the broader business community. In some ways they hark back to the background of Elvin – businessman first, sport lover a distant second. This has not always been typical in British sporting administration. The perception of 'jobs for the boys' has certainly not been far from the truth. Simon Cummins set up the International Sports Practice of Odgers Berndtson, one of the most well-respected global executive recruitment businesses, to buck this trend. Simon's background is itself unique, having been a headteacher for ten years, Head of the Prep School and a Member of the Executive Group at Millfield School in Somerset and run commercial schools across Europe. The business has placed many senior executives across Olympic and other spaces, including the Chief Executive of LOCOG, Paul Deighton.

'LOCOG is a completely unique culture,' Simon says, 'which reflects the need to build up to 6,000 people at its peak and then ultimately close operations down again to zero. We were looking for people who could handle the start-up scenario, who were both entrepreneurial but also adept at handling very complex, changing structures. The ability to interface with Government was clearly also important. We had the benefit of the broader Odgers network in order to compile a short-list which stretched far beyond sport. The initial list contained candidates from a very wide range of sectors.'

Odgers has gone on to recruit roles in the Olympic space such as the Chair of the Olympic Delivery Authority, Chief Executive of the British Olympic Association and Marketing, Commercial and Client Services Directors at LOCOG. Cummins says, 'For us this has been a process of educating the wider market. Bringing a wider scope of talent into London 2012 has opened the eyes of the sports business as a whole. Candidates already working in sport have rarely had the breadth and depth of experience and specifically the international exposure necessary to maximise the value of their assets – whether we are talking about the Olympic Games or Premier League football clubs maximising their value in Asia. The ability to understand the digital landscape and deal across regions is far easier to acquire in other sectors than it has been in a sports industry slow to wake up to modern day business practice.'

People strategy is certainly an area in which the London 2012 Organising Committee is setting best practice every day. For example, led by HR Director Jean Tomlin they are already thinking through how they support their employees in locating roles for 2013 onwards. The aim is that they have these identified by early 2012, so (just like the athletes themselves) they can focus on delivering when it counts come Games time.

Certainly, there should be no shortage of interest in candidates who have demonstrated their ability to deliver in a fast-changing, high pressure environment such as the Olympic and Paralympic Games. Come 2013, many sporting organisations will likely be dealing with financial and government instability after a life of secure Government funding up to London 2012. Cummins says, 'These candidates will be helpful to organisations that by 2012 may still be dealing with financial and government instability. For example, Olympic sports federations who will likely be coping with a severe drought in funding after 2012 will need to really understand how to use their assets in a more meaningful and creative way to maximise their value.'

Modern pentathlon, a sport created specifically for the Olympic Games, is one example of this. Peter Hart, Chief Executive of Great Britain's Modern Pentathlon Federation, says, 'Pentathlon GB receives significant funding for preparing all areas of the sport but at the same time we have to manage the growth and ensure that any projects are sustainable in the longer-term future. In 2013 the funding environment is unlikely to be at the same level as it is now. We are perceived as being a performance sport by the funding agencies which means that 90% of the annual funding is directed at around 40 elite members of the sport. This has implications for the remainder of the membership and volunteer side of the sports. We have managed this fairly well over the years but it does continuously challenge us.'

London 1948 delivered an extraordinary Games on a shoestring. The creativity of Elvin's commercial approach made the difference, from his understanding of the importance of media and television to the use of sponsors to add innovations to the event experience at no cost. Elvin's understanding of the importance of broadcasters and sponsors as the principal means of revenue generation but also marketing for the Olympic movement remains relevant to this day.

Once again London 2012 faces the challenge of a moving media landscape and new generations of consumers who will not be content to follow the Games in highlights shows on their televisions. Fortunately at this stage sponsors and broadcasters seem to be ahead of the game. London 2012's organisers have embraced the fact that in order to deliver a Games focused on legacy, the numbers have to add up. Just as Elvin was, they are business-people first and sports fans a close second. The blend seems to be working.

CONCLUSION

Britain's Olympic Legacy

Britain's driving role in the reinvention of the Hellenic Olympic tradition is one of the great untold sporting stories. Reigniting the Olympic flame required a series of innovative leaders to build the global phenomenon London awaits in 2012. Without the Cotswolds and Much Wenlock, De Coubertin would not have been inspired. Without the steady hand of London 1908, it is doubtful that the Games would have survived the impact of the First World War. Without Elvin's entrepreneurialism, they would likely have been viewed an expensive extravagance in a recovering world, rather than a means of recovery and renewal in their own right.

London 1948 was truly the first Olympic Games of the modern era. It demonstrated to the IOC and, critically, future host cities, that sport was capable of healing a population and supporting an agenda for health and wellbeing. It suggested that people really wanted to watch the proceedings and that media organisations would be willing to pay for the right to show them to the world. It hinted that business would one day pay huge sums to make associations with the events themselves. On that basis, winning rather than taking part started to become the primary athlete agenda, but more importantly, that of competing nations and their politicians. This ensured that athletes were to be prepared for excellence going forward and no longer left to their own devices.

Four visionary leaders between them created the blueprint for this, delivered the Games themselves and gave the gift of the Paralympic Games to the world. One of them, Elvin, managed to deliver a profit in a bankrupt nation which had little or no sporting infrastructure but did possess a latent passion for sport. Arguably this is one of the great sport business success stories of the 20th Century in Britain.

The achievement of London 1948 stands in stark contrast to Beijing 2008. This was an Olympic Games of unmatchable infrastructure, encompassing competitors from 204 nations and a viewership of billions of sports enthusiasts, sometimes estimated as half of humankind. However, had London 1948 not been a success, it is doubtful whether the movement would ever have got as far as Beijing. In the same way that London 1948 had to respond to Berlin 1936 and redefine the movement, so London now has the challenge of matching another immense show of political intent. The 2009 Berlin IOC Session reflected that, 'The Games of 1936 shone a magnificent light upon the City, but a long dark shadow upon the Olympic Games,' and therein lies some of the concern about the way forward in 2012. For every journalistic muttering about eligibility of athletes as truly amateur in 1948, now we have similar controversies surrounding drugs, or even athletes running under flags of convenience.

No matter who held the Games in 2012 and where they sat in the global economic cycle, the focus would not have been about demonstrating how good the Games are, but rather demonstrating the return to an Olympic and critically also Paralympic ideal. The Organising Committee's progress so far demonstrates that their legacy ambitions remain realistic, if still ambitious, in the face of such staggering levels of domestic and international public debt.

Rob Clarke, Head of Reward, Policy and Organisational Development at London 2012 sums it up neatly when he says, 'We hope that the legacy for London and the UK will be many things: re-engaging a generation of young people with sport, implementing a more sustainable model for staging the Games, a once-in-a-lifetime experience for a workforce of 250,000 people and a legacy of talented people capable of staging future major sporting events in the UK such as the Commonwealth Games in Glasgow in 2014 and potentially the football World Cup in 2018 or 2022.'

The London's Bid Team's commitment was to bring the Games back to its roots and inspire the youth of tomorrow. This lies in producing Bolts rather than Bird's Nests, and thinking not just of 2012, but 2036 too. There is no doubt that the spectre of public debt, international instability and a fractured British nation makes this more challenging, but it also makes the size of the prize significantly bigger.

In his speech to the IOC Congress on 5 October 2009, Seb Coe reflected on this challenge, saying:

'Throughout history great political, technological or artistic movements have come out of periods of great adversity. The United Nations from the Second World War, satellite technology from the Cold War, great jazz from the Great Depression. We meet today in another time of adversity. But in that adversity lies opportunity. The Olympic Movement has a once-in-a-generation opportunity, I would say a responsibility, to better define and imbed its timeless values. Never let a good crisis go to waste. This first Congress in 15 years must seize the moment to turn this bleak picture into an opportunity. If the 20th Century was about bringing sport to the world then the 21st must be about reconnecting young people of the world to sport.'

If we can be upbeat today about the likely impact of the modern Olympic movement on Britain, so there is reason to be cautiously optimistic about the legacy of London 2012 on the Olympic movement of the future. While the balance of global power is shifting, ultimately the United States still plays a pivotal role here. It was a very big gamble for the IOC to ignore a strong American bid from Chicago in 2016 after choosing London over New York in 2012.

Rick Burton's view of London 2012 from the other side of the Atlantic reflects the current state of flux in the United States' perception of the Olympic Games in general, and London 2012 in particular. He says, 'Some Americans currently see London 2012 as the Games New York lost. Others see them as the Games before Brazil (the Games Chicago lost in 2009 when bidding against Rio de Janeiro). Familiar as they are with swimmer Michael Phelps' eight gold medals in Beijing, they will turn to London to see what the world beyond their shores looks like. We can hope they might identify with a Muslim woman sprinter, an Indian marksman or a Chinese swimmer.

'Americans will turn their attention to the athletes. For the first time in many quadrennial moments, they will see in London, as they did in Vancouver, a city that they imagine is much like their own New York, Chicago or Los Angeles. It is a cosmopolitan, engaging, English-speaking, trend-setting, familiar place. And they will like what they see. Idealistic as it may seem, it is possible that Americans will rediscover the Olympic Games in 2012, much like a comfortable pair of reading glasses that allows them to magnify their love of sports and international culture…while keeping the delivery vehicle (a phone or laptop) within arm's reach.'

China may be on the rise, but no matter how much the IOC protests otherwise the ongoing global success of the Olympic and Paralympic movement depends on the United States. The nation has its own love affair with sport, although not always Olympic ones.

For the British, Olympic sport has always meant something special, just as one of the Olympic sports, football, means something unique to the Brazilians in the country that follows London… initially of course with the World Cup 2014 and then also the 2016 Olympic and Paralympic Games. Rio's statements around their bid shortly before the decision in Copenhagen made an explicit connection to the continued growth of their nation. The President of the Brazilian Olympic Association and the Bid Committee said, 'Rio is ready to deliver. Our proposed Games Plan for 2016 has been developed in alignment with our own city's growth plans and as pointed out by President Lula, also fits with the Government's vision for the country.'

Bids to host Games are no longer solely about the opportunity for the City to add to the future of the Olympic Movement. The Bid process is now also around the likelihood of the Olympic Games adding to the future of the host nation, something Rio grasped far better than Chicago. This is a powerful demonstration of the way in which London has changed the Olympic and Paralympic Games for good, even before hosting them.

Almost 400 years ago, the Olympic Games were reignited in Britain as a means of improving a small pocket of Cotswold society. Britain's gift to the world in 1948 was a business model for the 20th Century Olympic Games and the birth of the Paralympic Games. In return, the Games allowed Britain to just begin to discover sport's potency as a means of social change in a suffering nation. Finding ourselves in similar straits today, let us hope London 2012 can contribute to easing today's challenges. Beyond British shores, London 2012 has the opportunity to demonstrate that global events can bring local community together in a fractured world. It also has the potential to create a model for the future of a combined Olympic and Paralympic movement where global sporting events can be delivered by second as well as first world nations, with social and economic regeneration front and centre of their strategic goals in doing so. Here's hoping.

BIBLIOGRAPHY

Books

Ashley, Maurice, 1980, *The English Civil War A Concise History,* Thames and Hudson Limited

Baker, Keith, 2008, *The 1908 Olympics*, SportsBooks Limited

Barber, B. & Barker, B.,1989, *Tournaments*

Barnes, Simon, 2006, *The Meaning Of Sport,* Short Books

Barnes, Simon, 1989, *Sports Writers Eye: An Anthology,* Queen Anne Press

Bean, Anita, 1991, *Nutritional Guide to Sports and Fitness,* Quest Vitamins Ltd

Beattie, Geoffrey, 1997, *On the Ropes,* Indigo

Birley, Derek (Sir), 1993, *Sport and the making of Britain,* Manchester University Press

Beverland, Mike (Prof.), 2009, *Building Brand Authenticity: 7 Habits of Iconic Brands,* Palgrave Macmillan

Bland, A.E., 1948, *Olympic Story,* Rockliff

Burns, Francis (Dr.), 1981, *Heigh for Cotswold! Robert Dover's Olympick Games,* Robert Dover's Games Society

Busby, Matt (Sir), 1959, *My Story,* The Sportsman's Book Club

Callow, John, 2005, *James II,* The National Archives

Cleaver, Hylton, 1951, *Sporting Rhapsody,* Hutchinson

Collins, Mick, 2006, *All-Round Genius The Unknown Story of Britain's Greatest Sportsman,* Aurum Press Ltd

Courtauld, George, 2006, *The History of Britain and the World,* Ebury Publishing

Davis, William, 1976, *Punch on the Olympics,* Punch Publications Limited

Disley, John, 1978, *Orienteering,* Faber and Faber Limited

Dunphy, Eamon, 1992, *A Strange Kind of Glory,* Manderin

Dyson, Geoffrey H.G., 1981, *The Mechanics of Athletics,* Hodder & Stoughton

Finle, M.I. & Pleket, H.W., 1976, *The Olympic Games: The First Thousand Years,* Chatto & Windus

Gabrieli, Francesco, 1989, *Arab Historians of the Crusades,* Dorset Press

Girardi, Wolfgang, 1974, *Olympic Games*, Collins

Goodman, Geoffrey, 1997, *The State of the Nation The Political Legacy of Aneurin Bevan*, Victor Gollancz

Goodman, Susan, 1986, *Spirit of Stoke Mandeville The Story of Ludwig Guttmann*, Collins

Greenberg, Stan, 2003, *Whitaker's Olympic Almanack 2004*, A & C Black

Haddon, Celia, 2004, *The First Ever English Olypmpick Games*, Hodder & Stoughton

Hallam, Elizabeth M., 1986, *Domesday Book Through Nine Centuries*, H.M.S.O.

Hampton, Janie, 2008, *The Austerity Olympics When the Games Came to London in 1948*, Aurum Press Ltd

Harris, Tim, 2007, *Sport: Almost Everything You Ever Wanted to Know*, Yellow Jersey Press

Hart-Davis, Duff, 1988, *Hitler's Olympics:The 1936 Games*, Coronet Books Hodder and Stoughton

Hicks, Gill, 2007, *One Unknown*, Rodale

Hofer / Lennatz, 2009, *Serving the Olympic Idea The Berlin Session of 1909*, Deutsche Olympische Akademie

Imlach, Gary, 2005, *My Father and other Working-Class Football Heroes*, Yellow Jersey Press

James, Lawrence, 2006, *The Middle Class A History*, Little, Brown Book Group

Jarvie, Grant, Hwang, Dong-Jhy & Brennan, Mel, 2008, *Sport, Revolution and the Beijing Olympics*, Berg

Jefferson, Lenskyj, Helen, 2002, *The Best Olympics Ever? Social Impacts of Sydney 2000*, State University of New York Press

Jenkins, Rebecca, 2008, *The First London Olympics 1908*, Piatkus Books

Johnson, Paul, 1992, *The Offshore Islanders A History of the English People*, Orion Books Limited

Jones, Graham, 2009, *Thriving on Pressure*, Easton Studio Press

Killanin, Lord & Rodda, John, 1976, *The Olympic Games 80 Years of People, Events and Records*, Book Club Associates

Kynaston, David, 2007, *Austerity Britain 1945-51*, Bloomsbury Publishing Plc

Lee, Mike, 2006, *The Race for the London 2012 Olympic Games*, Virgin Books

Loades, David, 2007, *Henry VIII Court, Church and Conflict*, The National Archives

Matthews, Stanley, 2000, *The Way It Was: My Autobiography*, Headline Book Publishing

McCann, Liam, 2006, *The Olympics Facts, Figures & Fun*, Facts, Figures & Fun

McWhirter, Ross, 1972, *The Olympic Games 1896-1972 in support of the British Olympic Appeal*, Scott International Marketing Inc

Meyer, H.A., 1964, *Modern Athletics by the Achilles Club*, Oxford University Press

Miller, David, 1970, *Father of Football*, Stanley Paul

Nally, T.H., 1906, *The Aonac Tailteann and the Tailteann Games*

Oaten, H.J., 1947, *Olympiad 1948*, Findon Publications

Patten, Marguerite, 2004, *The Wartime Kitchen Nostalgic Food and Facts from 1940-1954*, Hamlyn

Payne, Michael, 2005, *Olympic Turnaround*, London Business Press

Phillips, Bob, 2007, *The 1948 Olympic: How London Rescued the Games*, SportsBooks Limited

Rex, Peter, 2006, *The English Resistance*, Tempus Publishing Limited

Riley, Henry Thomas, 1860, *Liber Costumarum*, City of London, London Metropolitan Archives

Rivers, James, 1948, *The Sports Book 2*, Macdonald & Co.

Ruckert, Henry, 1980, *Olympics for the Disabled Holland 1980 Commemorative Book*, Stichting Olympische Spelen voor Handicapten

Saul, Nigel, 1983, *The Batsford Companion to Medieval England*, Batsford Academic and Educational Ltd

Scruton, Joan, 1998, *Stoke Mandeville Road to the Paralympics*, The Peterhouse Press

Stenton, D.M., 1951, *English Society in the Middle Ages*, Harmondsworth

Stow, John, 1598/2005, *A Survey of London*, Sutton Publishing

Strutt, Joseph &Hone, William, 1885, *The Sports and Passtimes of the People of England*, William Tegg & Co

Swinglehurst, Edmund, 2007, *Family Life in Britain 1900 to 1950*, Futura

Thurlow, David, *Track Stats. (Quarterly Bulletin of the National Union of Track Statisticians)* Volumes 43/1 and 44/1, National Union of Track Statisticians

Tibballs, Geoffrey, 2004, *The Olympics' Strangest Moments*, Robson Books

Turner, Barry & Rennell, Tony, 1995, *When Daddy Came Home How Family Life Changed Forever in 1945*, Hutchinson

Various, 1636, *Annalia Dubrensia*, Facsimiles of originals by Scolar Press and Tabard Press

Wallechinsky, David, 1984, *The Complete Book of the Olympics*, The Viking Press and Penguin Books

Walters, Guy, 2006, *Berlin Games How Hitler Stole the Olympic Dream*, John Murray(Publishers)

Waterfall, Charles, 2008, *Coal Dust and Bevin Boys*, East Street Press (Bridport)

Watman, Mel, 1996, *Olympic Track and Field Athletics Guide*, Athletics International / Shooting Star Media, Inc.

Watman, Mel, 1968, *History of British Athletics*, Robert Hale Limited

Wilson, Harry, 1982, *Running Dialogue A Coach's Story*, Stanley Paul & Co. Ltd

Year Books, Magazines, Programmes and Academic Articles

Beck, Peter, 2008, The British Government and the Olympic Movement. The 1948 London Olympics, *International Journal of the History of Sport*, Routledge

Bolz, Daphné, 2010, Welcoming the World's Best Athletes: An Olympic Challenge for Post-war Britain, *International Journal of the History of Sport*, Routledge

Fletcher, David & Wagstaff, Christopher, 2009, Organisational Psychology in Elite Sport, *Psychology of Sport and Exercise Science*, Elsevier

Rogan, Matt, 2008, *Building the Business Case for Internal Sponsorship Activation*, Henry Stuart Publications

Various, 1949, *BBC Yearbook 1949*, Richard Clay and Company Limited

Various, 1948, *British Olympic Association Official Report of the London Olympic Games 1948*, World Sports

Various, 1951, *The Official Report For The Organising Committee For The XIV Olympiad*, The Organising Committee For The XIV Olympiad, London. 1948

Various, 1948, *XIVTH Olympiad London 1948 Opening Ceremony Official Programme*, Organising Committee for the XIV Olympiad

Various, 2009/2010, *Sport Business International Magazine*, Sport Business Publications

Wassong, Stephan, 2009/2010, International Society of Olympic Historians, *Journals of Olympic History* / International Society of Olympic Historians

Wassong, Stephan, Bijkerk, Tony & Lennarz, Karl, 2009, International Society of Olympic Historians, *Journals of Olympic History* / International Society of Olympic Historians

Archives, Museums and Specific Websites

www.bbc.co.uk/olympics

British Library

British Museum

British Olympic Association Archive

Cabinet Office Archives

Cambridge University Library

City of London, London Metropolitan Archives

Express Newspaper Archive

The Gibson Collection, Cornwall, for *The Arctic Times*

www.haltontennis.co.uk – Halton Village Tennis Club website

www.insidethegames.com – A fantastic destination for all Olympic fans

www.ifs.org.uk – Institute of Fiscal Studies

International Society of Olympic Historians archive publications

LA 84 Foundation Sports Library
Lloyds Banking Group Archive
Museum of London
www.london2012.com
Memorabilia and film collection of John and Dorothy Parlett
Much Wenlock Museum
National Archives
National Football Museum Preston
National Union of Track Statisticians publications
Punch Magazine Online Archive
River and Rowing Museum, Henley
www.sportengland.org
Thame Public Library, Oxfordshire
The Times Digital Archives

LIST OF INDIVIDUAL CONTRIBUTORS

Adrian Moorhouse — Olympic Swimming Gold Medallist, Seoul 1988, BBC Commentator & Lane4

Alastair Brownlee — Elite Mens World Triathlon Champion 2009

Alison Mowbray — Olympic Rowing Silver Medallist, Athens 2004 & Lane4

Andy McGrath — Associate Director of Performance, NHS South Central Strategic Health Authority

Ben Ashworth — Lead Physiotherapist, English Institute of Sport

Bobby White — Great Britain Handball Team Goalkeeper

Claire Blakeway — Head of Internal Engagement & Communications, BP London 2012 Partnership

Clare Strange — Three-time Paralympian, Great Britain Wheelchair Basketball Team & Lane4

Craig Edmondson — Head of Marketing, Premier League

Daryl Jelinek — Former Professional Rugby Union player, now General Manager London 2012 Partnership, Coca-Cola Great Britain

David Fletcher — Sport and Performance Psychologist, Loughborough University

Dominic Mahony — Olympic Bronze Medallist, Seoul 1988, Team Manager, Great Britain Modern Pentathlon & Lane4

Dorothy Parlett — Olympic Athletics Silver Medallist, London 1948

Dr. Mike Loosemore — Sports Physician at British Medical Institute, Great Britain Team Doctor, Olympic Boxing and Olympic Fencing, England Athletics Team Doctor

Georgie Harland — Olympic Modern Pentathlon Bronze Medallist, Athens, Sport and Performance Psychologist, Sports Engagement Manager, British Olympic Association

Greg Searle — Olympic Rowing Gold and Bronze Medallist, Barcelona and Atlanta, Current Team Member, Great Britain Rowing Team & Lane4

Ian Barham — Buckinghamshire Manager for the 2012 Games

Ivor Lloyd — Former Great Britain Rower, Managing Director, Dorney Lake Services and Chair, Leander Rowing Club

Jamie Doward	Home Affairs Editor, *The Observer*
Joel Ramsbottom	100m and 200m Sprinter
John Parlett	Olympic Athlete, London 1948, European and Commonwealth Champion
John Steele	Former Professional Rugby Union Player, now Chief Executive, UK Sport, shortly to become Chief Executive, Rugby Football Union
Juliet Slot	Formerly London 2012 bid and LOCOG Commercial team member, now Managing Director, Pitch Communications
Karen Earl	Chairman, Synergy and European Sponsorship Association, *Sunday Times* Sports Businesswoman of the Year 2009
Keith Evans	Chief Executive, British Retail Consortium Trading Division
Kevin Underwood	Director, Buckingham Group, Constructors of Handball Arena
Liz Yelling	Two time Olympic Marathon runner, Commonwealth Games Bronze Medallist and Director, Yellingperformance
Marc O'Brien	Managing Director, VISA UK
Marion Rogan	Buckinghamshire Lawn Tennis Association Committee Member, Tennis Coach and Marathon Runner
Mark Richardson	Olympic Athletics Silver Medallist, Atlanta & Lane4
Martin McElhatton	Former Paralympian, now Chief Executive, WheelPower
Martin Yelling	Great Britain Athlete, Duathlete and Triathlete now Multisport Coach, Media Commentator, Director, Yellingperformance and Presenter, Marathontalk
Marzena Bogdanowicz	Former Director of Marketing, British Olympic Association, now Managing Director, b-focussed
Morgan Garfield	Director, Ellandi LLP
Neil Gibson	Strategic Director (Communities and Environment), Buckinghamshire County Council
Nick Leighton	Director, Halton Village Tennis Club
Olivia Garfield	Group Director, Strategy, Policy and Regulation, BT
Paul Thawley	Former Senior Physiotherapist, British Medical Institute, now Director, Elite Physical Medicine
Peter Hart	Chief Executive, Pentathlon GB
Prof. Adam Carey	Elite Sport Nutritionist, Managing Director, Corperformance
Prof. Francis Farrelly,	Professor of Marketing, School of Economics, Finance and Marketing, RMIT University
Prof. Mike Beverland	Professor of Marketing, Bath University
Prof. Rick Burton	Former Chief Marketing Officer, US Olympic Committee, now David B. Falk Distinguished Professor of Sport Management, Syracuse University

Richard Hughes	B2C Commercial Director, EDF Energy
Rob Clarke	Head of Reward, Policy and Organisational Development at LOCOG
Sally Hancock	Director of Olympic Marketing, Lloyds Banking Group
Sarah Winckless	Olympic Rowing Bronze Medallist, Athens now Chair, British Olympic Association Athletes' Commission
Sean Collins	Former Great Britain Rower, now Managing Director, Thames Clippers
Simon Cummins	Head of International Sports Practice, Odgers Berndtson
Steve Attrill	Owner, Hive Beach Café, Burton Bradstock, Dorset
Sir Philip Craven	Five time Paralympian, Wheelchair Basketball World Champion 1973, now President, International Paralympic Committee
Steve Parry	Olympic Swimming Bronze Medallist, Athens, BBC Journalist and Director, Total Swimming
Sylvia Disley	Olympic Athletics Bronze Medallist, Helsinki 1952
Tim Benjamin	Olympian, European and Commonwealth Games Athletics Silver Medallist, now Personal Trainer and Athletics Coach
Tom Williams	Lecturer in Sports Science, University of Leeds, Athletics Coach, Presenter, Marathontalk, Director, Parkrun Leeds
Wil James	Head Quarter Psychologist, GB Holding Camp, Athens Olympic Games, current National Lead Psychologist for the England and Wales Cricket Board & Lane4

ABBREVIATIONS

AAA	Amateur Athletic Association
ACC	Allied Control Council
BOA	British Oympic Association
BOC	British Olympic Committee
BP	British Petroleum plc
BT	British Telecommunications plc
DLR	Docklands Light Railway
GDP	Gross Domestic Product
GLA	Greater London Authority
GOE	Government Olympic Executive
GPO	General Post Office
IFS	Institute of Fiscal Studies
ISMGC	International Stoke Mandeville Games Committee
ISMWSF	International Stoke Mandeville Wheelchair Sports Federation
IWASF	International Wheelchair and Amputee Sports Federation
LDA	London Development Agency
LOCOG	London Organising Committee of the Olympic and Paralympic Games
LTA	Lawn Tennis Association
NBA	National Basketball Association (USA)
NBC	National Broadcasting Company (USA)
NCU	National Cyclists Union
NGB	National Governing Body (ies)
NHS	National Health Service
NUTS	National Union of Track Statisticians
ODA	Olympic Delivery Authority
RFU	Rugby Football Union
RYA	Royal Yachting Association
SEEDA	South East England Development Agency
TCC	Transport Coordination Centre
UCI	Union Cycliste Internationale
UEFA	Union of European Football Associations
USOC	United States Olympic Committee

INDEX